D0529033

Using the WEB for Social Research

Craig McKie
Carleton University

McGRAW-HILL RYERSON LIMITED
Toronto Montreal New York Auckland Bogotá Caracas
Lisbon London Madrid Mexico Milan New Delhi
San Juan Singapore Sydney Tokyo

McGraw-Hill
Ryerson Limited
   A Subsidiary of The McGraw·Hill Companies

Using the Web for Social Research

ISBN: 0-07-552851-7

1 2 3 4 5 6 7 9 10   W   6 5 4 3 2 1 0 9 8 7

Printed and bound in Canada

Care has been taken to trace ownership of copyright material contained in this text. The publishers will gladly take any information that will enable them to rectify any reference or credit in subsequent editions.

Many of the names and symbols used by manufacturers to distinguish their products are trademarked. McGraw-Hill Ryerson Limited acknowledges the trademark status of these products. More specific credits may be found on the figure acknowledgments page, an extension of this copyright page.

Sponsoring Editor: Gord Muschett
Associate Editor: Margaret Henderson
Developmental Editor: Marianne Minaker
Production Co-ordinator: Nicla Dattolico
Cover and Inside Design: Dianna Little
Photo Composite: M. Tcherevkoff Ltd./The Image Bank
Typefaces: Arial, Impact
Printer: Webcom Limited

Canadian Cataloguing in Publication Data

McKie, C. (Craig), date —
        Using the Web for social research

Includes index.
ISBN 0-07-552851-7

1. Social sciences - Computer network resources.
2. World Wide Web (Information retrieval system).
I. Title.

H61.95.M34   1997   025.06'3   C97-930895-X

"The electron is the ultimate precision-guided weapon."

John Deutch, Director, Central Intelligence Agency, quoted in the **New York Times**, June 25, 1996 page B7.

"As to privacy, it exists no longer. We have sacrificed it to the cause of convenience; it is our burnt offering to Lord Electron."

Phillip Finch, **f2f**. New York: Bantam Books, 1996, page 3.

Table of Contents

PART ONE: FOUNDATION SKILLS 1

Chapter One	Establishing Relevancies 5	
Chapter Two	Setting Up a Personal Computer for Full Multimedia Use of the Web 17	
Chapter Three	The Basics: Connecting and Communicating 27	

PART TWO: ROUTINE USE OF THE WEB FOR COMMUNICATING AND LOCATING RESOURCES 39

Chapter Four	Internet Utilities: Basic 41	
Chapter Five	Using Paper Libraries and Their Reading Rooms 53	
Chapter Six	Internet Search Utilities: the Web Search Engine Family and WAIS 77	
Chapter Seven	Elementary Information Dispensing: Web Sites, USENET, Listservs 99	

PART THREE: SKILLS FOR EVERYDAY WEB USE IN RESEARCH 117

Chapter Eight	The World Wide Web: Basics 119	

Chapter Nine   Finding and Using Information for Research:
                        Defining Your Needs 133

Chapter Ten   Finding and Using Information for Research:
                        Finding Materials 151

Chapter Eleven   Finding and Using Information for Research:
                        Organizing and Presenting Results 169

Chapter Twelve   Discipline-Specific Research Examples 175

Chapter Thirteen   Providing Services: HTML and your Web
                        Site 193

Chapter Fourteen   Communicating: Other ways of gathering and
                        dispensing information197

Chapter Fifteen   Electronic Scholarship: Risks and Rewards
                        207

PART FOUR: APPENDIX OF TECHNICAL DETAILS AND INSTRUCTIONS 221

Glossary   271

Acknowledgements   277

Index   279

PART ONE

Foundation Skills

This volume is intended for students of the social sciences. Its examples are for the most part drawn from social science resources or materials which may well be of use to any student in his or her day-to-day research activities, whether in researching and writing essays, or accomplishing more advanced research tasks such as the acquisition and analysis of data sets.

Broadly speaking, the social sciences today embrace a number of disciplines which are distinct both from the Humanities (arts and letters) and from the physical and applied sciences (for example, physics and engineering). These distinctions may seem somewhat artificial now in light of their medieval origins but the boundaries continue to indicate real methodological differences. Not only is the subject matter of the social sciences distinct (human behaviour broadly understood) but also its research methods. You may think of the social sciences today as being made up of the following disciplines: psychology, sociology, anthropology, political science and geography. Often economics is added as well though there tends to be an arms-length relationship between it and the other old-line social sciences based on theoretical differences of approach to research. In addition, newer disciplines that combine elements of the main social sciences are often classified together with them, such as gender studies, Canadian studies, mass communication and even professional schools such as social work and journalism can be included under the general heading of the social sciences.

The nature of the research activity portrayed here is not strikingly different from that performed by fully fledged professionals in the social sciences. Of course, the World Wide Web represents a much larger body of resources than just resources for students and professors. It contains all manner of information for enlightenment, entertainment, diversion, and fantasizing. Part of the intrinsic problem in learning to use Web resources is searching for and finding the useful material buried amongst dross of all sorts.

The volume is divided into parts. The first part is addressed to questions of justification (why should I learn these skills?) and of basic process. There are obviously very many technical questions related to how your computer is configured and how the software is set up. By and large, these questions are addressed not in the main text but rather are relegated to a technical appendix. This appendix is composed of dense materials which are intended to help you understand (if you wish to) what the computer and the software are doing with your requests and the resources they acquire for you, and also to deal with common problems. With little or no understanding of what is going on 'under the hood' the student of today can walk into a university lab and use the Web tools. When it comes to doing this from a home computer, however, more detailed technical matters must be mastered. There are many books already in print which can help you in this respect; the technical appendix just covers problematic situations with the typical software setups on home computers. These initial difficulties can be overcome but they may require some informed tinkering on your part.

Part II has to do with basic processes of communication such as the use of e-mail, USENET newsgroups and listservs which all have roles in embedding your work within the context of easy global communication through the Internet. In addition, using the resources of libraries is still very much part of the research process.

Part III presents the core material of this volume: rapid routine use of the full array of electronic tools as integral parts of the social science research process in today's wired environment of borderless, instantaneous, and personal scholarship. Detailed examples are provided on the use of these tools, both in a generic sense and a discipline-specific sense. Mounting your own Web page as an active participant in the electronic culture is also dealt with. A concluding chapter in this last part deals with the implications of the advent of electronic scholarship and also with some of the hazards and pitfalls of this new electronic environment including hacking and snooping, and finally draws some conclusions as to what rapid Netification of the social science research process may mean for us all in the long run.

Since the tools and procedures are all new, none of us including the author can possibly know all the details and procedures. These will accumulate in the received wisdom only with the passage of time. But it is only by passing on new techniques and processes that the enterprise of research as a whole will be advanced. Hopefully the reader can participate in this process of tools and techniques discovery. It has been wonderful to see how very fast these have developed in the past few years. I would hope that the processes will continue to accelerate and be enriched in the years to come.

Needless to say, despite intensive care taken to forestall such things, there will be errors which escape my detection and make it into print, or statements which though once true no longer are. May I beg the reader's indulgence in advance for these gaffes. May I also extend effusive thanks to the anonymous reviewers whose attention to detail and persistent questioning have prevented some but by no means all excesses from being present in the finished version. Profuse thanks are also due Mike McAuliffe for assistance with the arcane business of Pagemaker templates.

Craig McKie

Realized in Ottawa and Toronto, Ontario; Prince George and Chilliwack, British Columbia; and Wolfville, Nova Scotia in the summer and fall of 1996.

CHAPTER

ONE

Establishing Relevancies

TEHRAN, Dec 20, 1996 (Reuter) "A senior Iranian cleric called on Friday for restricting Internet access because the global computer network fed 'poison' to the masses."

Ideas and words have no natural affinity for cellulose. They sit uneasily on a printed page such as this, becoming inhumanly fixed in time at the printer, and crumbling to dust after only a few decades as acidification destroys their paper medium's molecular bonds. None of this is preordained.

For millennia, ideas and words had their own life in the pressing necessity of oral tradition and practice. Fact and nonsense mixed with the telling, changing form and fashion while developing differing and conflicting versions of themselves without end, such that a story could have as many versions as there were people to remember and tell them again with a different spin. Stories could contain truth and falsehood mixed without embarrassment; indeed the importance accorded the distinction is relatively recent and seems still to elude fundamentalists of several religious stripes.

But in the face of the ancient way of doing things, the printing press created attribution, reputation, and the accumulating preponderance of evidence, and these in turn created professional scholarship.

Cellulose fibre, even though it is chemically a sugar, is remarkable in that it is not a food for many organisms. This accounts for its persistence. Even ruminants like cows require special stomach arrangements and a captive gang of specialized bacteria to make it useful as a staple food. Thus the indigestibility of wood fibre, combined with its equally indigestible clay binders, is responsible for the existence and persistence of paper and ultimately of books as a storage medium. Paper as a medium for words and ideas is also inherently indigestible for most young humans. It requires many years of instruction and drill to use it with facility and many never learn this skill. Paper-based words and ideas are hard to absorb in bulk, difficult to search efficiently, hard to remember, and are not open to change and revision. The detection of significant errors in a printed work cries out to the scholar in all of us for the creation of a new printed treatment which avoids these errors and more closely approximates our inherited reality. This process of revision has become the routine activity of science and the humanities, and most particularly it has sustained professional scholarship for several hundred years.

The tyranny of the cellulose regime in nature is responsible for the persistence and size of trees, and in turn for the importance of the tree in the trade in cellulose as a basis of the staples economy in much of northern Canada. We all have a vested economic interest in lumber, pulp and paper, and its derived processed and manufactured products. Its sale to others and to ourselves pays the bills. If developed societies have anything at all in common it is that they are built, literally and figuratively, of cellulose. It is one of the magic trio of structural inedibles: wood, inorganic minerals processed through the guts of ancient creatures and deposited to ripen in or as sedimentary rock, and refined base metals, all of which this country has in abundance.

We will meet in this volume the digital termite, the digital "document," consumer and digester of the print culture and all that sustains it, destroyer of worlds and reputations, and leveler par excellence. Revisable and reproducible at little or no cost, the "document" is distributable without charge around the world in as many identical copies as are required over all borders, time zones and political regimes without hindrance, censorship, or reprisal. It is the currency of vigorous debate and the grist for scholarship of a new and different sort, if for no other reason than the process of *peer review*, the cornerstone of all previous professional scholarly regimes and rationer of scarce cellulose space, defender of the status quo and conventionality and touchstone of scientific process, can be openly undermined. This is so simply because anyone with a modicum of World Wide Web skills can publish anything they want on any topic they want to write about at whatever length desired with whatever multimedia props are deemed desirable. Students are not barred from this process by virtue of their junior status. Indeed, they may have advantages if they can gain a superior command of the new electronic tools at an early stage and use those skills to good advantage during their time as students.

As has been repeatedly noted elsewhere, paper publications have often been the social glue that holds organizations together. Traditionally, these publications provided a means by which memberships could be defined and limited to those who paid for and received the paper copy. In a sense, possession of this form of periodical paper publication was a credential of membership. In addition to maintaining a social group, such publications supported negotiation between members and represented a stable record of debate. All of these latent functions tend to vanish in the digital world where mailing lists are fluid, free of charge, open to anonymous subscription and serve poorly as a permanent archival record of decisions.

 As a Web document consumer, the student and the scholar alike can acquire and use anything that exists in the Web environment which he or she has the capacity to view or listen to. Reputation can be generated by accumulating readers directly through Web publication, without the usual cost and editorial barriers of the print-based process. Reputation gained in this way may ultimately prove just as powerful as that gained by years of slogging through peer-reviewed but very low-volume refereed journals. A classic end run by "document" of professional barriers is now possible as it was made possible to a much more limited degree by television for such science personalities as David Suzuki and Carl Sagan.

Bill Gates is fond of the phrase "digital convergence" which he uses like a bludgeon to convey the sense that *everything that can be reduced to digital form will be*. He, for instance, is buying up huge photo archives and converting the images to digital files. The attractions of this conversion are simple. Take for instance the case of the learned journal with a few hundred subscribers, most of them libraries. The paper journal is late in appearing, often years after the articles in it were submitted for review, horrendously expensive to produce on paper, expensive to distribute, expensive to store on shelves, flammable, losable, stealable, and expensive to reproduce in the hands of the reader. Alternatively, what if the contents of the journal appeared only as Web documents? Who would be inconvenienced? True, some scholars would have to acquire some new skills on their computers. But in return, most of the production, distribution and storage costs would be eliminated, timeliness would improve dramatically, errors and typos could be fixed at leisure and on the fly, students could all have their own copies from which to cut and paste free of charge, etc., etc. This insight has not been lost on scholarly journal managers nor the granting agencies which pay much of the cost. Digital conversion is actually occurring! Financial cutbacks at universities and colleges have caused administrations to cut back or actually to cease the acquisition of new library books. It does not take much imagination to see where such desperate measures lead. They lead directly to a single shared dispersed electronic world library of all digital documents everywhere, linked by the Web.

This advance levels the playing field between junior and senior researchers. While it allows the work of senior social scientists to become richer and more diverse, the advantages accorded to today's students are much more impressive. The walls of the paper library no longer form the outer bounds of research possibility. While use of these conventional resources is still necessary and desirable, it no longer forms the core of research work necessarily.

Further, much valuable data and information is never published on paper at all. These unpublished but rich resources can now be economically stored in electronic form and given away to those whose narrow interests would make them valued resources. In the process, traditional notions of what libraries and librarians do are inevitably changed. Yes, this data must be organized and documented and there are expenses in doing this but they are nowhere as great nor as persistent as printing and storage on paper.

So Web publishing is not something you can take or leave. It is happening, driven by the same imperative for cost reduction that did away with the hand copying and illumination of manuscripts of a much earlier era. This means that a whole generation of professional scholars must now learn how to use "the document" and the sooner the better. The conversion will not stop and it will not go away. For students, the opportunity is offered to make this jump right away. Even first year novices can improve the content of small essays immediately with the judicious use of the new electronic resources.

WHAT IS THE WORLD WIDE WEB?

The Web is simply a very large number of digital "documents" residing on a very large number of interconnected Internet computers. These computers (each with its own address or "IP number" [IP stands for Internet Protocol]) are connected in a single global cooperative by wire, by fibre optic cables, by satellite links or by telephone lines. The manner of connection is not nearly so important as the fact that each member computer can exchange large amounts of digitized information freely across the world with any or all other connected computers. Distance has thus ceased to be the decisive factor in human intellectual life. As a result, the student can ill afford to ignore the power of the Internet to both disseminate and to collect and sift information in all its forms.

From the point of view of the student of a social science discipline, the Internet offers access to unimaginably large amounts of information, data, and interpretative material in a timely, cost-effective, and comfortable manner. Further, the user can easily become an active contributor to the body of knowledge on offer in the world with very little additional effort. Contributions can be made through the exchange of electronic mail with distant colleagues, through postings to the USENET newsgroups, and to topic-particular e-mail discussion groups (called *listservs*). Integrated with everyday study and work, the Internet offers an incomparable opportunity to actively participate in the accumulation and dissemination of a truly global body of professional social science knowledge, expertise, and opinion no matter which level one occupies in the status hierarchy at the outset.

Using the Internet is getting easier all the time, in no small measure because of the rapid adoption of the World Wide Web as a presentation standard for all manner of digital materials including text, graphics, programs, and even audio and video across the Internet. Use of "the Web" is based on a "point and click" approach in its full graphics form, and the use of the keyboard arrow keys in the less attractive text-only mode. Both methods are easy to master, hard to break, and are forgiving in the extreme for novices. And, when a resource is located, its location can be saved in a "bookmarks" file on your computer so that the address (or Uniform Resource Locator, the URL) need never be written down or committed to memory. The saved URL, which is stored together with a descriptive title of the user's choosing, can be easily recalled and used. The Web itself has become the contemporary equivalent of the great library at Alexandria, though it is much more robust than its predecessor because it is not flammable, nor is it subject to the intrusive influence of any single government. The Web is a liberated zone of free and, if necessary, anonymous expression, or, in the words of Hakim Bey, the "temporary autonomous zone".

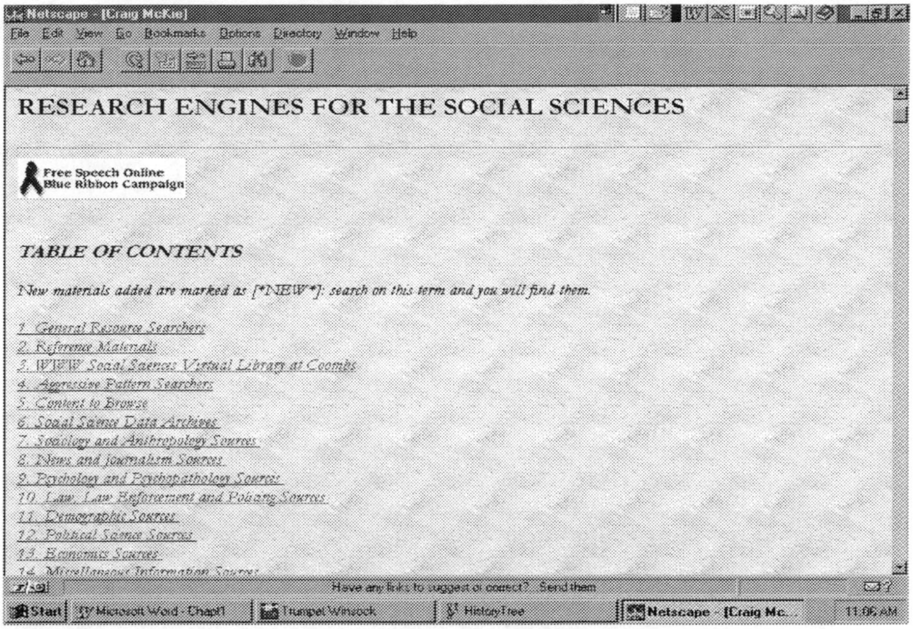

Figure 1 Typical Netscape Screen portraying my site of starting points for a search for social science resources. It may be found at http://www.carleton.ca/~cmckie/research.html

HOW CAN STUDENTS OF SOCIAL SCIENCE BENEFIT FROM THE INTERNET?

Social scientists, both finished professionals and learning students, can benefit in many ways from the use of the Internet toolset. In general, the Internet delivers better, faster, more timely communication with colleagues and sources of information than has ever before been available. It offers superior information resource gathering, enhanced collaboration, better dissemination of one's information, instantaneous informal peer review, and low barriers to publication of drafts and requests for comments. It can also be used to acquire huge public data sets from a multitude of national data services and international agencies. Fast searches of recent periodical literature are also available free of charge as are current information sources on contemporary geopolitical events. In addition, many of the world's great newspapers of record daily publish full electronic editions which are available to everyone free of charge. Taken together, these tools allow students of social science to become active participants in the events which shape and illuminate contemporary social processes and discourse. The availability of these tools and resources to anyone with a connection to the Internet is a marvelous addition to the set of skills offered to the world by social science as an institution.

In the future, new tools will be added to this toolkit. Already, experiments with slow scan television carried over the Internet have made it possible for professors in one continent to conduct interviews of colleagues in another "live" in the classrooms of each. Though the sound quality is excellent, the slow scan television is yet not up to commercial standards but the spontaneity of such exchanges of views renders the video quality of little significance. We can look forward in the near future to lectures delivered over great distances to students who would otherwise have no contact at all with leading world scholars. Also available are software packages which enable two-way telephone-like voice conversations between colleagues over the Internet that are free of charge and scrambled to prevent interception. In general, these new and experimental software advances are free of charge (for example, CUSeeMe television, PGPfone, and Nautilus).

TOOLS OF THE INTERNET....

Electronic Mail allows you to exchange information, files, and manuscripts rapidly and effectively (including files from the common word processing packages if suitably encoded). Many exchanges of messages can take place during a single working day. The effect is that of a conversation between interested co-workers. Also possible is active collaboration on a single project between several colleagues thousands of kilometers apart who may never have actually met each other. New collaborations become feasible; old ones become closer and more continuous. Because time zone differences can be overcome (conversations need not be confined to times when both parties are logged on), the range of possible collaborators is greatly expanded. Every user has his or her own unique e-mail address. It looks like *someone@somewhere.com*. The first term is the user's logon name and the second is his or her home machine's name. Use is as simple as composing a memo and sending it off to its destination with a few key strokes. It is however mandatory that you know the correct e-mail address of your intended recipient.

Electronic card catalogues of the world's great libraries (and some not so great ones as well) are in general available to everyone with an Internet connection. The obvious example is the Library of Congress in Washington whose catalogues can be searched easily through the Web. You can search for any resource such online libraries hold and locate copies of books which might subsequently be ordered by interlibrary loan, or locate obscure journal articles, copies of which can then be requested.

Listservs are dissemination engines. They are e-mailing lists that can send single e-mail messages (including attachments of many sorts of files if desired) to an unlimited number of recipients who are members of a list. Any member of a list can, with one message, address all of the members of the list. Listservs are maintained at a single location and to write to the entire list, all that is required is a single message to the listserv. Listservs can be started on almost any Internet host computer that has the required (free) software installed. In principle, any group of e-mailers who share a common interest can start a listserv on any subject imaginable. Lists can be open to all or closed to all but welcome applicants. Postings can be moderated (reviewed by an editor) or unmoderated; additionally, e-mail postings to the listserv can be encrypted so that the source of a posting can be truly anonymized if desired. In addition, there are features that allow compilation of daily message packages rather than or in addition to allowing the individual retransmission of submissions when they arrive. Some list owners also maintain archives of submissions.

Newsgroups - Another way in which information is circulated by Internet users is by posting to and reading of the USENET newsgroups (of which there are now thousands). Newsgroups are topic specific. One simply posts information or a question in the form of an e-mail message to a newsgroup or newsgroups which seem appropriate for your interests. Readers subscribe to newsgroups they wish to read using reader software such as *Tin* or *Free Agent*. Since posting and reading are independent actions, and there is no obligation to do either, it is never certain who may read your posting. In practice, some newsgroups are very well read, particularly where they have come to be a place for debates on topics that attract a large and active audience. You may post questions and receive advice from others very quickly, sometimes in a matter of minutes. In essence, strangers (who may post anonymously should they wish) may become your information agents in many remote locations simultaneously.

The **World Wide Web** is the most sophisticated venue of information exchange on the Internet. The user has access to millions of "Web pages" which may contain data sources, information and/or other onward "links". The resources of Web pages may be viewed with a Web browser (such as *Netscape*) or textually (with a text-based browser such as *Lynx*). It helps to know where to start. One good place to begin is Yahoo in California, a site started by two students at Stanford University. Its address is *http://www.yahoo.com*. It has a well-developed social science component of useful links. All addresses on the Web are in http format (**h**yper**t**ext **t**ransport **p**rotocol).

Telnet is the modern traveler's friend. When you have an Internet account and you are traveling, a friend or colleague with access to an Internet account wherever in the world you are can help you to *Telnet* to your home Internet account. You may then logon and use it as if you were in your own room, reading your e-mail for instance. There are no additional charges for this service no matter how distant the telnet connection is nor how long it lasts; its part of the toolkit. Often, you also use this tool to reach the electronic catalogues of libraries as well.

The older tools. There are several older Internet tools. Without going into detail here, they function to distribute free software, information and allow simultaneous real time conversations between dispersed participants. These tools are still valuable but their functions tend now to be "buried" in other more sophisticated software packages and are thus hidden from view. Some of these older tools are: *Gopher*, an information scrounger tool which predates the Web; *Archie*, a program designed to find you copies of shareware; and *FTP*, a transfer program which acquires copies of programs for you. In general, these older programs run in the UNIX operating system which, although the Web "floats" on a sea of UNIX, you may never directly encounter if you use a graphical browser such as Netscape. In this book, you will be shown UNIX commands from time to time as examples since many students and professors still do their day-to-day electronic work immersed in the UNIX operating environment.

WHERE TO START....

• Getting Connected

Every user needs access to the Internet by means of a "member" computer. Many students and professionals choose to do this by means of a personal computer, a modem and a telephone connection to an Internet "host" computer. In the academic context, a connection may be provided in a number of different ways: Ethernet cable, internal telephone systems, fibre optic connections, and so on, either through a lab, home, or office computer. Each, though, provides a "pipe" between the Internet and the user's machine. Connections come in many gradations of quality. Since faster is better, faster also tends to involve more expense. In the future, very fast connections (by which is meant high-volume connections) will become commonplace, perhaps through the shared use of the coaxial cable that now is only used for the delivery of television cable services to households. Obviously, the quality and quantity of high technology infrastructure available to the user is a function of the relative wealth of his or her region of the country.

• Learning the skills

One of the charms of the World Wide Web is that it is to a large and growing extent self-documenting. Once "there," you can easily locate free learning materials to further develop your skills. However, getting 'there' is still a formidable hurdle. While it is possible to learn in isolation from printed reference material, it is best to learn from or have routine access to an experienced user. Becoming an "information apprentice" seems, on experience, the best way to learn the tricks, the shortcuts and the "magic" instructions. In part this is so because the Internet runs for the most part using the UNIX operating system at its base. This system is as arcane as it is beloved of Internet programmers; commands are not intuitive and often could never be guessed by the novice. Direct instruction by a trusted and knowledgeable colleague is the best solution. Often, it takes just a few hours of tutoring to overcome the initial barriers and enter the self-documenting zone of the Internet. While this initial step requires a degree of faith, the novice will be richly rewarded by newly granted access to the developing world of shared data, knowledge, research advice, publication and hopefully wisdom.

• Routine use

Once you have reached your goal of easy use, you may well find that the Internet toolset becomes a part of everyday life, moving far past strictly educational use into all aspects of personal existence. Having easy access to the world's newswire services in real time and major newspapers and newsmagazines before they are published tends to do that. Embracing this sort of change in learning style is deeply enriching on a personal level and brings us all a little closer together.

- ## Your Own Mailing list to establish and maintain contact

Once you have identified members of your own particular Internet community, no matter where they might happen to live in the world, it is possible for you to establish your own mailing list or listserv to remail messages from any member of your list to all members of the list. USENET postings and listserv messages inviting colleagues to join a new listserv on some narrow specialized topic is a normal part of the world's information traffic nowadays.

- ## Maintaining a WWW site to publish your own information, reaching a global audience

Once you have access to an Internet service, whether run by yourself or by others, and once Web server software is installed, it is quite simple to begin to publicize information on any topic through your own Web page. Editing tools are available on the Web to help you master and construct HTML documents for your Web site. HTML (which stands for **H**ypertext **M**arkup **L**anguage) is the basic dialect of the Web. One of the best ways of learning how to do this is to look at the HTML code which other users are employing on their web pages. All Web browsers allow you to view the source coding for others' pages. Copying of features which appeal to you is an easy and effective way to get started. It is also useful to register your Web pages once they are constructed and available with some of the many registries of Web pages. This will allow users around the world to locate and visit your site based on your brief description of its contents. In addition, there are page-seeking Web robots (such as AltaVista) which actively search out and catalogue the contents of new Web pages all the time.

SETTING UP YOUR OWN INTERNET SERVICES

You may wish at some time to actually establish and maintain your Internet services on a machine over which you have exclusive control. In order to do this, many elements of hardware, software, and registration have to be put in place. For instance, you must obtain a computer over which you have authority and which has the technical capacity to serve as an Internet host. It need not necessarily be powerful and expensive though each helps in some respect. Such a computer must be provided with a high-speed network feed from some other member machine on the Internet. It must also be given a unique IP address by some registration authority such as the INTERNIC, one of the central network information centres. In addition, it must have access electronically to a router computer that has a current copy of the IP addresses of other Internet member computers. Further, specialized software such as UNIX, Web server software, and e-mail software must be installed and properly configured. In general, a high level of sophisticated knowledge is required to carry out these tasks. Should you choose to assume this responsibility, you will also have to take necessary precautions to guard the security of your site since attacks by hackers can be confidently predicted. While there are security software tools and expertise available to you, you may well find that the routine keeping of system logs is a requirement and that trouble can develop at any time of day or night. (A low-budget version of this software universe called Linux is available for modest personal computers running in a low-volume context.) You, as system administrator must also decide how external users will access your service, whether by Telnet, dial-up access, or exclusively as external Internet Web users visiting from other Internet hosts. Committing to offer dial-up services to others may itself pose formidable technical and expense challenges.

OTHER RESOURCES YOU MAY OFFER

You may use your Web site to offer virtually any form of digital resource to other users. You may for instance make available databases, papers you or others have written, software you wish to give away or announcements you may wish to publicize. The situation with respect to copyright on Web documents is not at all clear and there is little guidance available. In general, normal good citizenship on the Web includes not appropriating the work of others for your own gain without permission. Having said that however, it is the very essence of the Web that copying of files takes place without hindrance. Indeed, that is the main attraction of the World Wide Web as it has evolved.

WHAT IS AVAILABLE THROUGH THE WORLD WIDE WEB?

Although the World Wide Web is of fairly recent origin (it was first imagined then realized by Tim Berners-Lee at the CERN particle accelerator in Switzerland as a means of sharing the results of remotely generated physics experiments), virtually all major institutions in the Western world have rushed to establish their institutional presence on it. This presence includes most of the major educational institutions. They have established Web sites to display course offerings and supplementary readings, faculty contact information, library catalogues, and other promotional and helping materials. At the academic department level, much more detailed information on course offerings and requirements is often available as well, in some cases already supplanting traditional printed pamphlets and brochures.

Increasingly, data and research resources are available too, not just to students and faculty of the posting institutions but to anyone with Web access. You may for instance wish to see how Prof. X in Europe teaches his course in symbolic interactionism. Hopefully his course outline will be found on a Web site somewhere. Additionally, courses are beginning to be offered for credit in this manner. Course requirements are posted and student submissions arrive from distant parts in electronic form. Electronic discussion groups take the place or greatly augment small group classroom discussions. The mechanics of actually taking such courses for credit and paying the required tuition fees have yet to be fully worked out but experiments in this direction are beginning. It is quite likely that future students will acquire course credits from many dispersed educational institutions while in residence at a single school, raising complex questions of assessing transfer credits, tuition payment sharing and so on. You may even be able to receive a degree from a university you have never physically attended.

What amounts to a reserve shelf of required readings and supporting materials for specific courses can also easily be constructed, particularly if you have access to a modern high-quality scanner. These machines together with optical character reading software can swiftly acquire textual material and convert the text to Web format electronic files (HTML) with some speed. Whether or not this compromises the 'fair use' provisions of copyright is an open question. Traditionally students and scholars are allowed to make one copy for personal scholarship. Since any number of students can access the same single electronic copy of a document simultaneously on a Web site, the traditional bottlenecks of the paper reserve shelf in the library are circumvented. Indeed, it is not even necessary to have a copy of the "document" in question on your reserve shelf site. You may simply include an active link (a URL) which points to the location where it can be found. Interesting new material found by students can easily be added to the list as well, making the enterprise a dynamic and interactive one. Where this leaves copyright issues is very much up in the air. As mentioned, traditionally every scholar is entitled to make one copy for scholarship purposes. This clearly refers to a physical copy. In the context of electronic documents however, the big question is whether this scholarly right of fair use extends to the Web. A related question is how could violations be litigated given that the document or the students could reside in different provinces or countries? We will leave these issues to the lawyers and proceed with our studies.

Given the wide availability of Census data and opinion research data on the Web for secondary statistical analysis, specific tables or findings (or even files of custom-written SPSS code for creating a novel variable) can be added to a site as information is discovered as well. Raw data sets, files of control commands, and output tables can all be included as resources at a site. These are of great value to senior students looking for thesis topics which involve secondary data analysis.

Differences in the file formatting of resources is a continuing problem, however. There are currently approximately 200 different document formats in active use on the Web though about ten predominate (e.g. .zip, .tar, .gif, .jpeg, .wav, and so on in addition to common word processor formats such as .wp and .doc). These formatted files must be handled correctly after arrival on your PC (or your computer lab's PC) to decode the intrinsic content. While there tends to be a specific decoding tool for each file format which must be correctly used to break out the content, recently general purpose software has appeared which is much more flexible and capable. A program called *Keyview* for instance promises to be able to decode most of the current file formats in use. It does indeed seem to be able to do this but one first has to know about Keyview's existence, know how to obtain and install a copy on one's PC, and how to configure it to work properly. There will be more on this program and this general decoding problem in a later chapter.

This file format quandary highlights a more general problem: as a Web user with a research question, the solution is often obscure and needs a fair bit of detective work to solve. In this book, I hope to be able to short-circuit some of this tedious detective work, preclude some of the obvious errors a novice will make, and in general make the process of obtaining research resources from the Web easier. The problems a user will encounter may be understood as being of several generic types: 1) obtaining a stable connection to the Internet in order to search and acquire resources; 2) learning how to use the Web tools once a stable connection is established; 3) finding the research resources you are looking for; and 4) using those resources successfully by decoding them and handling them in a useful manner. Responsibility for imagination, interpretative skill, and accomplished writing remain as ever in the hands of the scholar. There is little prospect for change along these dimensions.

IMPORTANT DEFINITIONS:

TCP/IP:
All information passes between the computer you are using for Web services, the **Server/Host** of your service provider, and the Internet using the **Transmission Control Protocol/Internet Protocol** or **TCP/IP** for short. This protocol governs the way "packets" of information are broken up, packaged, labeled, transmitted and received. It is the universal language of the Internet. You as a user do not have to deal with it directly; software programs do that for you.

IP address number:
Your unique identifier on the Internet is your IP (Internet Protocol is the "address" of your computer). It is always in the form of four sets of three or fewer numbers separated by dots (as in the IP number 1.1.1.1). These numbers are assigned following the terms of an international agreement and you cannot assign a valid IP number to yourself. Your service provider will assign you one; or may, in place of giving you a unique IP number, use a system in which a temporary IP number is assigned as you login each time. Either will work, though for using services such as person-to-person voice communication over the Internet a permanent personal IP number is much better.

URL:
Uniform Resource Locator; the "address" of a Web site, as in

http://www.carleton.ca/~cmckie/research.html

THE REMAINDER OF THIS BOOK

This brief tour of the Web and the larger Internet will hopefully have given you a short glimpse of the incredible potential of the Web and of the kinds of skills required to integrate the new digital materials into scholarship. The remainder of this book will explore this skillset, dealing in some detail with the kinds of skills needed to be a confident and flexible user of the new information resources.

CHAPTER

Setting Up a Personal Computer for Full Multimedia Use of the Web

"...the entire Internet contains from 2 terabytes to 10 terabytes. A typical public library with 300,000 books, by comparison, has about 3 terabytes of data."

The Washington Post, September 22, 1996. p. H1.

In the beginning was the word, or more properly, lots of words sitting in inaccessible public files on computers around the world. What Tim Berners-Lee did when he invented the World Wide Web was to develop a way in which remote computer users could look for those files, find them, and then read them by first copying the files to their own computers and then looking at their contents with competent viewing software. With Tim's now-archaic WWW browser, a remote user could locate documentary resources and acquire literal copies. What the files contained initially was text.

In the fullness of time, it occurred to many people around the world independently that there were other kinds of digital files which could be dispensed in the exact same manner. Digital files could contain raw data for secondary analysis, photographs, maps, digitized speech, movies, newspapers and magazines, data from remote sensors automatically recording temperature readings, indications of earthquakes, traffic conditions on the San Bernardino Freeway in suburban Los Angeles, and surf conditions on beaches all over the world. A file could also contain a recent view of yourself sitting at your desk if you so desired to make a spectacle of yourself with a

$200 black and white television camera dispensing its pictures to the world. The Web now contains far more than words in plain text files. But in order to gain access to the non-text content (which one could think of as the value-added component to the Web), you have to have a capable computer and capable software to use with it. In addition, the computer hardware must contain devices to handle sound files and make them audible through speakers of the conventional sort, and equipment which renders photographic images faithfully in high definition and a full range of colours on a high-quality monitor or flat display panel.

The possession of this specialized computer equipment and accessories raises the price of participation in the Web (though to a much lesser extent than was the case a couple of years ago), and it increases the complexity of the software operating environment on your computer. There are more programs, operating or not as required, and they have to talk to each other on the fly and in a constructive manner. There are now for instance more than 100 'plug-ins' or helper programs for the Netscape browser alone. The choice in graphical browsers has now come down to Netscape (which is by far the most prevalent one) and Microsoft Internet Explorer which is increasing in prevalence and which comes as part of the Windows95 installation package.

In your Web research use, you may have at your disposal a fully equipped lab with up-to-date computers. Because of the classroom-like environment of labs, however, it is unlikely that these computers will have sound cards and amplified speakers installed. Similarly, they will be unlikely to be equipped with CD-ROM drives for loading software or playing games and/or music. These shortfalls are intentional in most cases to preserve the quality of the academic environment in the lab. Since universities and colleges are now chronically short of money for purchasing new computers, the machines you are allowed to use may be lacking in other respects too. They may be slow, be unable to render photographic quality images on their monitors, and may lack any means to store files except perhaps on a diskette which you supply. Suffice to say that lab computers are seldom state-of-the-art and are often broken because of the heavy use they receive in continuous service. However, many students now purchase computers for their homes with the intention to do their research while connected to the university or college's server over the telephone line using a modem. While computers for sale today tend to come equipped with modems and CD-ROM readers, speakers and sound cards and so on, actually configuring them to use with software can be quite tiresome. This is doubly true if you yourself are trying to upgrade an older computer. Some useful information for such upgraders and tinkerers is included in the technical appendix to this book.

With a home computer which has a word processing package installed, and bibliographic capture software such as *BioBase*, you can cut and paste literature citations and references into files on your own computer for future use. The fact that you control what gets saved on your home computer and where it is stored is a substantial advantage to you when compared to using a lab computer from time to time.

Thus there are two aspects to the full multimedia experience for you the potential or actual computer owner and user. The first aspect deals with computer hardware and accessories and the second aspect deals with the suite of software "helpers" which augment the function of your browser program which is now often Netscape. We will consider the hardware first and leave the software constellation to others, keeping in mind that in university and college labs you will probably not be allowed to install any additional software, a restriction which of course does not apply to your personal computer at home (or to a laptop or notebook computer which you carry around with you during the day).

HARDWARE: THE MANY FACES OF THE INTERNET

The first personal computer provided for me by my then-employer was an Apple III. It had 128k main RAM memory and its processors worked at a rate of about 1.2 MHz. It cost in excess of $10,000 in 1982 when it was new (or at least twice as much in current 1996 dollars). My present computer has a Pentium processor which runs fully one hundred times as fast, with more than one hundred times the main RAM memory available to it. And it cost much, much less than the old Apple III. But even if that old Apple III were still around and still working (you had to pick it up by the front panel and drop it occasionally to reseat the chips!), it would not be entirely useless for Web browsing purposes since it could have provided slow text-only access to the Web resources. Some service is better than no service and you can accomplish quite a bit with a slow, text-only computer if it has a modem to connect you to your server or provider of Internet service. Generally, such service is provided by universities and colleges in Canada to accredited students and faculty by means of special phone numbers which you dial with your modem from home over an ordinary telephone line. Note that the quality of service can vary dramatically from institution to institution where quality is a function of the speed of data transfer and the frequency of busy signals.

There is no particular type of personal computer which is required for connecting to the Internet and thus to the Web from home. Very old small memory machines (for example an old Apple II) will do the job in text-only service but very, very slowly if connected to the right kind of modem through the serial interface port of the old computer. In general, if you are using this sort of obsolete equipment, you will be limited to low-volume, text-oriented kinds of activity. You may also become very frustrated at the slow pace at which your screen display changes following the issuing of a new command. In order to work in the text-only environment you would also in all probability have to become familiar with the UNIX operating system and the functional programs which run on it such as the *Lynx* Web browser, the *Emacs* and *Pico* text editors, the *Tin* newsreader and so on. Most students (and to be fair about it most human beings) find learning UNIX a humbling experience much to be avoided. Still, if that is the price of admission for prospective researchers who have no other way of gaining access, it may well be worth it. Signing up for a text-based community *freenet* service if there is one where you live may actually be advantageous to you and it also might well be worth the effort. Though freenets are text-only at least for the time being, they have the singular advantage that menus disguise the UNIX commands and you thus need not learn them. UNIX is often referred to as a purposefully arcane system in which no commands are intuitive and functions have nonsense names. This is true; however basic UNIX commands can be mastered with effort.

More up-to-date personal computer equipment consists of two broad categories of machines: IBM-compatible and Apple Macintosh equipment. In addition, there is a third broad category of workstations such as those manufactured by Sun Microsystems and Digital Equipment which are fully capable of sustaining an excellent Internet connection. The latter workstations are typically found in circumstances where advanced computing is already taking place, for example in an advanced university lab. In each of these three broad categories, very capable software exists for sale or free of charge which will allow you to use the computers for Internet purposes. More information on this software can be found in the technical appendix.

In terms of the installed base of computers, IBM-compatible machines form a large proportion of the total with Apple Macintosh machines generally forming less than 10%. Advanced workstations have not yet become very widespread because, being much better and faster computers, they tend to cost a great deal in comparison with the personal computers in the first two categories. Though physically unimposing (advanced workstations often occupy less space on desktops than IBM-compatibles), they possess enormous computing power, and the more expensive models are clearly superior in performance to room-filling mainframe computers of two decades ago. Today, these workstations form the heart of university lab and dial-in services. They generally work in the background supplying files to the much less capable computer you are using upon your request. They also look after communications with the Internet for e-mail posting and receiving and fetching Web documents.

The important points about these three main types of computers are that each type of computer is fully Internet capable given a Network connection of some sort, and secondly, that each has a distinct "species" of supporting software which the user must buy or otherwise acquire and install correctly. The software for one "family" will not work on a member of another "family" of machines. Therefore, you can anticipate having to obtain and install the specific "species" of Internet software which is appropriate to your type of computer. And once having acquired a computer and the software, it then makes sense to add subsequent computers from the same "family" in order to avoid having to get a second "species" of software as well.

One final point on this matter is that there exist hybrid systems. One such hybrid is an IBM-compatible running a UNIX host program called *Linux*. In most respects, *Linux* running in this fashion mimics the activities of a large workstation machine running UNIX. It might be thought of as a low price copy of workstation UNIX service. This type of operation is not easily installed by beginners; the installation disk pack tends to run to 50 or more diskettes and it must be configured to a particular setting once installation is completed. This configuration is a task for experts although high school students working with high quality equipment and with a lot of advice and assistance from experts have been known to complete the task. Resisting the temptation to play with Linux is probably a wise move unless you are an expert and very few human beings are at this stage in history.

Machine attributes such as available RAM memory, the speed of internal data transfer and the size and speed of the hard disk (if any) inevitably have an effect on performance of a personal computer in Internet service. Most users now will probably be running their Internet sessions in the Microsoft Windows 3.1 operating environment for some time to come, with conversion to Windows95 occurring gradually. One quirk of Windows is that the serial port drivers which "push" the information in and out of the serial port were slow in the original versions of Windows 3.1 and variants. New and improved port drivers for Windows (such as *cybercom.drv*) are a necessary augmentation to get full performance from many advanced modems. Finding and installing these new drivers maybe difficult in these cases and often this requires the active assistance of an experienced person with this sort of knowledge. Since such persons may be in short supply, it may be necessary to accept somewhat lesser performance than anticipated until the necessary changes are made. Once you are able to get connected to the Internet, you will find that it is alive with a variety of USENET *newsgroups* which can provide instruction on how to deal with this sort of problem. In addition, there are Web sites which dispense this type of help to all users free of charge.

In terms of personal computer equipment which people are now using in Internet service, we can establish four broad classes of hardware:

Type A: Fully capable multimedia computers. These have a great deal of RAM memory (16 megabytes and above), a high-volume, fast central processor, a large fast hard disk (1.2 gigabytes and above), video accelerator cards (at least 1 megabyte of RAM memory is required for full colour) to sustain high-resolution full-colour displays on large SVGA monitors (15" and above), a high-speed modem (28.8 bps or faster), and a 16-bit audio card and speakers with a microphone for use with the audio processing card. All major manufacturers and all computer "species" have models in this category. Most such packages also have a CD-ROM drive which, although it does not pertain directly to Web use, may prove essential in future for the loading of software packages.

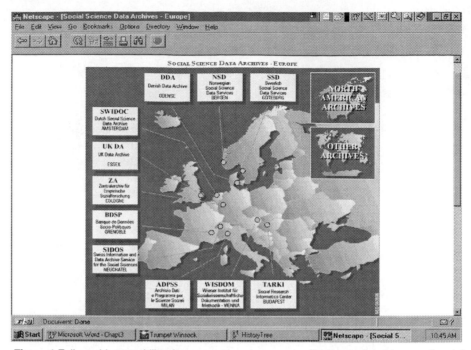

Figure 1 Full graphics capability gives you access to resources like this, a clickable map of social science data archives around the world. It can be found at http://www.nsd.uib.no/cessda/europe.html

Type B: Marginally capable multimedia computers. These tend to be older model computers with slower central processor chips, and lesser variants of the features possessed by Type A machines. They will be noticeably slower in operation, and they may not be capable of photographic rendition of full-colour images. Typically, university computer lab machines fall in this category. They also typically lack hard disks and audio cards and speakers (for obvious reasons) and may have no capability for storing data locally other than on a wholly inadequate floppy disk drive. Nevertheless, they can be useful for the research enterprise if their limitations are accepted. Printing the results of a search may also be problematic if the lab printer facility is heavily used. The lab may also lack the ability to reproduce graphic images on paper. Charts and graphs that you may have developed at a remote facility such as the CANSIM database (Statistics Canada's storehouse of hundreds of thousands of time series data) must then be stored for printing elsewhere and/or in another manner.

Type C: Text only monochrome display computers. This type of computer would have been typically found in computer labs and offices in 1990 and are still to be found in many small university and college labs. They are restricted to text-only operation and lack any means to present graphical or sound file elements. Images they acquire can however be saved for viewing on another more capable machine.

Saving and moving these files necessitates acquiring some skills in the UNIX operating system. Using the text-based Lynx Web client, they can be used for many text-oriented research activities. Usually, they connect by some means to a server which is running UNIX. The user is forced to employ difficult-to-learn UNIX text editors such as *Emacs* or *Pico* and e-mail programs such as *Elm* or *Pine*. Learning to use the UNIX file system is also difficult. However, those who wish to establish their own Web sites (and even those with high-quality multimedia computers) must of necessity operate within this UNIX environment while establishing their file structure and converting their documents and other files for public availability through the Net. For this reason, some passing acquaintance with UNIX becomes essential for all Web users sooner or later if they wish to be active contributors to Web content. With older text-only equipment, the point where UNIX knowledge becomes essential comes much sooner. There are a great many helpful resource files available to UNIX novices on the Web which will help you overcome this challenge.

Type D: The Rest. It is possible to conduct some semblance of systematic research activity with almost any old computer that has a modem and a potential connection to a server. Even if that server has only e-mail services and no link to the Web at all, it is possible to use e-mail to conduct Web searches and to further use e-mail to collect those resources without the use of a Web browser at all. Though a labourious process, it does work. Users without access even to Internet e-mail but who rather have some limited outflow system for e-mail such as the Fidonet system can follow this strategy. Though it cannot be recommended, if there is nothing else available to you it can be much better than nothing. You do however have to learn where to send you e-mail requests, where the gateways to the e-mail system are, and how your requests for files should be formatted. We will cover the techniques of this barebones access later on.

THE MINIMUM FUNCTIONAL PACKAGE

Notwithstanding the above section, in order for your system to work well in the multimedia environment (or at all) you need to have a minimum of hardware and software installed, configured and working well with each other. Here is a checklist of the materials and services that you need

You Need....

• a modem of sufficient speed to sustain your work (14,400 bits per second rate or faster) if you are not already connected in some way, for example through a local area network.

• an Internet service account: either a text-oriented account with menus, a UNIX shell account; or a SLIP/CSLIP/PPP account, or TIA/SLiRP connection. The latter types of software connect your machine directly to the Internet and are faster and thus superior. Commercial service providers will generally either provide the barebones software you need to get started or will tell you what you need and where to get it. Much of this software is free of charge and can be obtained on the Internet itself. Some examples of useful or required software are:

- terminal software (e.g. *Procomm*) for text-oriented work if your service provider provides a text-oriented account or a UNIX shell account.
- browser software (e.g. *Netscape*) for graphic-oriented Web browsing.
- a personal computer of sufficient quality to sustain the text and/or graphics activities you wish to carry out.
- helper programs (e.g. a *Winsock* for using a SLIP/CSLIP/PPP connection; a *Telnet* client, and other Netscape "helper" clients discussed in the technical appendix).
- printed instructions from your service provider on how to make and sustain a connection; and the telephone number of the customer service line which you can phone when problems arise. You might paste a copy of this telephone number on the corner of your monitor.
- If you intend to use Netscape or a comparable graphics browser, you will need to know the numeric (IP) address of a nameserver [a computer which keeps track of addresses of Internet hosts], a mail relay machine (SMTP) [a computer which forwards and receives e-mail on your behalf], and hopefully a newsgroup serving machine (NNTP) [a computer which forwards and receives USENET newsgroup postings on your behalf]. These addresses are necessary to send information requests, use e-mail, and to receive and post to newsgroups.
- If you intend to use the graphics-oriented World Wide Web, you will need a personal computer with a video card and monitor that has enough resolution and colour capacity to render the images accurately. This generally means that you should

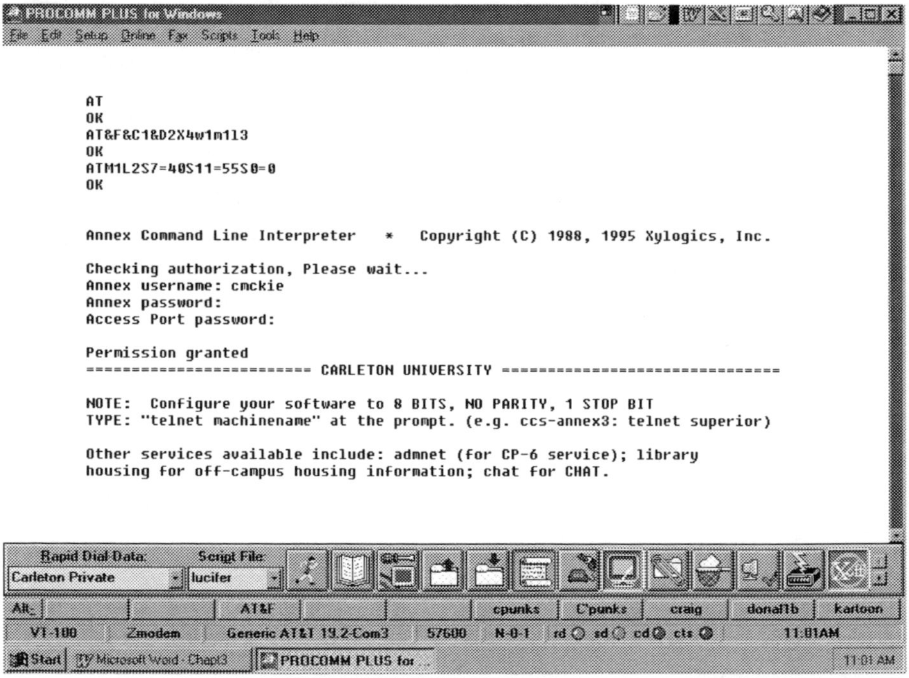

Figure 2 An example of a text-only session on a UNIX host using Procomm Plus for Windows as the terminal program.

have a video adapter card with 1 megabyte or more of video memory and an SVGA monitor. If you don't have this, then images received will be presented in false colour with poor resolution. With the appropriate video hardware, it is possible to get almost photographic quality resolution from Web sites.

WHAT'S THERE TO BE FOUND ?

The Web is not an orderly array of files or documents. It does not accumulate like a paper library, if only for the reason that files are constantly changed and updated. A file of a given name may not be the same file 5 minutes from now if it is revised in the meantime. This is particularly true of news and public affairs sites which provide wire service text or audio files from newscasts for instance. Whole chunks of information are changed and updated each hour or day and new streams of material added continuously. In addition, sites change their addresses and file structures as they grow and migrate. For this reason, there could never be the equivalent of a card catalogue of resources on the Web. The dynamism of the database must be taken into account in searching strategies and one must be prepared for surprises. Happily, there are numerous automated searching sites which are available to help you find what you want. Once having found what you want, you cannot assume that it will be there in exactly that form two months from now.

Obviously, this volatility also affects the citation process. The aim of traditional citation and bibliographic procedures is to ensure that future readers can locate source materials you cite and discuss in order that they can view these sources independently and form their own opinions if necessary. Since with Web resources these locations are impermanent you must provide your reader with rather more detailed information than was the case in the past as to what you found, where you found it, and when you found it in order that it can be searched for at a new location some time in the indefinite future. It is therefore apparent that you must take down this citation information at the time you see it initially and in full detail. A pop-up program for capturing information on the fly with cut-and-paste techniques is available as shareware. It is called BioBase; the data entry screen will be shown in a later chapter.

Some content, for example postings to the USENET newsgroups, vanishes in less than two weeks, though it is to some extent archived. Other material at stable Web sites may persist much longer though subtle changes and additions may be occurring unbeknownst to the average visitor. For this reason, citing a Web document as a source must done in such a way that the date of acquisition features prominently. Actually recovering a document as it was when you cited it, however, may be to all intents and purposes impossible because of the churn factor. This non-recoverability

erty issues as well such as copyright, privacy, and dangerous knowledge, which have as yet not been addressed at all as they emerge in the Web environment.

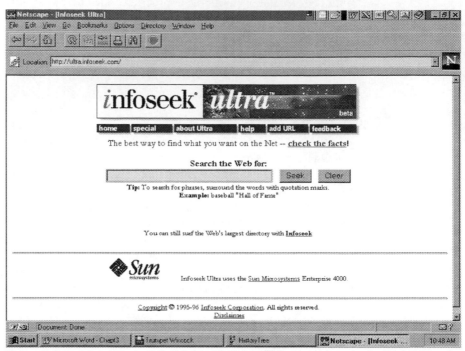

Figure 3 A partial answer to the question 'How do you find resources on the Web?' Search engines like Infoseek Ultra help you locate what you are searching for and allow your browser to follow links to the resources it has located.

We will now move on to questions of making your computer do the trick and actually help you work on and complete social science research projects.

SITES SHOWN IN THIS CHAPTER...

Social Science Data Archives - Europe   http://www.nsd.uib.no/cessda/europe.html
Infoseek Ultra   http://ultra.infoseek.com/
Research Engines for the Social Sciences http://www.carleton.ca/~cmckie/research.html

CHAPTER

THREE

The Basics: Connecting and Communicating

"Today's schoolchildren are growing up in a world that is linked through a global web of communications networks. They live in a society that produces information at an ever more rapid rate. Physical distance poses fewer barriers to communication than before, while instant access to relevant information becomes more and more crucial."

Ann Vedantham and Laura Breeden, **Internet Research**, vol.5, no.1, 1995, p.30.

Without a doubt, one of the single most useful research tools provided by the Internet is electronic mail or e-mail (pron. ee-mail). It allows you to communicate with anyone, anywhere in the world providing they also possess an e-mail account of their own, or one they can borrow for the purposes of sending and receiving messages.

ELECTRONIC MAIL

In its simplest terms, the process is one in which you compose a message to send to somebody using a text editor. A text editor can be something as large and ubiquitous as *WordPerfect* or *Word*, or a lesser known editor such as *Emacs* or *Pico* in the arcane world of the UNIX operating system; there are dozens of text editors available, many of them free of charge. Using *WordPerfect* or *Word* poses special difficulties for e-mail because they both want to use the 8th bit (or "high") bit which will *not* pass through the e-mail system. If you choose to use word processors for preparing electronic messages, you must save your messages in text (ASCII) format only in order to avoid the problems associated with formatting characters routinely used by word processors. This difficulty is discussed in the technical appendix under the heading MIME attachments. You can also use the Windows clipboard to cut and paste plain text into your mail program.

Once your text is composed, you then post this text to the e-mail address of the person through an e-mail gateway address. More often than not, this will be your Internet host computer running something called *SMTP* (Standard Mail Transport Protocol). But you are not limited to sending each text to one person. You can easily also send the same text to a group of persons, or a whole mailing list of persons whom you wish to read what you have written, even if you don't know their names and e-mail addresses, but only that they subscribe to a particular issue-centric listserv.

Once it arrives at its destination, your e-mail message is deposited in the incoming mailbox of the recipient to await pickup and reading. The incoming mailbox is just a file to which e-mail messages are added. These messages will in turn be read by the recipient at his or her convenience using other aspects of their mailer program, aspects which deal with the reading and filing of incoming messages. If everyone were logged on to the Internet all the time, an electronic mailbox might not be necessary. But realistically, most of us are not logged on all the time and the messages must be stored pending your turning your attention to reading the mail.

There is nothing mysterious about the process of writing the message. People have been doing this for centuries to exchange views, sentiments and basic information across distance. The great difference between e-mail and regular correspondence lies in the fact that delivery is virtually instantaneous and the recipient need not be logged in or even awake to receive the message when it arrives. The e-mail transaction is therefore asynchronous (as between sender and receiver) but its instantaneity means that there can be many exchanges of information in a single day. The exchange process becomes more a dialogue and less a speech. And this *process is ideal to support research inquiries*. You are not restricted to e-mailing people you know; you must only find out what the intended recipient's address is. There are utilities to help you do this.

In order to send someone e-mail, you must first obtain the e-mail address of the person you wish to contact. The simplest way to do this is to phone them and ask; you need only do this once. There are other methods of finding out the correct address but they are not always successful.

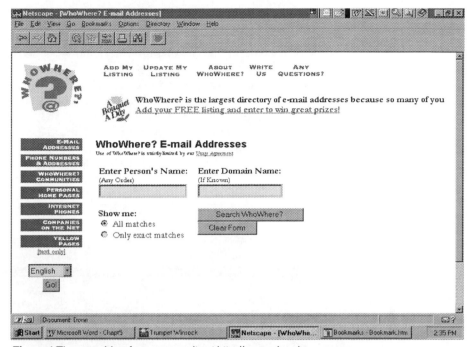

Figure 1 The searching-for-persons site at http://www.whowhere.com

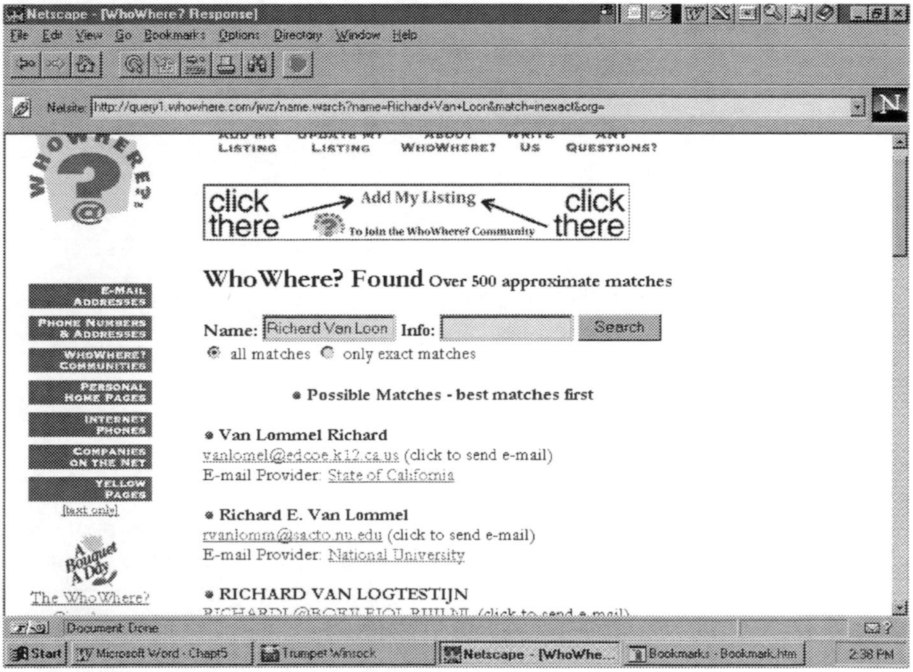

Figure 2 Searching nowhere.com for the mythical Richard Van Loon comes up with 500 near misses which you can peruse in case any of them is the person you want.

There are three broad categories of e-mail text handling software tools:

1. **UNIX e-mail** and editor programs (such as *Elm* and *Pine*, and their companion editors *Emacs* and *Pico*). These have been in existence for years and were in use long before e-mail became a standard tool of researchers. They are, being UNIX tools, difficult to learn and unforgiving of ignorance. Nevertheless, many thousands of research professionals communicate this way routinely. It is not impossible. A short exposition on UNIX e-mail will be found later in this chapter.

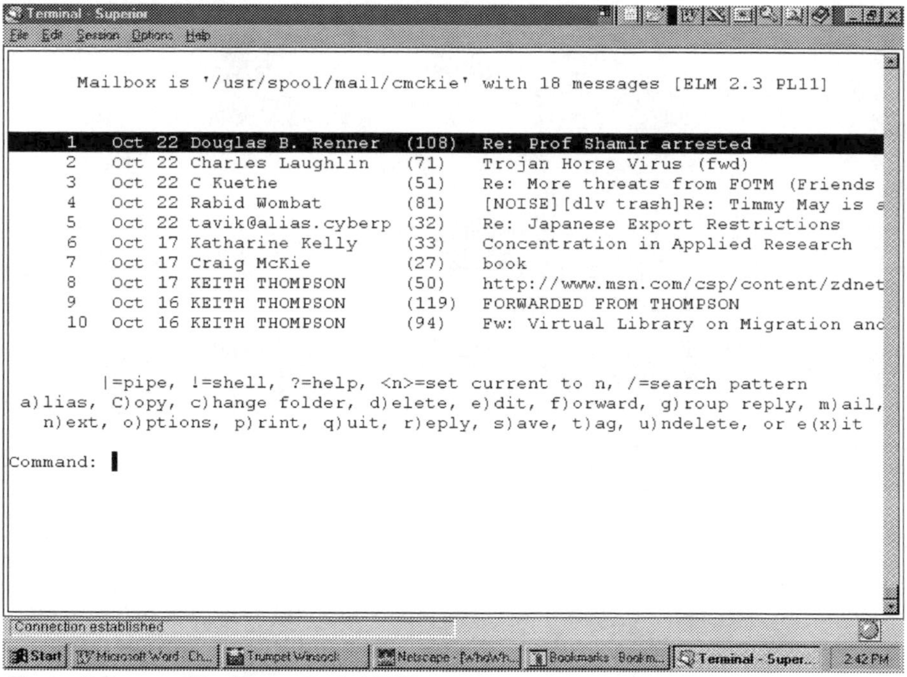

Figure 3 Screen of the Elm mailer in UNIX

2. **TCP/IP based** programs for e-mail and newsgroup management such as *Forte Agent, Eudora, Pegasus* and the internal *Netscape* mail and news facilities. Of these programs, only those that have a cost attached to them can be considered full-featured (including for instance MIME attachment decoding discussed in a later section in this chapter). Several of these retail software products have reduced capability shareware versions such as *Forte Free Agent* and *Eudora Lite*. Overall, the retail full-featured programs are without a doubt the best, easiest to use and most powerful communications tools available for posting and reading purposes. They have fully manipulable address books with alias lists for group postings, and in the

case of Agent, full filtering of incoming newsgroup articles and e-mail to automate the disposal of e-mail and posts from unwanted sources).

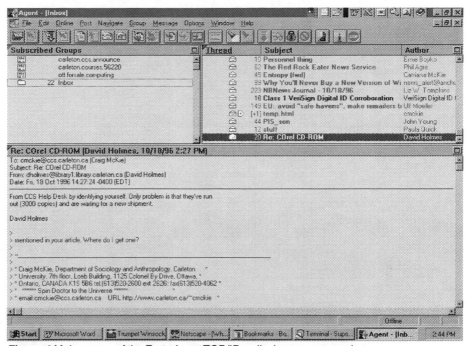

Figure 4 Main screen of the Forte Agent TCP/IP mailer/newsgroup reader.

3. Most **freenets** provide a simple editor/mailer system in which all the functions you need are integrated in one complete package bundled together with a simple file storage system.

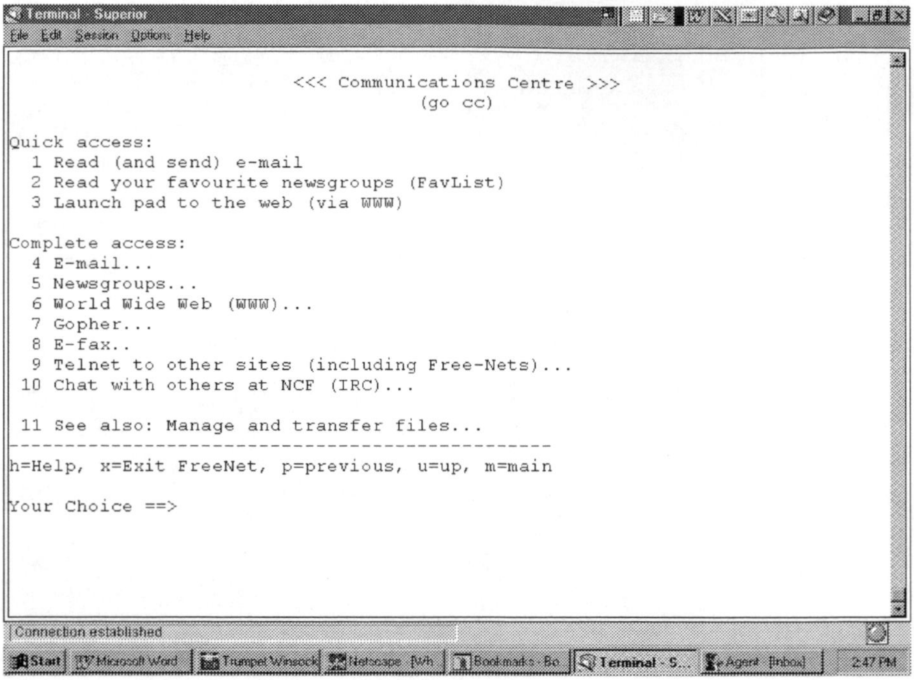

Figure 5 Mail screen of the National Capital Freenet.

If you are purchasing a connection from a commercial service provider, it is very likely that you will be given a shareware electronic mail editor/mailer such as *Pegusus* or *Eudora Lite* to use. While you do have to configure them to suite your purposes, they perform well in most circumstances. You might however wish to spend a modest sum and upgrade to the full retail version of *Eudora Pro* or *Agent* for instance. You will the notice the difference in flexibility and ease of use.

Almost any text editor will allow you to compose an e-mail message made up exclusively of text and numbers. Providing this message is saved in a plain text format file with no control or formatting characters (such as *WordPerfect* and *Word* routinely supply unless you tell them not to by saving in ASCII text format), the file is then sent to a mailer program such as *Elm* or *Pine* in the UNIX system using your terminal program (such as Procomm or one of its variants or HyperTerminal in Windows95 for instance). It can also be cut from your word processor and then pasted into the message body of a *Eudora* or *Pegasus* or other similar TCP/IP mailer message which is probably the simplest thing to do. The message will then be transmitted to another user of Internet e-mail providing a valid address is supplied. If for any reason the address is invalid, it will be returned to you with a note saying why it was rejected.

Simple spelling errors in addresses account for the greater proportion of these "bounces". For this reason, a good address book facility in your e-mail program is a great boon. Good ones capture addresses from incoming e-mail messages to add to your address book. That way, errors due to mistyping tend not to occur.

In everyday practice, once you are familiar with the routine, you compose your message *within the mailer program,* or using a text editor of your choice *outside the mailer program* if you wish and then somehow paste the text into a mailer "envelope", and then you transmit the finished message by telling your mailer program (sometimes referred to as a mailer *daemon*) to send it to a valid address via your Internet host. The host then sends your message on its way in digital form via the electronic highways of the Internet as a series of *TCP/IP* packets. [The mechanics of transmission of these information packets are discussed in the Technical Appendix.] Note that *there is no confidentiality nor guarantee of privacy whatsoever with electronic mail*. If you want such privacy, you *must* encrypt your e-mail using a robust encryption algorithm. The topic of e-mail privacy will be dealt with in sparing detail in Chapter Fifteen.

In general, if you are dealing with a commercial Internet service provider, you should expect to be provided with the software you need to carry out routine activities such as electronic mail. If you have acquired UNIX shell account service at your college or university, you may well have to learn how to use a UNIX editor such as *Emacs* or *Pico*, and a mailer program such as *Elm* or *Pine*. In general, *Pico* with *Pine* is the easiest combination to use if you are just beginning. While simple text-oriented menu-run frontend systems for UNIX are becoming more common, they are by no means yet widespread in academic circles.

As mentioned before, e-mail messages may be composed *within* a mail program (examples: *Elm, Pine*) using a text editor which comes with it; or messages can be composed on a host machine (the service provider's machine which intermediates between your personal computer and the Internet) using its text editor first (if there is such a facility at your host) and then submitted as a file to the mailer. Or messages can be composed from within World Wide Web browsers like *Netscape* that have a text editor built in and then sent on to the mailer network computer providing you know its name or its IP address. The mailer program (or *daemon*) on your service provider's host communicates with the Internet using a protocol called SMTP or simple mail transport protocol.

Note that in some applications such as those offered by *freenets* or other local non-profit community Internet access services, the mailer program may be customized to appear slightly simpler for the user than the examples beneath. Freenets exist in many communities across North America; you can find out if one is available to you by phoning the computer center of any local university or college and asking if there is one in your community local calling area. Some Internet service providers and most freenets offer a customized and simplified text editor to use with their mailer systems. These may not correspond exactly to what is described here but they will do the same things, albeit in slightly different ways. However it may be composed, the text portion of the message is just simple text. It is also possible to e-mail encrypted text messages for decoding by the recipient, encrypted program files, encrypted pictures and sounds, and indeed virtually any file which can take digital form (reduced to binary code) providing it is properly prepared for transmission. But doing these "extras" requires more preparation than simple text e-mail. Thus, if you have a WordPerfect or Microsoft Word file with text markup "tags" in it (in other words the "normal" WordPerfect or Word file), you may, if suitable encoding preparation is done, send it by e-mail too, as a MIME attachment, described in the technical appendix.

Once composed, the message must be correctly addressed (i.e. to a valid e-mail address). The mailer then makes and places an "envelope" of origination and destination information to enfold your text. Such labeling information is essential for transmission but it is supplied automatically for you and requires no work on your part. This is one of the main jobs of a mailer program such as *Elm* or *Pine* or the mail forwarding feature in *Netscape*. Other standalone (and free) mail programs like *Eudora* or *Pegasus,* both of which assume a TCP/IP connection is present and working, can do the job too. All of these mailer programs provide "envelopes" for the transmission of text messages and most also receive incoming mail addressed to you, display it for you to read, file messages and/or delete them as the case may be.

If you are using electronic mail with a graphics-oriented mail program such as *Eudora* or *Pegasus*, it will be quite clear what you should do to compose and send or to read incoming mail even if you have never seen the program before. The graphic interface they use contains extensive help files and examples in addition to menus of common task requests. Either program should be easy for the novice to use. However, if you are using a UNIX shell account or even an account on a freenet, the process becomes a little more difficult since a more hands-on approach is necessary.

RESEARCH APPLICATIONS USING E-MAIL

There are several ways in which e-mail can be used for research purposes. The first and most obvious way is to send e-mail queries directly to persons with knowledge to share. When e-mail was new and access restricted, the volume of e-mail messages was low enough that you might reasonably expect a response every time. Unfortunately, this is no longer the case and many persons are now highly selective in which e-mail items they choose to read. For this reason, it is very important that the subject line contain the essence of your message. In many respects, the hope of getting a constructive response now rests on the clarity of the subject line.

Or, you can locate relevant listservs and subscribe so that the stream of queries and information from the listserv will flow to your e-mail account. You can participate actively in discussion on the listservs and become part of the exchange process. As a working example, there are several social science listservs operating in the world (such as METHODS-L and teachsoc). There are various sites on the Web which maintain lists of listservs by subject and you could consult one of these lists by going to my research resources page (at **http://www.carleton.ca/~cmckie/ research.html**) and finding the link for the Liszt list of listservs (or go directly to it at http://www.Liszt.com/) for example.

Alternatively, if you have a specific question to ask, you can either post directly or indirectly to a suitable USENET newsgroup (covered in Chapter Seven) and you will probably receive some responses if the question is not completely offbase. If you have no access to the newsgroups themselves, you might ask that responses to questions be e-mailed directly to your account and not to the whole newsgroup; or else use the service at http://www.reference.com to receive the newsgroup postings by e-mail.

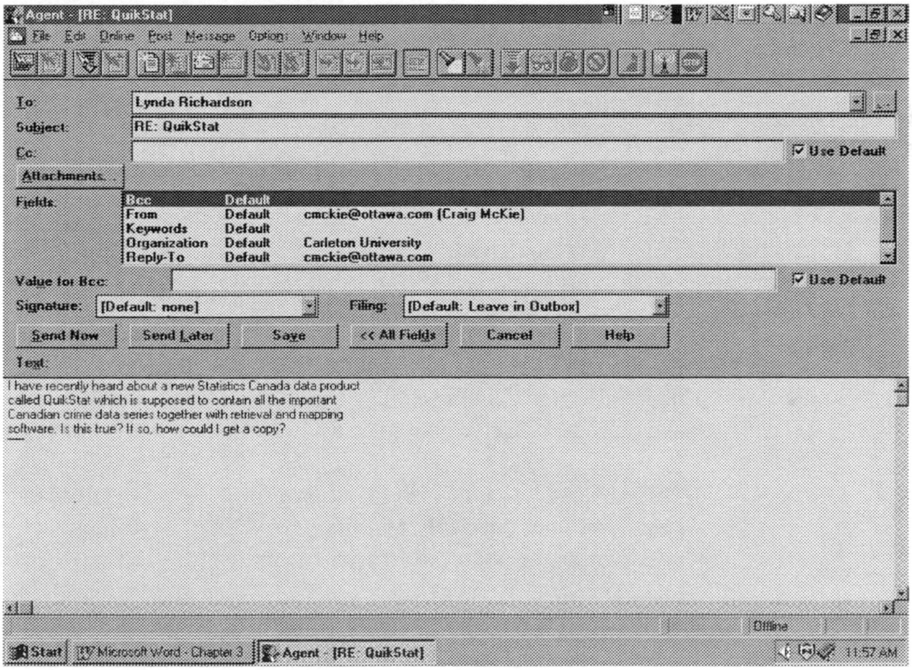

Figure 6 A typical e-mail request to find research resources.

SOME SIGNS OF TROUBLE

Whenever you are doing anything with the Internet, a certain part of your life is a little less secure than it was before you started. For instance, the first time you post to a newsgroup, your e-mail address will be added to the register of such addresses in conjunction with the posting. Further, from the information on your sig file, strangers may be able to reconstruct some elements of your life such as your likely

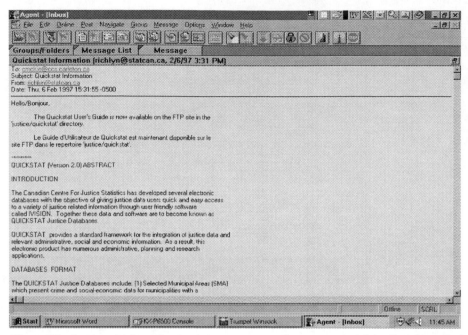

Figure 7 And a prompt informative (and also pre-prepared) response containing the information I requested.

phone number and maybe your street address and postal code by consulting one of the North America-wide phone number, name and street address concordance CD-ROM products available for less than $100 at your local computer store. Even without the CD-ROM, it is possibly to use databases on the Web to find much the same material. Once in possession of this information, credit reports are only a phone call and a modest service charge away.

This means that you a) could get unwanted e-mail from strangers who know more about you than you feel comfortable with, and b) some phone follow-up activity is possible. For these reasons, some people on the Net have chosen to disguise their real identities by use of pseudonyms, aliases and anonymizing remailers. Note the recommendations concerning signature (sig) files in the Technical Appendix. It could be that your sig file inadvertently gives away enough information so that much of the rest can be filled in.

Probably nothing of this sort will ever happen to you. But it is not imprudent however to consider these issues before you make up the contents of your sig file, or send your first posting to the newsgroup or listserv. The tools have incredible potential; but the advance does not come without a certain cost in personal privacy.

The movement to universal e-mail has now moved past the initial freenet stage. Free dial-up accounts were for a period of time in 1996 available to each and every U.S. resident who agreed to have paid advertising including in their messages. A company called Freemark Communications made the offer to all U.S. residents with access to a computer with a modem in September 1996. As their press release put it, "We've created the world's simplest e-mail, making it easy for anyone to take advantage of [the] benefits, and the fact that the service is free is a huge advantage for a company's bottom line." While Freemark soon went out of business because of a lack of advertising revenue, others have taken its place based not on free dial-up access which is available through the freenets, but on Web sites which offer free e-mail accounts.[1] There are no charges of any kind nor is there a limit as to the number of messages sent or received.

Another innovation is the permanent e-mail address. One of the problems with e-mail in general is that when you leave a school or a job behind, you also leave behind access to your e-mail account. One way around this is to have a generic e-mail address which will redirect incoming e-mail to your new e-mail address. When you move, you change the redirection to your new account and the transition is painless and seamless from the user's point of view, and more importantly from the view of your correspondents. One such service is offered free of charge in the Ottawa, Ontario region by a local service provider whose announced intention is for everyone in the Ottawa area to have a personal e-mail address which is stable over time. You can see the terms of this service and view the application form at http://www.ottawa.com. It also allows individuals who are working independently in their homes to have an apparent corporate or institutional identity. For instance, you could set up an address of convenience as MegaCorp@ottawa.com and all mail sent to that address would end up in your personal freenet account elsewhere. This sort of public representation of identity can be manipulated and is in and of itself an interesting social phenomenon. Using forwarding like this, you could have incoming e-mail bounced through several accounts effectively masking your identity; and if one of the bounces left the country, say to a freenet account in Cleveland, Ohio, it would be very difficult for anyone to follow the electron trail to your basement.

We now move on to Part II of this book which is concerned with basic communications and information distribution systems which can be put to very good use by social science students of all sorts.

Sites shown in this Chapter...

Whowhere?   http://www.whowhere.com
The National Capital Freenet   telnet.ncf.carleton.ca

Notes

[1] See http://www.usa.net for instance.

ROUTINE USE OF THE WEB FOR COMMUNICATING AND LOCATING RESOURCES

The Internet began as an entirely text-based system using UNIX commands to move files around the world. A set of software utilities which worked on a text-only basis was developed to facilitate this form of communication. In this Part, we will review some of the more basic tools for research work using the Web. Some of the earlier text-based tools will be mentioned since they still work and on occasion they must be used directly. For the most part now, their operations are subsumed within the normal operations of browser software such as Netscape. Some readers will be able to try them out in their older standalone form (and "older" in this context means a couple of years ago) if they have access to a UNIX shell account, while others who have an exclusively browser-based service will not. The important thing is however that all of these text-based utilities continue to appear as functions in the graphics Web environment though many are now hidden from view in a graphics browser like Netscape.

Hidden or not, they are still important, particularly the *Telnet* command for remote computing. It remains one of the single most useful of the Internet tools and it can be used in primitive text-based systems and in graphics-oriented Web browsers as well.

After the initial chapter in this Part on the basic utilities, we will move on to the characteristics of the new library facilities on campus, considerations of the search engines of the Internet (in Chapter Six) and then the Internet "broadcasting" utilities such as USENET in Chapter Seven.

CHAPTER FOUR

Internet Utilities: Basic

"There is little fundamental difference between the way we teach today and the way we did one hundred and fifty years ago. The use of technology is almost at the same level. In fact, according to a recent survey by the U.S. Department of Education, 84 percent of America's teachers consider only one type of information technology absolutely "essential": a photo copier with an adequate paper supply."

Nicholas Negroponte, **being digital,** N.Y., Knopf, 1995, p. 220

The central tool for research, as for other purposes on the Web, is the Internet browser, now usually Netscape Navigator or Microsoft Internet Explorer. These tools have within them subtools for looking at Web pages, playing sounds, showing pictures, in addition to reading USENET newsgroups (the subject of a later chapter) and sending and receiving e-mail. In the case of the latter two dimensions, the tools provided are rudimentary and many Web users prefer to acquire other specialized software tools to deal with these activities such as the TCP/IP e-mail programs described in the previous chapter and in more detail in the E-Mail Details section of the Technical Appendix.

TOOLS FOR THE WEB

In order to use a browser, you have to have additional TCP/IP software which forms the communications channel between your browser and the Web, often through a modem and over a telephone line if you are doing your work from home. The Technical Appendix contains additional details on how this software is configured to work for you. TCP/IP software such as Trumpet Winsock or the TCP/IP software which is shipped as part of Windows95 are often difficult to install and debug. But in this chapter, we will assume that these matters have been worked out and that your browser and its attendant software components such as a *Telnet* program or a terminal program such as *NetTerm* are installed and operating correctly. If they are not you may wish to refer to the Technical Appendix for assistance.

By and large now, the browser software will look after tasks such as acquiring new software from FTP archive sites, which only a couple of years ago required the use of specialized tools and a lot of arcane knowledge about how the Internet works. Similarly, the browsers can deal with the older generation of Gopher information sites without any difficulty at all. All in all, most of the early generation of Internet programs and functions are now subsumed in the graphical browser's list of capabilities. Doubtless, though, some students will still be using text-based browsers such as *Lynx* which, though text-based, have much of the functionality of the graphics browsers.

Having said this however, browsers are not limitless in their abilities and often need "helper" software to perform the activities necessary to the research enterprise. Helper software for instance is needed to view various kinds of files one is likely to find on the Web. One example of this is the *Acrobat* Reader necessary to view documents in .pdf format. These documents retain all the font and graphics characteristics, such as colour, from an original printed document. The Acrobat reader is made available from many sites by the Adobe company which makes and sells the software to actually construct .pdf documents (which is called the *Acrobat Distiller*). Below is an example of an Acrobat document.

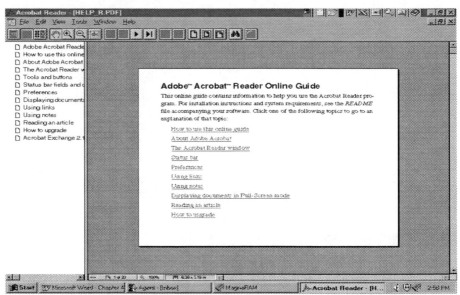

Figure 1 One example of an Acrobat .pdf document shown by the Acrobat viewer, in this case the Acrobat manual itself. It can easily be printed out on paper if desired as can any Acrobat document.

What the Internet does best is to move copies of large files around the world at high speed. There is no inherent limit to the number of copies that can be made from one "original" nor is there degradation in the subsequent copying of copies in contrast to what happens in the physical photocopying process. In the case of Acrobat documents, the literal appearance of the original page is also preserved complete with any and all pictures or graphics which might appear on a given page, right down to the correct colour scheme. On the Web the process of copying and moving is free of charge to the end user. Where exactly this leaves copyright, attribution rules, and other assorted holdovers of the traditional print culture is not at all clear.

In order for this distribution of knowledge to occur however, a user has to make a syntactically correct request for a known file at a known location on the Web. When Netscape or another similar browser does the task, the mechanics for requesting and receiving the file are buried beneath the surface and you don't see what is happening. However, this underlying process is essentially the same as the older manual process of acquiring files using the FTP (File Transfer Protocol) tool but the user does not see the commands being issued and fulfilled. In the end, the file or resource requested is deposited on the computer you are using and you may do with it what you wish.

Though you use FTP indirectly for the acquisition of files, it is in fact an operating arm of the Web browsers. What the browser software does in practice is to issue FTP requests on your behalf, looking after the syntax of the requests for you so that you do not have to worry about dealing with the arcane FTP command set. So, FTP plays a critical role in the operation of the Internet though it is less visibly present as time goes by and more of the control of the syntax of commands is taken over by the more sophisticated user products such as the Web browser[1]. Most sites keep detailed logs of who is browsing through their facilities, at what time and for what purpose. In order to assure true anonymity, you must "launder" your request through an anonymizing site. This step might just be justified when you pick up your copy of the Anarchist's Cookbook for instance. It might just forestall a visit from men in dark suits in the future.

USING ARCHIE TO FIND A FILE

As the holdings of FTP sites multiplied geometrically on the Internet a few years ago, it became necessary to have a tool which would search out the location of files for you. The tool devised at McGill University to do this was called *Archie* (styled roughly after 'archive searcher' but taking advantage of the name of the well-known comic book character[2]). The Archie search is specific for a particular file, program or other digital resource of known name which is suspected to exist on an FTP site somewhere in the world. The command line version of Archie is available to you to use if, for instance, your service providing host runs an Archie client for you. The syntax is very simple: **archie somefile**. If you do not have an Archie client available, but are running a TCP/IP application in support of your browser, you may acquire your own archie client software free of charge from an FTP site. Alternatively, you may Telnet to a remote Archie client or better still, use one of the forms-based Archie clients with a web browser such as Lynx.

EXAMPLE OF AN ARCHIE SEARCH.....

{yourhost:1} archie lviewp1a.zip

Host ftp.bhp.com.au
    Location: /internet/www/clients/ms-windows/mosaic/viewers
        FILE -r—r—r—   304843 Jan 11 14:02 lviewp1a.zip

Host ftp.deakin.edu.au
    Location: /pub/Web/clients/ms-windows/mosaic/viewers
        FILE -r—r—r—   304843 Jan 11 03:02 lviewp1a.zip
    Location: /pub/Web/helpers/ms-windows
        FILE -r—r—r—   304843 Mar 11 07:37 lviewp1a.zip

The Archie search will, if successful, return a number of locations where the file you want can be found. You may then acquire a copy of that file with your browser using the addressing information you have. For instance, you could supply the following URL to obtain a copy of Lview with your browser: ftp://ftp.deakin.edu.au/pub/Web/ clients/ms-windows/mosaic/viewers/lviewp1a.zip. Although this site is in Australia, the browser will obtain the copy for you with some speed. You would then have to take whatever steps are necessary to install the software on your computer.

If you have a Web browser such as Lynx or Netscape, you can use a much easier form of Archie called *Archieplex,* which operates entirely from forms. There is such a site at the following address: http://www.lerc.nasa.gov. Here, you can use the forms both to specify the name of the file you are looking for, some other options such as case-insensitivity in spelling, and where you wish your search to be carried out. Here is what the screen looks like when searching for a later version of the same program, Lviewp1b.zip.

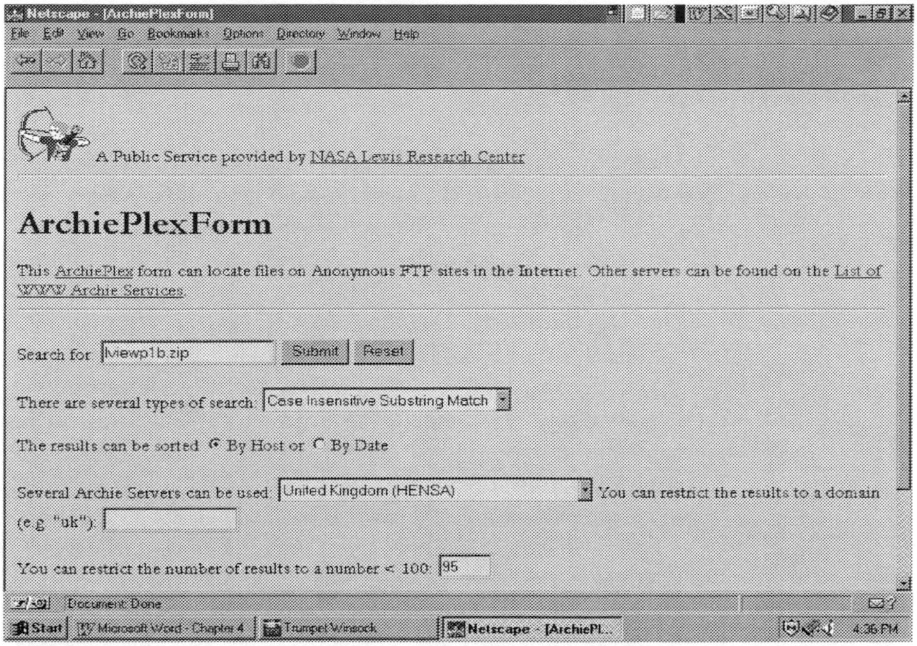

Figure 2 The primary search screen for Archieplex at NASA. Note that you can control many aspects of the search with this query form, including the sites chosen for the search. This site is very busy during normal working hours in North America.

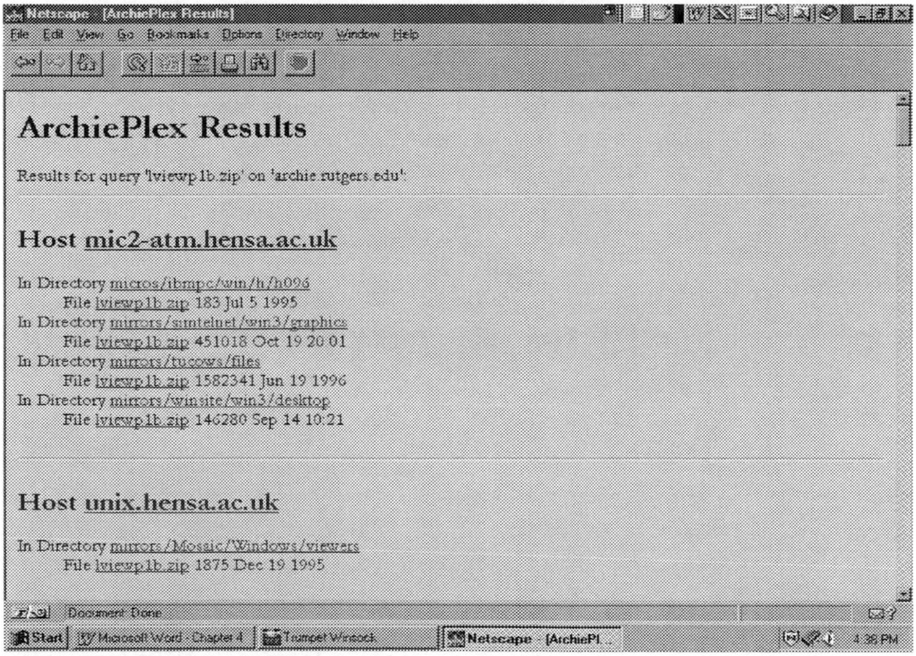

Figure 3 The results of the search showing the locations where the requested file can be obtained by FTP.

BASIC PROCESS FOR TELNET

Another fundamental tool of the Internet is *Telnet*. Although the graphics browsers have become more and more prominent in the set of tools used on the Web, the older Telnet tool is still indispensable for many applications. It can be used from within your graphics browser if you tell it where to find the appropriate software in the "preferences" menu. Telnet allows you to establish a direct text-based connection to a remote computer in order to become a local user at that site. Thus, if you have an account at Site A and another account at Site B, you may logon at Site A and Telnet to your account at Site B, logon there and use the second account as if you were actually sitting in a computer lab at Site B. By Telnetting to a site and logging in, you acquire as many privileges as any other local user. The advantages of this arrangement are obvious. If you are traveling and wish to read your e-mail or do work on your home computer account, provided you can borrow an account at the site you happen to be at whilst traveling, you can Telnet to your home account and do anything you would normally do with your home account. Also, if you have more than one account, you may telnet from one account to the other account no matter where it is in the world, allowing a certain independence from local laws and ordinances.

There are also Telnet sites at which you may logon as "guest". Notable amongst these are the community freenets which now exist across North America. Other public sites include the catalogues of many major libraries (see the next chapter on library use) and the Weather Underground site at telnet://madlab.sprl.umich.edu:3000. Though these direct uses of the Telnet tool are important, more and more the Telnet operation is 'buried' in the operation of other tools such as a Web browser. Part of the setup of a browser program is to let the browser know where it can find a Telnet program when it needs it. If you don't have a copy, your first task would therefore be to acquire one.

EXAMPLE OF TELNETTING TO A SITE WHICH ALLOWS "GUEST" LOGONS......

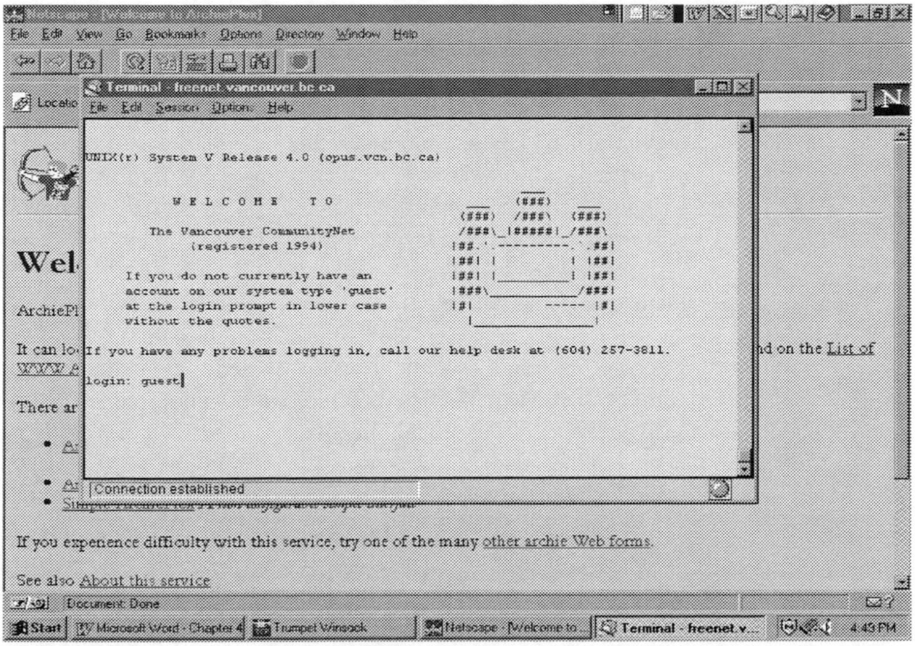

Figure 4 Telnetting to the Vancouver freenet from within Netscape using the Telnet client which comes with Winsock. Note that I log in as "guest" since I don't have an account at this freenet.

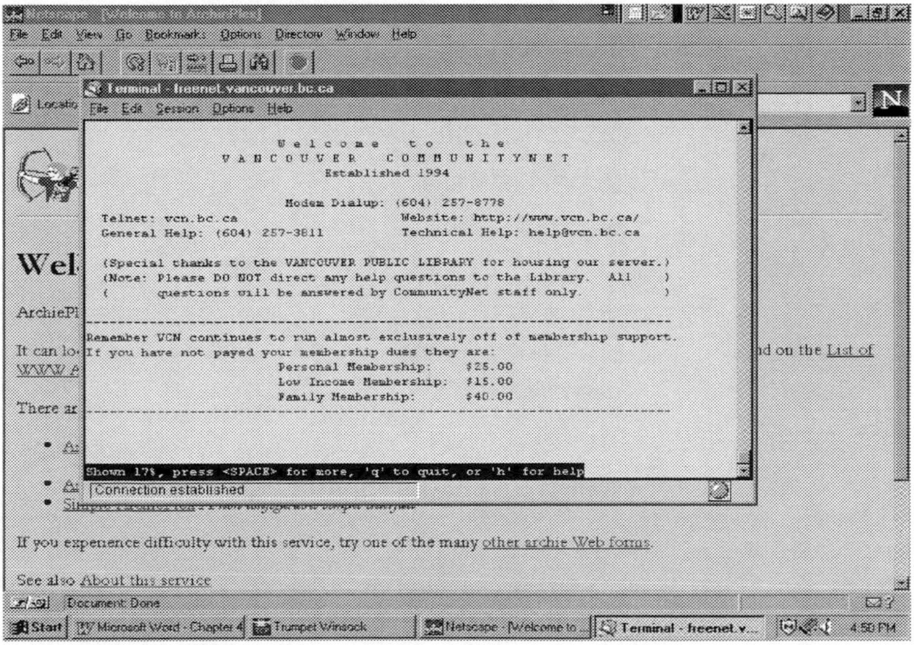

Figure 5 I have now logged into the Vancouver freenet as a guest. Since it is a text-based service, all interactions will be typed though I can copy and paste text to the Windows clipboard if I want to.

Whether operating *Telnet* from a UNIX shell account or from within a graphics browser like Netscape, the basic commands of Telnet are simple and straightforward. You *Telnet (address)* and once you "arrive", you are told that ^] is the escape character. This means that if you get stuck and want to break the connection, you should hold down the **Ctrl** key while pressing the] key at the same time. Having done this, you can then **quit** the session, **close** a connection, or **display** Telnet status information. If a remote Telnet site does not respond to your request to connect, your Telnet client will eventually give up trying and tell you that it has.

Instead of using the Telnet tool directly, you may also use the *Gopher* tool (a direct ancestor of the Web) to Telnet, and of course you may also use a Lynx browser or Netscape to Telnet as well, always provided there is the requisite Telnet client software available to it. A copy of Telnet, for instance, comes in the Winsock package of software but you can use other pieces of software such as NetTerm (which will operate either in text mode or as a TCP/IP client) and *Ewan* a TCP/IP Telnet client. In the Lynx text-only Web browser client, you first type **g** and then type in the Telnet address you wish to visit (such as *telnet://freenet.vancouver.bc.ca* as in the previous example).

HERE IS ANOTHER EXAMPLE OF TELNET, THIS TIME TEXT-BASED AND TO BOOKSTACKS INC., A BOOKSTORE IN CLEVELAND...

{yourhost:1}
Trying 192.148.240.9 ...
Connected to books.com.
Escape character is '^]'.

Book Stacks Unlimited, Inc.
Cleveland, Ohio USA

The On-Line Bookstore

Modem   : (216)861-0469
Internet : telnet books.com

Enter your FULL Name (e.g SALLY M. SMITH) : John Smith
Calling from (CITY, STATE, COUNTRY)? Moose Junction

BOOK STACKS Welcomes John Smith
Calling From Moose Junction

Is this correct (Y/N)? Y
Please enter a Password to be used for future logons.

Each time you logon you should use the same name and password.
Your password may be up to 8 characters long. You may use any printable
characters (a-z, 0-9, !@#,./<>?;':"-$%*()_+). UPPER and lower case
characters are the same.

Note: Only ******* will display during subsequent logons.

Your password? ******
Re-enter New password to verify: ******

_____   NEW   USER   INFORMATION
_____

ONLINE BOOKSTORE

Book Stacks Unlimited, Inc. is an online Bookstore and Readers' Conference
System accessible by modem or Internet from anywhere in the world.

You can search for books by author, title, ISBN, or keyword, or just browse
the 'shelves' by subject. Pick the titles you want, place your order, and we
will ship them directly to your home or office. Currently, we have over
240,000 titles.

PHOTOS AND FILM CLIPS

Part of what the Web has to offer you is the ability to view still photos and film clips which are downloaded from the Web and viewed from within your browser, or with the assistance of browser helper programs. There are many different formats for storing and shipping graphics files on the Web (and this is true of audio files and real-time broadcasts as well). Browser software can handle still photos and exhibits such as maps very well with built-in software. If however you want more control over the way stills are presented you might wish to obtain a copy of a shareware program called *Lview*. It handles many more types of file formats than does browser software and in addition it is able to convert the exhibits from one format to another, resize the graphics and otherwise modify the files you acquire. Since the program is shareware, it seems like a good idea to get a copy.

The situation with respect to film or video clips is more confused. There are several prominent formats including *.mpeg*, the most prevalent. In general, the browser will want you to acquire and install helper software such as Mpegplay and QuickTime programs to view the clips you acquire. The quality of reproduction of these short movies varies enormously, as a result of differences in the quality of the source and from hardware differences in the computers you choose to look at them with. Contemporary computers tend now to come with full-screen video reproduction abilities, but only for certain file formats. A bit of study, acquisition of special player software, and installation by you are often necessary before you can play all the video files that are available on the Web.

COOKIES

Both Netscape and Microsoft Internet Explorer employ cookies. These are short information files which are exchanged between your browser and a remote host in order to simplify and validate identification of visitors and their preferences. If for instance you have an account at a Web site, say with your tastes in information already specified, the cookie material deposited on your computer will serve to identify you and your tastes the next time you visit without you having to type all the information in again. Cookies are time limited. They can last for a short period of time (6 hours on the *New York Times* site) or can last months. They can be modified with new information by "setting" a new cookie on your computer should your account information or your tastes change.

Initially when cookies first appeared, some concerns regarding confidentiality were raised since in effect, you are allowing a remote computer to deposit a file on your machine. These security concerns have now been dealt with to some extent and Netscape, for instance, now warns you when it has been asked to receive a cookie file from a remote Web site unless you tell it not to in the preferences menu.

When cookies reside on your computer, they can be inspected with a text editor by you or anyone else with access to your computer. Since account names and passwords often appear in cookies in plain English, it is wise to keep this type of exposure in mind when acquaintances or strangers use your computer. As a matter of practical necessity however, many Web sites now *require* you to accept their cookies in order to gain access to their resources. The plus side of this situation is that you don't have to go through the typing exercise on subsequent return visits. The negatives have to do with compromising your privacy to some degree.

Predictably, the author of the Cookie Monster software which orchestrates the transfer of information cookies, Nicolas Berloquin, has received demands from the Children's Television Workshop that he change the name of his program[3].

HELPER SOFTWARE

Throughout this book we refer to "helper" programs which are more often than not free software distributed via the Web from specific shareware sites such as http://www.shareware.com (the Virtual Software Library), Jumbo shareware [http://www.jumbo.com] or Ziff Davis [http://www.downloadnow.com]. At these sites, you specify your operating system (Windows 3.1, Windows95, Macintosh etc.) and then search for the specific name of a program you want, or search under functional headings for the choices available. Once selected, the software is sent to you via the *FTP* utility (file transfer protocol) in some fashion or another. Netscape has the capability to do this internal to its own operation (it is buried as functional code in

Netscape, but only for downloading and not uploading, at least in early versions) but you can also operate a version of *FTP* [e.g. *winftp*] on your own. To some extent, this is a chicken and egg problem since you have to have some means of doing *FTP* in order to get other versions of the program.

A shareware terminal program called *NetTerm* is particularly useful in this respect. It can act both as a terminal program working with a modem in your personal computer and also as a TCP/IP terminal program. It contains a *FTP* client plus the protocols necessary to support most kinds of file transfers (e.g. zmodem). It can be customized with respect to screen colour and text colour (though learning how to do this is a bit of a hit and miss affair) and it can be set to connect to a remote host with a single click of a button. There are versions available for both Windows 3.1 and Windows95 and they tend to look and work the same. I have had problems, however, using NetTerm on computers with high speed Pentium processors (typed characters tend not to be portrayed accurately).

Additionally, you need archive decompression programs to take apart the shareware packages after they arrive. Practically all files available for downloading on the Web are packed and compressed in some fashion. Some methods are unique to the UNIX operating environment while others, for instance, *zip* and *unzip* exist happily in most operating systems. Among the programs which are useful or essential to have are *Pkunzip* (for taking apart zip archives) or its easier-to-use cousin *Winzip, Stuffit Expander* (which reconstitutes .sit and .hqx archives, which are in the main of Macintosh origin though someone may send you a word processor file you can use in the format at some point), *uudecode* (which unpacks uuencoded files) and possibly *Arj* for .arj archive files as well. A program called *Keyview* contains all of these utilities and many more; there is a license fee for using it but it may prove very useful to have, since in a sense it covers all your bases in a single easy-to-use package. Note that some archive files may have been both zipped (to reduce their size and combine several member files into one archive) and uuencoded (to create an e-mailable file).

When you wish to reverse the process and send somebody else a group of files, the process essentially is run in reverse to create a single package to be conveyed to your correspondent.

You may notice that some shareware programs come in two versions, the ordinary version and the "lite" version. The "lite" versions are usually stripped down editions of the full program, or versions in which some features are disabled. These are intended to demonstrate the virtues of the full program, use of which usually entails the payment of a license fee. You may also encounter beta versions of programs not yet fully released. They are generally free of charge but may not have been fully proven. You are allowed to use these versions without charge but they may contain a stale date past which they will no longer work at all.

Some programs, and in particular Netscape itself, come in self-expanding zip files. These archives are distinguishable by their executable suffix [.exe]. If you download the Netscape installation archive for instance, you would in Windows 3.1 first move it to a vacant temporary directory, "run" the package to decompress it (this unpackages

Figure 6 Using Keyview is as easy as starting the program and clicking on open and pointing it at the file you want unpacked. It handles almost all known compression and storage formats automatically. It can be integrated with your browser to work with it to unpack files as they arrive from the Web. There is a license fee for using this program after an initial trial period expires.

all of the many files needed for installation), and then "run" a program called **setup.exe**, which is one of the unpacked files, to install the program. In Windows95, two steps are combined; merely run the archive .exe file and the whole installation process will occur. Many software packages now come ready for the process just described.

Sites shown in this Chapter...

Archieplex	http://www.lerc.nasa.gov/archieplex
Vancouver freenet	telnet://freenet.vancouver.bc.ca
Bookstacks	telnet://books.com

Notes:

[1] FTP can infrequently be used by you to transfer a file from your account to some remote site. In general, remote sites do not make a public area available for inbound transfer but if, for instance, you did want to give a copy of a file to a friend, and that friend was willing to allow you to use his or her logon name and password, you could use FTP to logon at their computer, then **put** the file to their account. The process is essentially the same except that you use the **put** command instead of the acquiring **get** command.

[2] There are other related Internet utilities called Veronica (which searches gopher sites) and Jughead (which does whole text searches). All of these are named for companion comic book characters.

[3] John Freed, "Internet Q&A", **New York Times**, Sept. 27, 1996

CHAPTER FIVE

Using Paper Libraries and Their Reading Rooms

"The riddle is this: if our property can be infinitely reproduced and instantaneously distributed all over the planet without cost, without our knowledge, without its even leaving our possession, how can we protect it? How are we going to get paid for the work we do with our minds? And, if we can't get paid, what will assure the continued creation and distribution of such work?"

John Perry Barlow, "Selling Wine Without Bottles: The Economy of Mind on the Global Net," http://www.eff.org/pub/Publications/John_Perry_Barlow/HTML/idea_economy_article.html as of Sept.7/96.

Paper libraries have existed as research resources for students for hundreds of years. Often superficially resembling temples of old, each university or college library contains some but never all of the fruits of scholarship, some of which goes back thousands of years in time to observers and observations made well before printing in its contemporary form was invented. Notwithstanding this long and rich history of storing knowledge on cellulose in specifically designated warehouses, the way students use these facilities and the uses to which students put the material has changed dramatically in the last three decades.

At the beginning of that period three decades ago, information concerning the publications housed in libraries was kept in card catalogues, one set for authors and titles, and one set for topics. In addition, annual paper guides to the periodical academic literature were (and in some cases still are) published annually in volumes for each discipline called abstracts. These abstracts contain a brief description of the content of each academic article in the relevant academic periodical literature for a particular discipline. Thus there were long annual series of bound volumes for the Psychological Abstracts and the Sociological Abstracts for example. If a student went through these volumes year by year looking through each index under topic keywords, he or she could locate the abstract for pertinent literature the whole text of which could then possibly be located in the stacks of paper editions of journals (if they were not out for binding). Once located, the article could be read, digested, copied by hand in part onto paper. A selection of such articles, woven together with passages from pertinent books would form the literature review section of students' essay submissions.

If the books or articles could not be found in the library they could always be ordered through interlibrary loan and would physically arrive some weeks later. This picture was altered somewhat by the appearance of relatively cheap photocopying in the early 1970s which greatly reduced the hand copying involved but essentially the process remained the same until about ten years ago. Scanners and cut-and-paste word processing programs and small portable computers together with cheap photocopying reduced hand copying to a minimum, even making the taking and recording of references quite easy and efficient with bibliographic pop-up programs such as *BioBase*. Then everything else in the library began to change all at once. The elements that changed follow in successive sections.

SUBSTITUTION OF ELECTRONIC CATALOGUES FOR CARD CATALOGUES

Canadian colleges and universities moved quickly to substitute general electronic catalogues with keyword searching for their old card catalogue systems; the electronic catalogues subsequently becoming available over the Internet to outsiders. Using the Library of Congress Web site for instance makes available information on a huge collection of books which would not appear in the collections of local academic libraries.

Most university and college library catalogues are now available for searching electronically by anyone with an Internet connection. In the example shown in Figure 1, the electronic catalogue at Carleton University Library is shown. We can use it to search for titles containing our chosen keywords. Selecting the appropriate keywords to use is therefore of pivotal importance; it is an important part of our research strategy discussed beginning in Chapter Nine.

In the library catalogue shown in Figure 1 the user can do Boolean searches (using ands, ors, and nots). In the example shown in Figure 2 we do a Boolean search for "juvenile" and "justice" (a recurrent subject matter example in this book) since in this example we want both terms to be present.

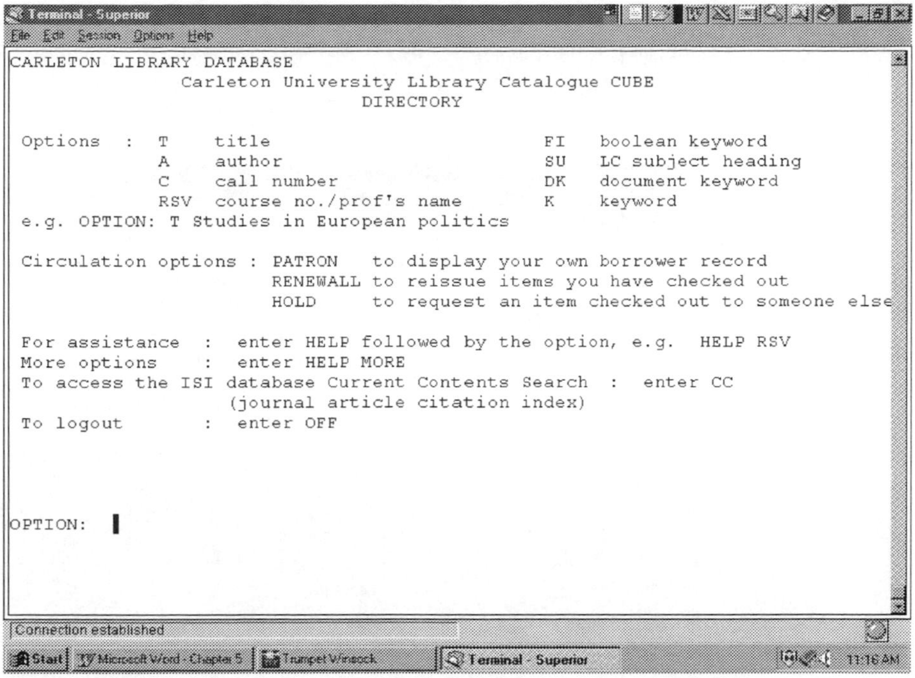

Figure 1 The electronic catalogue of holdings at the Carleton University Library

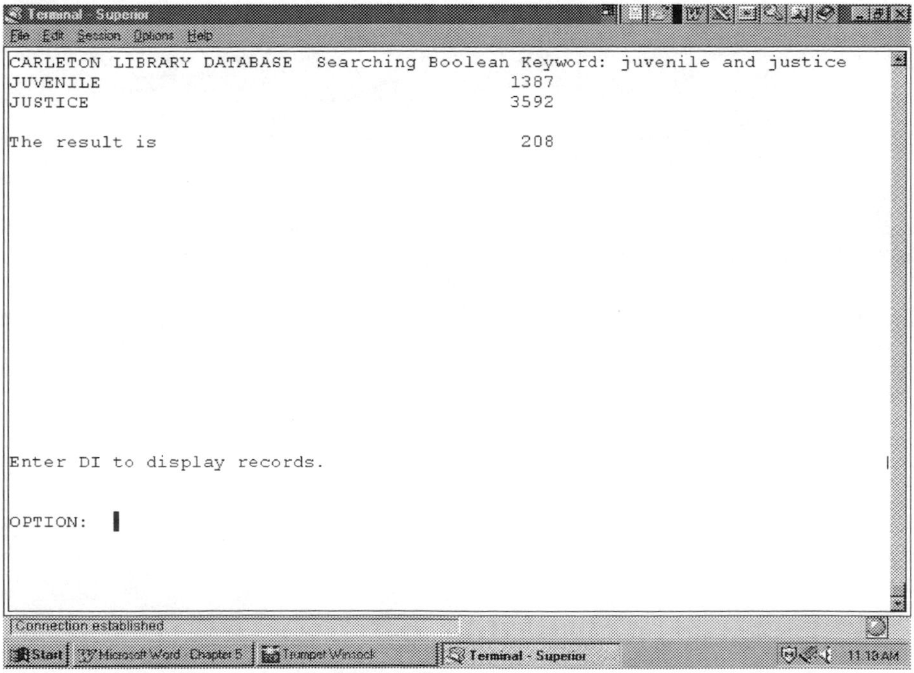

Figure 2 The results of a search for titles containing both the terms "juvenile" and "justice".

This sample search for resources at the library returned 208 documents currently held at the library. All 208 could be viewed separately and sequentially. The first of these is shown in Figure 3 below.

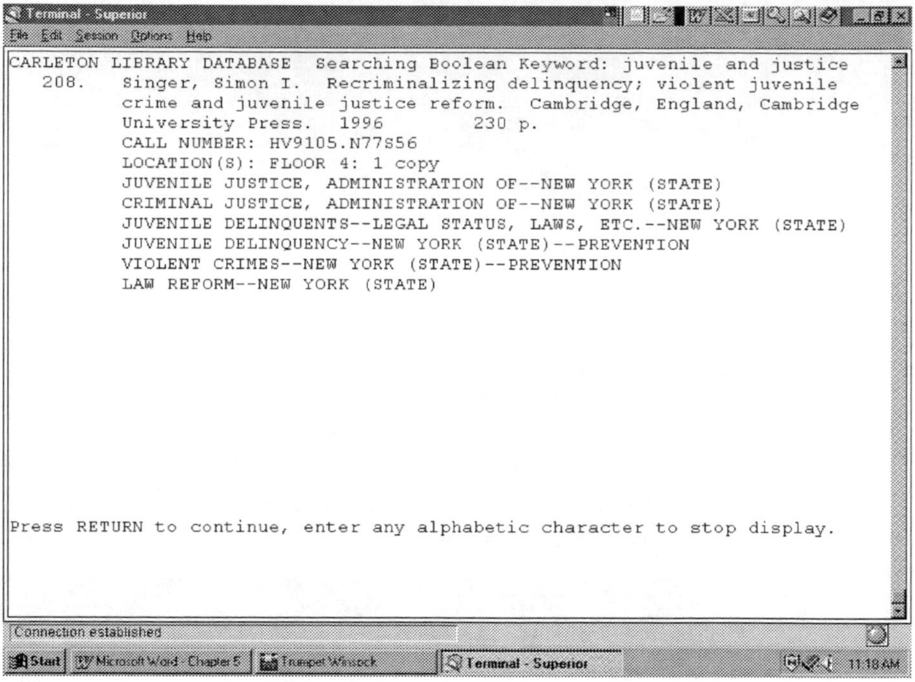

Figure 3 The first of 208 references to documents concerning juvenile justice held by the Carleton University library.

You may well want to do a more exhaustive search on your topic, for example using the resources at other Canadian university and college libraries or the Library of Congress. Shown in the figure below is the Library of Congress Web site. Generally speaking, the Library of Congress holdings are the most exhaustive in the world.

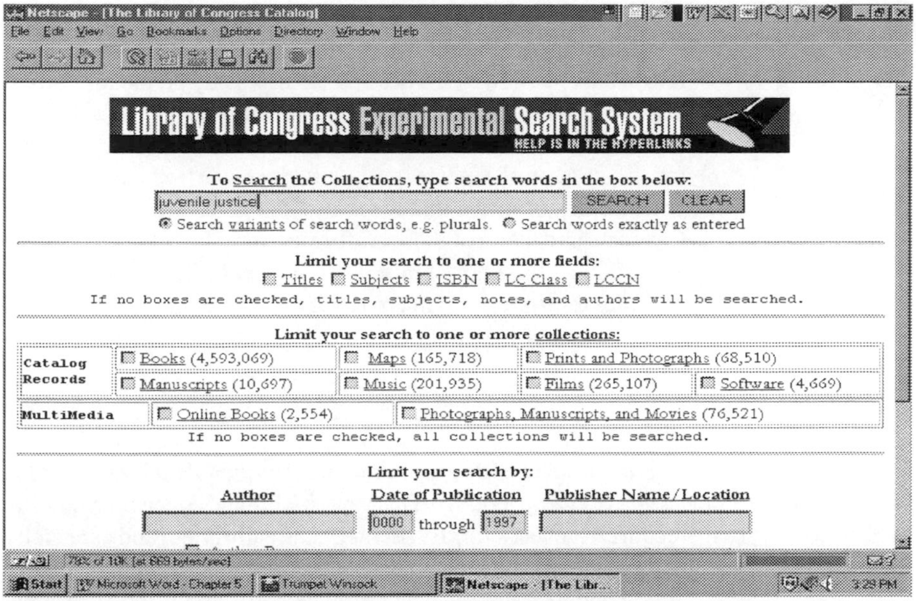

Figure 4 The main Library of Congress Web site form. Great flexibility of search patterns is allowed here.

Again using the juvenile justice working example, the Library of Congress proves to have an abundance of material available. You can then narrow the search to fit your research purposes.

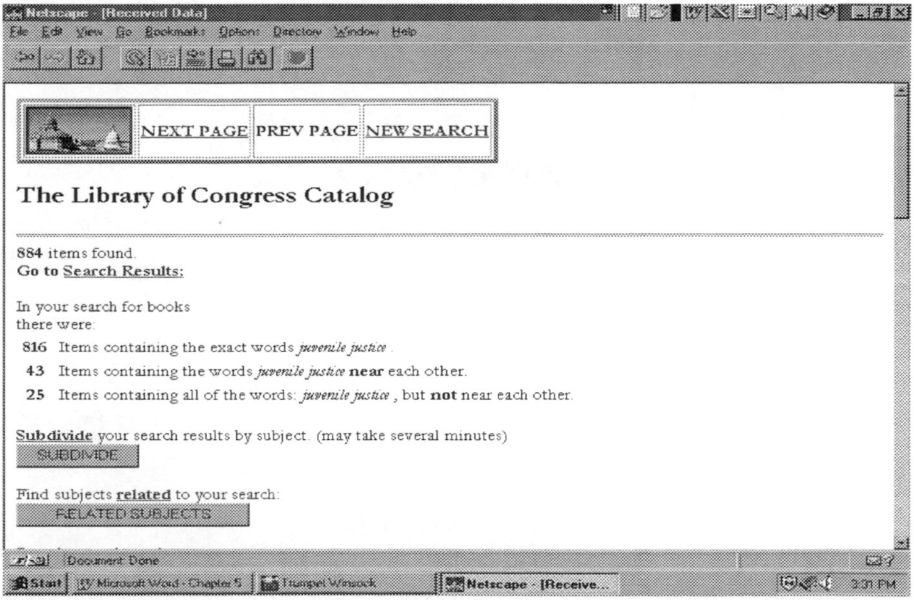

Figure 5 The harvest of a search for juvenile justice resources at the Library of Congress site.

The search of the Library of Congress Web site (http://lcweb2.loc.gov/catalog/) produced a large number of books in its collection (816) with exact matches, and many more that are close to the desired term. It is by no means certain, however, that your library will have these items in its collection; you may have to order them by interlibrary loan in order to read them. Be sure to take down detailed citation and cataloging information on the items you want since this information will have to supplied to your library in order that a request for an interlibrary loan be made. Libraries in Canada share their catalogue information so that if a copy of a document you want is housed in a Canadian library it can generally be obtained for you. It may take some considerable time for it to arrive physically at your location.

HYTELNET

There is a special kind of Telnet connection (**Hytelnet** — which does not require a guest or other account). This type of Telnet connection goes to a common cultural resource such as a library. In fact, many libraries (and especially ones in universities and colleges) now make their catalogue and data archives materials available in this way. Though gradually being replaced by Gopher and Web sites, it is still common to rely on a Telnet connection to gain access to remote library catalogue systems. Hytelnet is a special set of software designed for this purpose.

While it is possible from the prompt to connect to such a library directly, it is now common to use a menu location where all the major libraries of the western world are listed. Visiting one of these libraries is then a simple matter of selecting a link and pressing the Enter key. Such a menu is located at http://www.cc.ukans.edu/ hytelnet_html /START.TXT.html.

EXAMPLE OF HYTELNET ACCESS.....

hytelnet

        Welcome to HYTELNET version 6.6
          October 10, 1993

          What is HYTELNET?
          Library catalogs   *<==choosing this option*
          Other resources
          Help files for catalogs
          Catalog interfaces
          Internet Glossary
          Telnet tips
           Telnet/TN3270 escape keys

HYTELNET 6.6 was written by Peter Scott
E-mail address: aa375@freenet.carleton.ca

Data transfer complete*

hytelnet
On-Line Library Catalogs

The Americas   *<==choosing this option*

Europe/Scandinavia

Asia/Pacific/South Africa

Data transfer complete*

hytelnet
The Americas

Brazil
Canada
Chile
Mexico
United States   *<==choosing this option*
Venezuela

Data transfer complete*

hytelnet
United States

Consortia   *<== choosing this option*
Other Libraries
Law Libraries
Medical Libraries
Public Libraries
Community College Libraries
K-12 Libraries

Data transfer complete*

```
                          hytelnet (p1 of 2)
                     United States Consortia

    Abilene Library Consortium
    Access Colorado Library and Information Network
    Boston Library Consortium
    Colorado Alliance of Research Libraries
    C/W MARS: Central and Western Massachusetts (via CARL)
    C*O*N*N*E*C*T: Libraries in the Greater Hartford Area
    DALNET (Detroit Area Library Network)
    Fenway Libraries Online, Inc.
    Florida State University System
    HELIN (Higher Education Library Information Network)
    Houston Area Library Automated Network (HALAN)
    ILLINET On-line Catalog
    KELLY: Regional Online Catalog for WESTNET
    M.A.I.N.: Morris Automated Information Network (New Jersey)
    Maricopa Community Colleges
    MARMOT Library Network
    Maryland Interlibrary Consortium
    Nevada Academic Libraries Information System (NALIS)
    OhioLink
    OLLI: University System of Georgia On-Line Library Information
    — press space for more, use arrow keys to move, '?' for help, 'q' to quit
```

THE ADVENT OF ELECTRONIC LITERATURE SEARCHES

Using such tools as Sociofile, Current Contents, and the Silverplatter products, it is now possible to carry out fast and comprehensive searches of the academic periodical literature to augment your library catalogue searches. These sources (generally on CD-ROMs available at the library on dedicated computers) together can deliver a comprehensive list of periodical literature on a given topic covering relatively recent publications, or if desired or necessary covering a longer period of time. In addition, a growing number of periodical academic journals are published on the Web.

As an example, we will search Current Contents on the topic of juvenile justice. Current Contents is a commercial product and it may not be available to you at your library. However, it or a substitute might be available on paper, or at a public library nearby. The results of such a search are shown in the figure opposite and above. Each item can be viewed separately. There is generally a short abstract which describes the item's contents, cataloguing information, and as is the case with the reference shown in the figure opposite and below, a location where you can find the actual article to read.

```
Terminal - Superior
File  Edit  Session  Options  Help
CURRENT CONTENTS DATABASE   Searching Keyword: juvenile justice
    1. JUVENALIS................................................     1
    2. JUVENCUS.................................................     4
    3. JUVENILE.................................................  4,373  <-
    4. JUVENILEAND..............................................     3
    5. JUVENILEBROWN............................................     1
    6. JUVENILECHINOOK..........................................     1
    7. JUVENILECHRONIC..........................................     1
    8. JUVENILECYNOMOLGUS.......................................     1
    9. JUVENILEDELINQUENTS/.....................................     1
   10. JUVENILEDERMATOMYOSITIS..................................     2




TO DISPLAY enter DI for entry at <-  or DI and line no. at left, e.g. DI 6
TO CHANGE standard display, add S (SHORT) or TA (FULL) e.g. DI TA or DI S 7
TO BROWSE enter B for backward, or enter F for forward
OPTION:



Connection established
Start | Trumpet Winsock | Netscape - [The Library... | Terminal - Superior | Microsoft Word - Chapter 5 | 4:05 PM
```

Figure 6 A Current Contents search for resources on juvenile justice.

```
Terminal - Superior
File  Edit  Session  Options  Help
CURRENT CONTENTS DATABASE   Searching Keyword: juvenile
    1. JUVENILEDELINQUENTS/
        LET US PREPARE TEACHERS TO WORK WITH JUVENILEDELINQUENTS/
                            GERBEEV IV
        IN: RUSSIAN EDUCATION AND SOCIETY 1994 NOV  Vol.36  No.11  Pages 17
        - 26
        CARLETON LIBRARY DOES NOT HOLD THIS TITLE
        UNIVERSITY OF OTTAWA LIBRARIES HOLD THIS TITLE
        IURICHKA II,









Use GET to retrieve a record from a group of multiple hits, e.g. GET 19

OPTION:




Connection established
Start | Trumpet Winsock | Netscape - [The Library... | Terminal - Superior | Microsoft Word - Chapter 5 | 4:04 PM
```

Figure 7 A sample item retrieved from the Current Contents database. Pressing the return key at this stage would produce an abstract of this article.

GOVERNMENT INFORMATION IN ELECTRONIC FORMAT

The publication of masses of government reports, information, and raw data either to an unrestricted audience on the Web, or in the Canadian case, through the Data Liberation Initiative to members of the Canadian university consortium (which numbered 54 universities and colleges across Canada at the time of writing) has altered substantially the means and methods for obtaining government reports and information resources.

More and more, information from government sources, both in Canada and from abroad, will be found only in electronic format. Librarians who work in the government documents section of your library will help you obtain access to this information.

DATA SETS FOR SECONDARY ANALYSIS

The past few years have seen a fast-spreading availability of thousands of data sets complete with codebooks, questionnaires, etc. through library data centres and archives to accredited students and faculty members of universities. Resources available include Census data and other extremely valuable resources such as archives of opinion surveys going back many years, all in easy to use form with statistical packages such as SPSS and SAS. Again, a trip to the library is necessary to find out how to use these new and valuable resources.

CD-ROM BASED ANSWER-GENERATING PROGRAMS

Libraries now also tend to have available CD-ROM based products such as E-STAT on computers in the library ready for student and faculty use. E-STAT is a program which has current Census data combined on a CD-ROM product from Statistics Canada. It generates information and maps based on the Canadian Census in such a way that it can be used analytically and understood by virtual novices.

POPULAR JOURNALS AND NEWSPAPERS

University and college libraries used to have large selections of newspapers from around the world which would arrive by mail days or weeks after they were published. These papers have now largely vanished from the reading room to be replaced by whole text versions on the Web. The same is true for current periodicals of serious commentary such as *The Atlantic Monthly*. In their place are Web versions of these publications. The advantages to the user are numerous. These electronic editions are available immediately upon publication, you can cut and paste the contents electronically, and most importantly there is no charge to the reader nor to the library.

Following are some examples of what is available. Most of the world's major newspapers now have electronic versions and in subsequent chapters you will find examples of other newspapers and news services from around the world. Secondly, popular periodicals are available too. A site which collects these is shown in Figure 9.

Figure 8 An example of one prominent Canadian newspaper's electronic full-text edition which is available free of charge. Articles can be captured from this as from any other electronic document using cut and paste techniques.

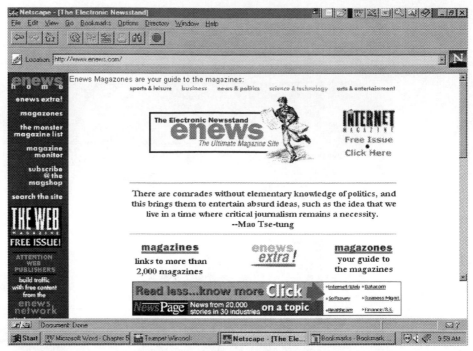

Figure 9 Not only are newspapers available in electronic form but so too are hundreds if not thousands of periodicals of varying quality. This site, The Electronic Newsstand, advertises 2000 such editions.

Figure 10 Here is one example of the whole-text electronic edition of a quality periodical, *The Atlantic Monthly*, which is read by students and faculty members all over the world. It publishes long and insightful essays on contemporary social conditions.

ACCESSING UP TO THE MOMENT NEWS CONTENT

Finally, there is the matter of truly current, current affairs contents. There is now a profusion of real-time news and public affairs sources available on the Web. Since most of the material is textual in nature, it can be viewed and used successfully using a text-oriented browser such as *Lynx*. Of course, the appearance of the material is enhanced with a graphical browser. In the specific case of the *New York Times* summary (http://nytimesfax.com), the eight page daily product actually is typeset in standard *New York Times* fonts and looks like the real thing, as does the Web site version, which is updated at least twice during most business days to reflect breaking news. The opposite is true of the appearance of the *Electronic Telegraph* (http://www.telegraph.co.uk/et/) the electronic counterpart of the *Daily Telegraph* newspaper from London, shown in Figure 12. It does not in the least resemble the paper product and is a wonderful example of good graphics design on the Web. Registration as a user at a news site has become normal. You establish a user login/password pair. In most cases (e.g. *The Daily Telegraph, Times of London*, the *Los Angeles Times* being some examples), these accounts are free. However, in the case of the *New York Times* electronic edition, an attempt is being made to charge non-U.S. visitors a monthly fee for access. There are several strategies around this: have a U.S. resident friend register for you, become a U.S. resident by means of opening an user account at a U.S. freenet, or use one of the open-user accounts established by public-spirited Net citizens discussed in a later section.

Figure 11 The *Los Angeles Times* Site. One of the most graphically slick sites on the Web. You must register to use it but registration is free. This site gives you access to the Associated Press and provides a utility called Hunter which will search the AP wire for you. Overall, a tremendous source of information. This site carries a slightly delayed version of the Associated Press (AP) news wire.

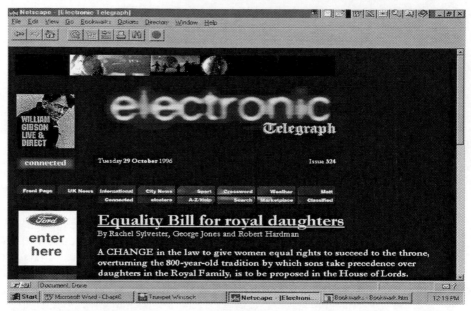

Figure 12 A gift to you from the ex-pat Canadian owner Conrad Black, the *Daily Telegraph* site (registration required but free) provides possibly the slickest design on the Web. Full contents of today's issue are available. Since it comes from England, it's available in the early evening in North America and well before "tomorrow's" *New York Times*. Though not shown here, the *Times of London* also has an excellent electronic edition.

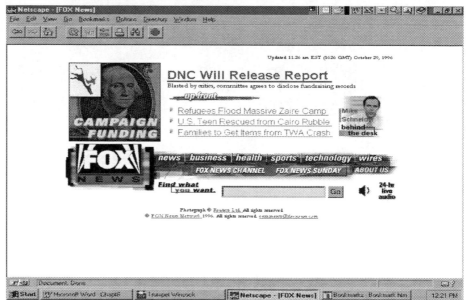

Figure 13 A gift to you from Rupert Murdoch, the Fox Network news service is mounting a good web page with the wire services (no Hunter however) but it does feature a live audio and video track of their broadcast, ads and all. You need the RealAudio or RealVideo software and a sound card to use it. The audio is acceptable over a modem at 14.4kbps and better with 28.8kbps. Note that this site also carries a short list of the latest items from the Associated Press (AP) wire service.

As mentioned above, most of these services require that the user register the first time access is attempted. Since this is the case, it is wise to think of an account name and password combination to use at all of the sites so that remembering the magic words is not difficult. In addition, some helpful soul has visited most of these sites and registered a generic logon account name (cypherpunks or cpunks) and password (also cypherpunks or writecode or cpunks) and you may use these combinations in a pinch. They work at many sites most of the time. Since you are gaining access to current items from the Associated Press wire service and also Reuters wire service, this account/password requirement is a small price to pay for access. There are no other charges. Here are some examples of available Web addresses and sites and a bit of what you can expect to see there:

This time in text format to demonstrate that the product (current news is just as effective this way, the following box shows the Yahoo site (http://www.yahoo.com) which carries the Reuters news wire service. Choosing *headlines* clickbox at the Yahoo site, you gain access to a summary of items from the Reuters wire service:

Live Wire - News from Reuters Online (p1 of 2)

[Yahoo | Write Us | Search | Info]

Live Wire - News and Headlines

News [Summary] - 6 new stories and headlines updated Tuesday August 1 5:00 p.m. [new]

International [Summary] - Headlines last updated Tuesday August 1 10:52 a.m.
Business [Summary] - Headlines last updated Tuesday August 1 2:00 p.m. *<=== choosing this option*

Politics [Summary] - Headlines last updated Tuesday August 1 2:38 p.m.

Sports [Summary] - Headlines last updated Tuesday August 1 12:00 p.m.

Entertainment [Summary] - Headlines last updated Tuesday August 1 5:56 a.m.

TUESDAY AUGUST 1 4:58 P.M.

News Summary

Headlines

    * Westinghouse to Buy CBS [new]   **<== choosing this option**
    * Hurricane Bozo Strengthens, Nears Florida [new]
    * Reno: Koresh to Blame for Waco [new]
    * Clinton Threatens Vetoes
    * Aide: Foster File Missing
    * OJ Defense Focuses on Leaks [new]

TUESDAY AUGUST 1 4:58 P.M.News Summary

    * Westinghouse to Buy CBS - For the second time in as many days, a
      major television deal is in the news. Westinghouse Electric Corp.
      says the CBS television network has accepted a $5.4 billion,
      $81-per-share, buyout offer. The deal had been widely anticipated.
      It comes on the heels of yesterday's surprise announcement that
      the Walt Disney Company was buying Capital Cities/ABC for $19
      billion.

    * Bozo Strengthens, Nears Florida - Hurricane Bozo is gaining
      strength as is bears down on Florida. Forecasters say the storm,

Another useful site for up to the moment news is Nando News (http://www.nando.net/nt/world/). This site in North Carolina has a comprehensive set of fairly up-to-date news items. It is not consistently updated but it tends to be quite timely:

World - Last updated Aug 1, 1996 - 20:36 EDT (p1 of 7)
 World

Top Story

    HOUSE VOTES TO LIFT BOSNIA ARMS EMBARGO
      * WASHINGTON (Aug 1, 1996 - 19:01 EDT) — Rejecting both a veto
      threat and a warning it would "Americanize" a savage war, Congress
      approved legislation Tuesday to lift the arms embargo against
      Bosnia so the Muslim-led government can better defend itself.

World News Summary

A little-known pro-Iranian Palestinian group which refuses to recognize the Jewish state has claimed responsibility for last week's suicide bombing which killed six Israelis on a bus.... Drivers in

The Yankee News Desk (http://www.tiac.net/users/magyver/news.html) has several feeds: the first is the summary file of latest news from the ClariNet news service (a pay-per-view service) — but the tearsheet is free of charge. The site also has feeds for the Reuters news summary, the Associated Press news wire, and the ABC radio news files in RealAudio format (listenable on both PCs and Macintosh computers with the necessary free software installed) among other materials such as sports and features.

The Yankee News Desk (p1 of 5)

[IMAGE]

News & Information
Sources

NEWSFEEDS

[INLINE] ClariNet Tearsheet (News)   **<== choosing this option**

[INLINE] Reuter's News Summary

[INLINE] AP Wire (Searchable)

[INLINE] ABC News (Audio)

[INLINE] WorldNews Today

ClariNet Tearsheet: U.S. and General News (p1 of 11)

ClariNet * ClariNet Tearsheet: U.S. and General News

CLARINET TEARSHEET: U.S. AND GENERAL NEWS

These top general and U.S. news stories are brought to you by ClariNet
Communications Corp., publishers of the ClariNet e.News electronic
newspaper. The e.News is the first and largest newspaper on the
Internet. This tearsheet is a small portion of the live news,
distributed around the clock, that the e.News offers.

Updated Tuesday, August 1, 1996, at 1:00 pm Pacific time.

* Clinton vows to veto environmental bill
* N.Korea criticizes U.S. over Korean war events
* Phillip Morris has lung cancer
* Clinton vows veto of House telecommunication bill

The next site is Edupage, a periodical summary of press clipping summaries of items of interest to those who wish to keep up with advances in computer technology and associated legal and legislative issues. It may be found at the following address: gopher://ivory.educom.edu/00/edupage.new.

****
Edupage, a summary of news items on information technology, is provided
three times each week as a service by Educom — a Washington, D.C.-
based consortium of leading colleges and universities seeking to
transform education through the use of information technology.
****

TOP STORIES
    Computer Associates Gets The Go-Ahead From Justice
    AT&T Cutting Global Information Solutions
    Neural Net Software Sifts Information
    New Data On Interactive Customers
    FCC's PCS Auction Plans Hit A Snag
    The Chemistry Of Computing

ALSO
    Texas Instruments Out Of Chips
    Shifting Sands At MCI
    Gates Goes To Ottawa
    FCC Lifts TV Prime Time Limitations
    Quadruple Number Of School Computers Urged

Another source of classified news items can be found at Tribnet in Tacoma, Washington at the following address: http://www.tribnet.com/news.htm

Welcome to TNT News Pages (p1 of 2)

[LINK]

In order to read our news stories, you must
register with us as a TRIBweb member.
THIS IS FREE and only takes a few seconds.

If you have already registered, you may continue on into the news
areas by entering in your userid and password when prompted.

Business News Computer News Editorials Education News Electronics
News
Entertainment News Family News Food Stories General Features Health
News Home & Habitat Local News Search over 900 Movie Reviews Music
News National News O.J. Simpson News Personalities & Famous People
Recipes 75 + Restaurant Reviews Science News Seniors News Sports
News State News Television Stories TV Listings Travel News Weather
Report World News YAP/Teens Stories
Data transfer complete*

(p1 of 9)

[IMAGE]

BUSINESS NEWS FOR TUESDAY AUG 1

07005 AFL-CIO's Kirkland: The working man's intellectual / Labor
leader to step down today

07087 Mutual funds trying to redo documents in plain English

07085 Spy stores: Retailers offer an array of high-tech eavesdropping
devices

07083 MARKET SUMMARY: 2nd thoughts about Microsoft depress price

07031 BUSINESS BRIEFLY

07033 For Warren Buffett, a tidy profit of $2.1 billion

07035 Disney buys ABC in mega-deal   <=== *choosing this item*

(p1 of 6)

DISNEY BUYS ABC IN MEGA-DEAL

Evan Ramstad / The Associated Press

BIZ E1

BW PHOTO / Marty Lederhandler / Associated Press: Michael Eisner,
Disney chairman, left, and Thomas Murphy, Capital Cities/ABC chairman,
outline the deal on Monday.

SIDEBAR (CHART) / The Associated Press: Horse trading in TV shows (E5)

 NEW YORK - Dear Peter, Barbara and Ted. Welcome to the Wonderful
World
 of Disney.

The Walt Disney Co. realigned the hierarchy of global media Monday
with a $19 billion deal to purchase Capital Cities/ABC Inc., owner of
the nation's leading television network.

The combination will pass Time Warner Inc. in size as the world's top
purveyor of entertainment, bringing in more than $17 billion annually

Finally, there is a collection of news items from England at a site called Futurenet UK News (http://www.futurenet.co.uk/News/today/index.html). No registration is required at this site.

FutureNet : News : Index (p1 of 4)

[IMAGE]

[NEWS] FUTURENET WORLD NEWS

Welcome to FutureNet World News, a daily newswire bringing you top stories from around the world, and today's happenings here in the UK. This is a free-access service, updated at around 1pm BST.

1 August 1996, last updated at 12:42

PROVIDED BY [UK NEWS]

New - FutureNet Computing News

A daily newswire bringing you information technology stories from around the world.

FutureNet : News : Index (p2 of 4)

TODAY'S TOP STORIES

POLICE INVESTIGATE MAFIA PLANS TO BLOW UP COURTHOUSE

PORTILLO WARNS AGAINST RASH THREATS OF AIR STRIKES<== *choosing this item*

ARRESTED MAN SEEN WITH MURDER VICTIMS

WEATHER SET TO STAY IN 90S TILL END OF WEEK

PRE-GAMES PREVIEW FEATURE ON LINFORD CHRISTIE

NAMES OF BRITAIN'S FANTASY CHIP SERVERS REVEALED

TODAY'S NEWS

* World News (9 items)

* FutureNet Computing News (145 items)

FutureNet :
News - PORTILLO WARNS AGAINST RASH THREATS OF AIR STRIKES
(p1 of 3)

[IMAGE]

[INDEX] [PREVIOUS] [UP] [NEXT] WORLD NEWS

PORTILLO WARNS AGAINST RASH THREATS OF AIR STRIKES

1 August 1996 at 07:15:59

By Charles Aldinger, Reuters, Washington.

Defence Secretary Michael Portillo has warned against making rash
threats to use massive air strikes to protect the Muslim safe haven
of Bihac.
Mr Portillo spoke after discussing the Bosnia crisis with his US
counterpart William Perry at the Pentagon in Washington.
Mr Perry said the North Atlantic Council, the political arm of NATO,
could make a decision as early as today on how the alliance might
help protect Bihac from attacks from Bosnian and Croatian Serbs and
rebel Muslims.

With this range of sources available on the Web free of charge, it is easy to see how developing events can be assessed with news materials *as they are happening*. In the case of major world events such as a large earthquake, new pointers are likely to be found on these sites where additional information can be found to supplement and expand on the facts of the event as they occur. With the Web, it has become very much easier to stay informed on world events. Also, dependence on a single source of information such as the local community newspaper is much reduced.

SUMMARY OF THE LIBRARY TOUR

From this brief tour, it can easily be seen that the university or college library is in the midst of an historic transition. Where once it was a paper warehouse with physical keys to finding materials, much of the searching and finding of research materials now takes place electronically. For example, in order to consult the Carleton University catalogue (a resource available to everyone in the world with an Internet connection), I need not leave my home or office. Neither am I restricted by time of day nor whether the library is physically open. Interestingly enough, when the Library of Congress first appeared as an online resource, it did keep office hours. There being no point at all to this restriction, it was quickly dropped.

In addition, much reference material and an increasingly large component of the periodical literature is now only available in electronic form, or available in both electronic and paper form. The changing of the economics of academic publication (many fewer low volume specialized academic books are being published and they are much more expensive than in the past) has had the result that new acquisition budgets for academic libraries are being restricted. This means fewer and fewer new books appear in the stacks each year, and the relevance of those that remain from previous eras grows less and less for contemporary research. This creates much more contention for scarce course readings at the reserve desk and adds to the imperative to use course Web sites for supplementary readings.

With these factors in mind, the present day student must increasingly make use of electronic searching resources and ultimately of electronic research resources themselves. The logic of the transition from paper to electronic documents is inexorable, noy only from the point of view of cost, but also with respect to ease of unrestricted access to multiple copies which the student can retain.

Sites shown in this Chapter...

Carleton University CUBE catalogue	available through Hytelnet
The Library of Congress	http://lcweb2.loc.gov/catalog/
Hytelnet	http://www.cc.ukans.edu/hytelnet_html/START.TXT.html
The Toronto Star	http://www.thestar.com/
The Electronic Newsstand	http://www.enews.com/
The Atlantic Monthly	http://www.theatlantic.com/
The Los Angeles Times	http://www.latimes.com/
The Electronic Telegraph	http://www.telegraph.co.uk/
Fox News	http://www.foxnews.com/
Reuters	http://www.yahoo.com/text/headlines
Nando news	http://www.nando.com/
Yankee news	http://www.tiac.net/users/magyver/news.html
Tribnet	http://www.tribnet.com/news.htm
Edupage	gopher://ivory.educom.edu/00/edupage.new
FutureNet	http://www.futurenet.co.uk/

CHAPTER

SIX

Internet Search Utilities: the Web Search Engine Family and WAIS

"Every computer interface, from the old command lines to virtual reality spaces, has used a single focal point that lies in the general area where the user's head is. Every aspect of these interfaces is adjusted to match that point, from font size to window placement."

Ashley Dunn, "Seeing the Forest of Knowledge for the Trees of Data."
New York Times electronic edition, October 23, 1996.

When starting a piece of research using the electronic tools of the Web, one is confronted with a number of choices and problems. Obviously, the *first of all* is how to find useful resource documents and data. But assuming you can find a useful resource, one of the next obvious questions thus raised is referencing what you find. The obligation to provide directions to a resource you are using is as old as scholarship itself. In the new electronic world however, documents change and disappear over time. This raises consequential problems of referencing since there clearly is no way to guarantee that the referenced resource is a permanent one. The obligation is thus transformed into the requirement for an audit trail. What should go into the audit trail and how should it be recorded? The first principle is that the source information be recorded at the time of collection; there may be no going back later to pick up the information.

In the older world of cellulose scholarship, bibliographic rules and styles abound. Recording references is a matter of handwriting or typing, typically on file cards. In our attempt to break the ties with past scholarship practices here, we must then deal with the problem of how to record references on the fly and a subsequent problem of the contents of citations in your own published work. Taking the introductory inscription above at the beginning of this chapter for instance, you will notice that it is drawn from the electronic edition of the *New York Times* and *it has no page numbers*.

This is a typical electronic citation problem and is unavoidable since page numbers presume the existence of physical pages upon which to appear — and electronic texts typically are not paginated at all. But first, the problem of how to record bibliographic resources electronically.

USING BIOBASE

The answer to the initial problem of on-the-fly recording of citation information is *BioBase*, a Windows program for recording references to articles and other literature on virtual file cards with the standard information fields identified. It is an elegant shareware program which can be popped up at any point in a search procedure to record a reference. Note that it does require the presence of the Microsoft visual basic environment file (the most recent available is vbrun400.dll — separate versions for Windows 3.1 and Windows95 — for depositing in your c:\windows directory). It is available at the Microsoft FTP site[1] as a self-expanding file. BioBase is currently distributed as a zip file called bbase20.zip; unzip it into an empty directory and then make an icon link to it. It is intuitive in operation and free of charge. While it was originally developed for biologists, it is universal in application and usefulness.

If you leave BioBase running on the desktop (perhaps loading it automatically each time Windows starts), it is simple to use the copy and paste features of Windows to acquire information in footnotes, reference lists, news articles or books you are reading and capture the relevant details on the virtual file cards. The data on these "cards" can later be reformatted for any purpose you want. Just as a reminder, if you highlight an address or a phrase and then choose the 'copy' option from the Edit menu in Windows, the phrase or address can be inserted anywhere else using the Shift-Ins key sequence, or the paste menu option. Thus if you find a URL that looks interesting, you can copy and then paste it into the GoTo address bar in your browser, or use the Shift-Ins key combination to paste it in. If the link turns out to be useful, you can then save it to your bookmarks file without ever having to type the address. Similarly, you can copy and paste whole chunks of text into a document you are preparing in your simultaneously open word processor. As a rule of thumb, no piece of text should ever be typed more than once in the modern computing environment. Copy and paste can completely do away with tedious recopying and is a great boon to researchers. Remember however that when you take a chunk of an online text document to insert in your document under preparation that then is the time to pop up BioBase and take the reference information such as it is into your bibliographic records. The source document may simply never be open and accessible to you ever again.

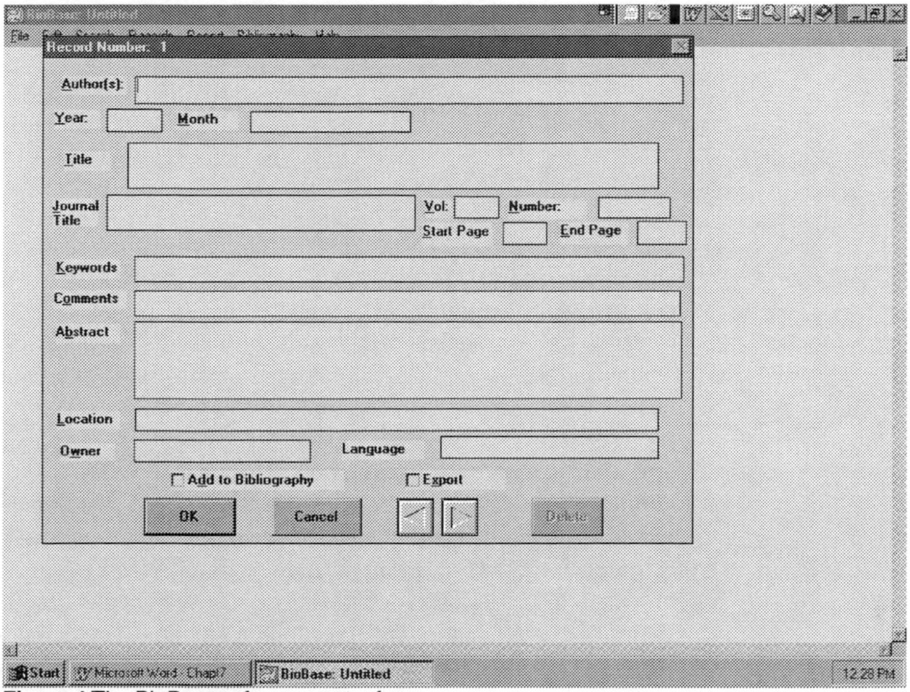

Figure 1 The BioBase reference entry form

SOURCE CITATION REFERENCE GUIDES

There is as yet no standard means of citing electronic resources in standard manuscripts. There are however a number of attempts to come to grips with this situation. Indeed, this is one of the first and most recurrent questions raised by students in today's classrooms. There are a number of style sheets which attempt to deal with the problem, for example, that of the American Psychological Association. See, for instance, pages 218-222 in the APA Publication Manual, 4th edition, address e-mail and CD-ROM referencing.[2]

Other specific problems lie with citing data sets or other novel resources you have acquired (acquisition and use of data sets being the subject of a later section). The best source available on this topic is "How to Cite Computer Files," by Laina Ruus & Anna Bombak. You can obtain a copy of this document at http://www.princeton.edu/~data/News/cite. Other materials which will be of use are: the aforementioned APA style guide at http://www.uvm.edu/~xli/reference/apa.html, and a document from the Princeton University library which deals with citing CD-ROM search and other associated activities at http://www.princeton.edu/~data/News/bobray.

WEB SEARCHING

As the title of this volume suggests, there is an overflowing wealth of potential research resources available on the World Wide Web (on the Internet generally). These are passive resources put up and made available by all manner of organizations and individuals around the world. In addition, there are more active resources such as data archives which may be able to send you whole data sets which you can then use with SAS or SPSS to produce entirely new tabulations and correlations for your own analytical enterprise. You may on occasion also interactively submit data requests which are processed remotely and the products are then shipped to you over the Web. An example of this would be Canadian socio-economic time series data which can form the basis of HTML charts prepared for you remotely and then presented on your screen for your viewing and permanent capture.

First though, a necessary distinction between sites, texts, and data. In general, Web searches deal with Web addresses, names of sites, and names of documents. For searching *within* text documents for particular words or phrases, one is somewhat restricted in conducting a generalized search but WAIS (which stands for Wide Area Information Service) text documents can be searched for keywords and texts. The Champlain search engine developed for searching Canadian government documentation also deals with the internal text components of text documents. Data may be searched at a number of different levels down to the wording of individual questions asked, in many instances. For example, Canadian Gallup Poll questions can be searched across the entire collection for specific question topics.

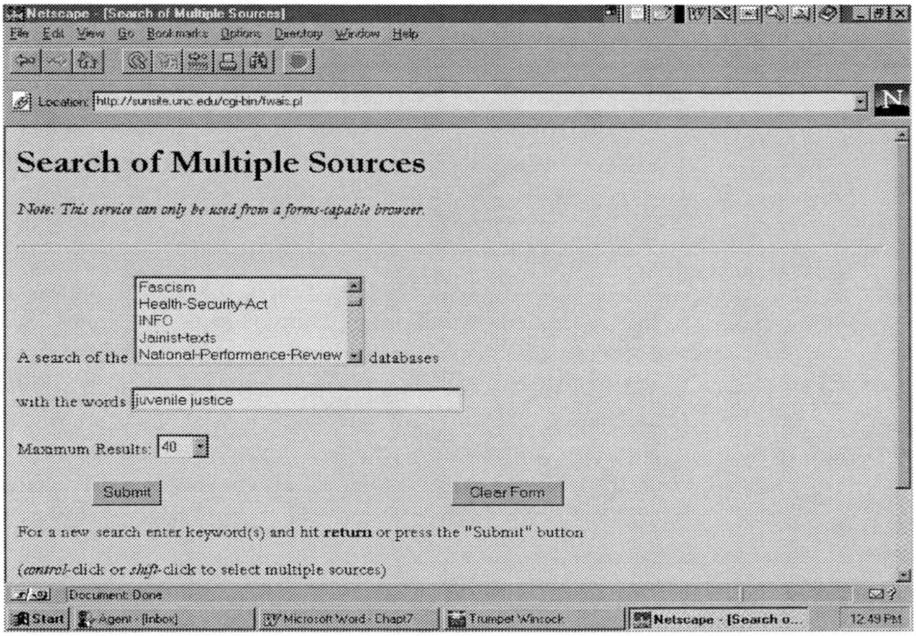

Figure 2 An example of a WAIS search form.

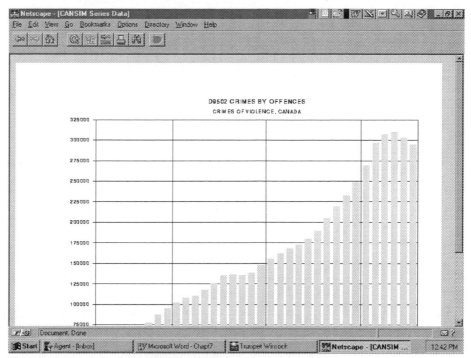

Figure 3 An example of a CANSIM chart requested as a bar chart.

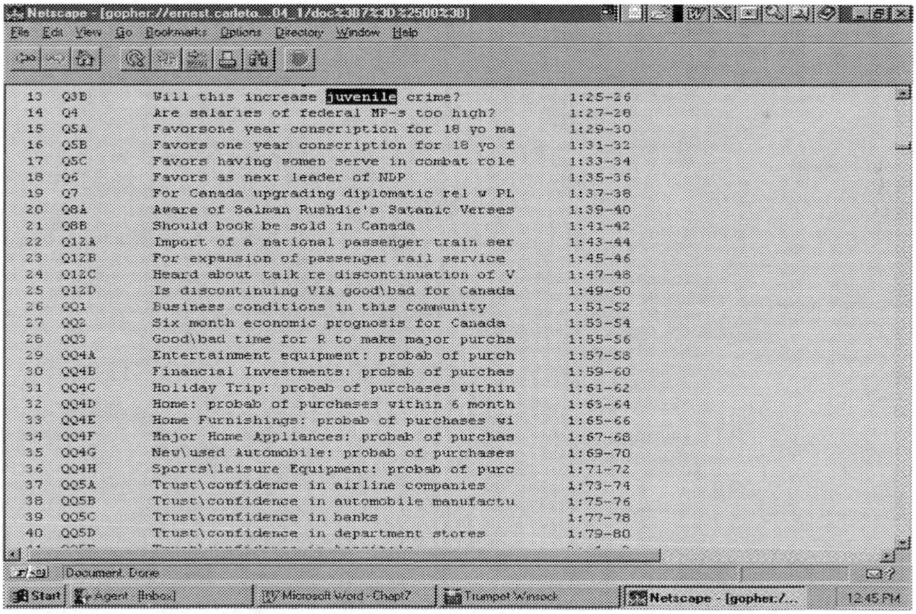

Figure 4 An example of a search of Gallup polls for questions relating to juvenile crime. This search turned up a question asked in 1989. The search was done on the Gallup database at the Library Data Centre at Carleton University.

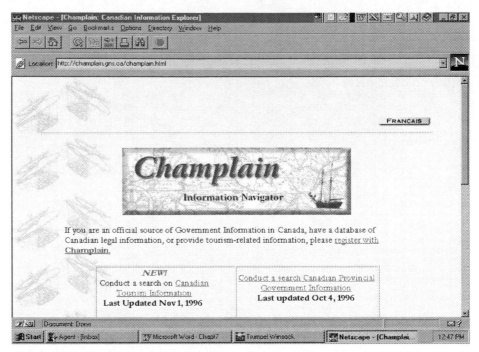

Figure 5 The Champlain search engine at Industry Canada. It searches the text of documents prepared for all three levels of government in Canada.

WEB SEARCHERS

At the highest level of abstraction, the search for relevant Web sites and document titles, there are a large number of competent search engines. Each employs a different strategy and may turn up different materials. They tend to generate extremely large numbers of relevant Web sites, so many now allow complex search terms with Boolean (if, and, or) logic. Resources located now tend to be ranked as to how closely the resource comes to what you asked for. In this context, a 100% rating would appear to be exactly what you asked for.

There is a special site which describes the various search engines and what type of search each is particularly well suited for. It is located at http://www.windweaver.com/index.htm. You should consult it when formulating your research strategy.

A large selection of search engines can be found at my research page site at **http://www.carleton.ca/~cmckie/research.html**. I usually recommend using several when doing a general survey of what is available for a social science research project. Specifically I recommend starting off the process with AltaVista, and Ultraseek but there are many more worthwhile places to start. This section of the research page is shown in the figure below.

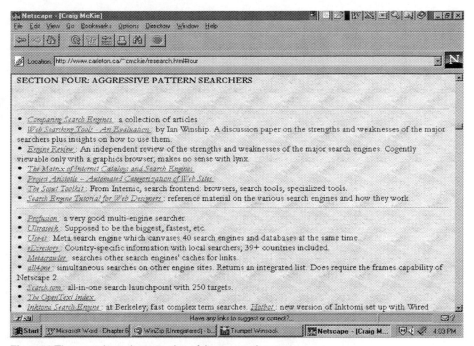

Figure 6 The search engines section of the research page.

Each search engine operates with a slightly different classification algorithm, and the means and methods by which each searches for new or altered sites also differ. Some search deeply in the material itself while others base their classifications on what is in the title or the first paragraph of text. It is therefore prudent to use several in a general search for resources. You may be surprised with how different the materials each turns up actually are.

WebFerret

If you have Windows95 installed on your computer, and it has a TCP/IP connection to use, then you can get a copy of WebFerret. This is a Windows95-only TCP/IP application which is alas not available for the Windows 3.1 user. It simultaneously searches five different major search engines and gives you a complete list of hits, rank ordered by apparent closeness of fit to your requirements. Distributed as a self-expanding file called WebFerretXXXX.exe where XXXX is the current version number. It is a fast and efficient piece of Network software and it is too bad that there is no version for Windows 3.1.

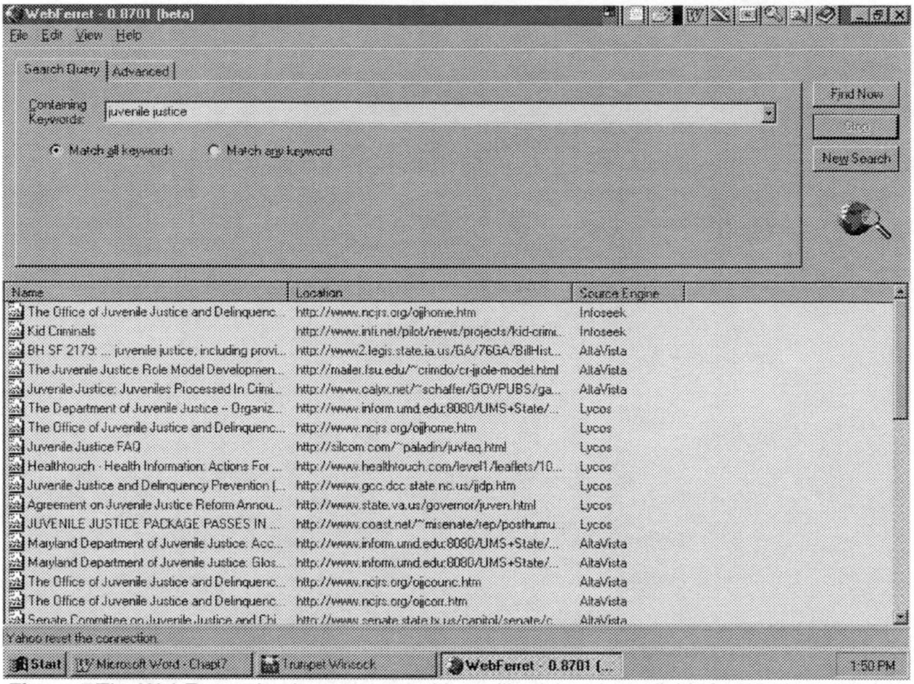

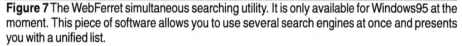

Figure 7 The WebFerret simultaneous searching utility. It is only available for Windows95 at the moment. This piece of software allows you to use several search engines at once and presents you with a unified list.

If you wish to use the major search engines individually, you can do this too. Since each major search engine is optimized for a particular kind of search, it is prudent to try several with the same basic search strategy. As noted earlier in this chapter, you will find a long list of these search engines on my research page at **http://www.carleton.ca/~cmckie/research.html**[3]. You might want to make a note of this address and add it to your bookmarks file. Having the page available means you don't have to remember the addresses of the major (or the minor) search engines. As of this writing, the major search engines list prominently includes: AltaVista, Inktomi, Ultraseek, Lycos, and the Yahoo site (which has a specific section for Canadian material at Yahoo Canada). These are very big, high volume searching sites, most of which have automated "Web beaters" which systematically examine all the known Web sites in the world for new or altered pages, capture the addresses and some aspects of the content. These synopses form a huge database which you then search with the appropriate search form.

Without going into much detail here, the best way of learning how to use these major searchers is to start using them. Search for some topic of interest such as "juvenile offenders" for instance and see what turns up in each of the search engine attempts.

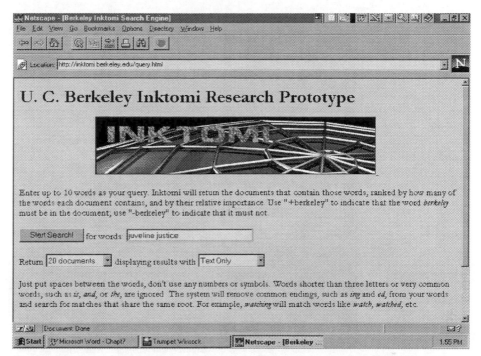

Figure 8 The Inktomi Search Engine. The name refers to an aboriginal word for spider web.

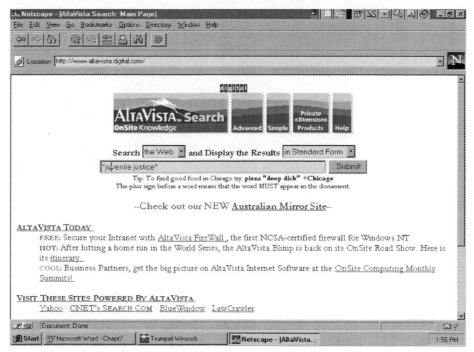

Figure 9 The AltaVista Search engine supported by Digital Equipment.

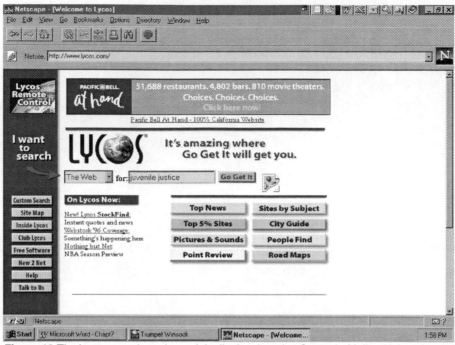

Figure 10 The Lycos search engine, originally developed at Carnegie-Mellon University and now a separate corporation.

DATA RESOURCES

There is a network of social science data archives in the world. They are repositories for deposited raw or packaged data sets which are usually accompanied by documentation and often come with SPSS or SAS control line data sets, or are actually packaged and documented export files ready to use. In Figure 1 in Chapter Two, we saw the home site of the European data archives system. In Canada, there are many such archives located in the larger Canadian universities. They tend to share resources amongst themselves so that a particular large data set need not be permanently stored at more than one site. These university archives have their own professional association (the Canadian Association of Public Data users: CAPDU at http://www.sscl.uwo.ca/capdu) which in turn is linked to an international counterpart (the International Association for Social Science Information Services: IASSIST at http://datalib.library.ualberta.ca/iassist). The major data repositories of the western world are to be found at the University of Michigan in Ann Arbor (ICPSR) and at the University of Essex in England. Most countries now make available Census information and other official survey data at little or no cost to accredited academic researchers. They go out of their way to provide user advice and assistance as well.

We will return to the use of data archive holdings in Chapter Ten. For now, it is sufficient to be aware of their existence and of the importance of their data holdings.

The library data centre at Carleton University for instance holds all Gallup polls conducted in Canada and still in existence back to their inception in 1949. The meta-database is searchable for all questions ever asked and such searches can be conducted on the Web if your request is transmitted through an accredited academic institution. Likewise, everything on the CANSIM database of Statistics Canada time series data, which is housed at the University of Toronto Library data centre is likewise browsable if you make your request from an accredited Canadian academic address. Other databases, such as those maintained by UNICEF, the World Bank, or the IMF are simply available to anyone at all.

CARL UNCOVER

The literature search has been part of the academic research activity for a long, long time. The rationale is simple: you must find out what others have written about your topic, see what data they may have examined, assess the value of their previous work, and finally formulate your own specific research questions in light of this previous work. In order to know what has been done, it was until fairly recently the case that you as researcher had to refer to paper volumes which contained abstracts of other people's published work. Abstracting volumes were and still are produced on paper in most disciplines.

However, electronic utilities began to appear at least ten years ago which have radically changed and expanded the literature search. Service companies such as Current Contents publish both paper reviews of current literature tables of contents and extensive archive CD-ROMs of hundreds of thousands of scientific and literary papers which can be searched for relevant materials. Large summary sets of archival CD-ROMs are now available. These tend to be very expensive and not all university libraries have them in stock. Some discipline-based reference CD-ROMs have also appeared such as *Sociofile* for sociology; and a company called Silverplatter produces a range of disciplinary literature CDs periodically. Your institution's library may subscribe to some or all of these products. They are valuable resources and should be used routinely.

Unfortunately, network licenses for these CD products tend to be much more expensive than single user licenses so you may have to physically go to the library to consult them. Alternatively, you may have to secure a login/password set on your library's server to use them remotely. The same holds true of the law reviews now coming into increasing use in law schools and in legal practice. One alternative is to use UnCover, a service offered by the Colorado Association of Research Libraries to anyone who cares to use it.

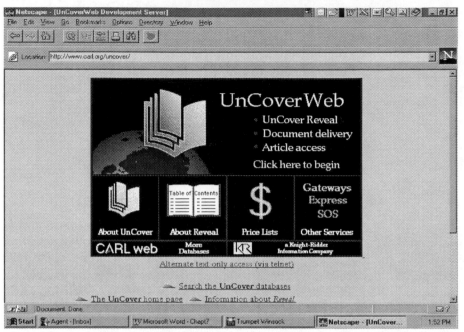

Figure 11 The Web version of CARL UnCover. It is always busy as scholars do literature searches on the free (open access) part of the service. The Telnet (text-based) version of the service is more easily available than the Web version. If the Web-based service is full, a screen will be presented offering Telnet access. Take it and use this alternative. The figures following show an example search using the Telnet avenue of approach.

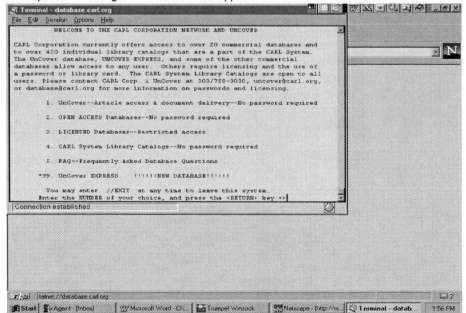

Figure 12 The CARL UnCover Telnet welcome screen. Choose option one, UnCover Article access

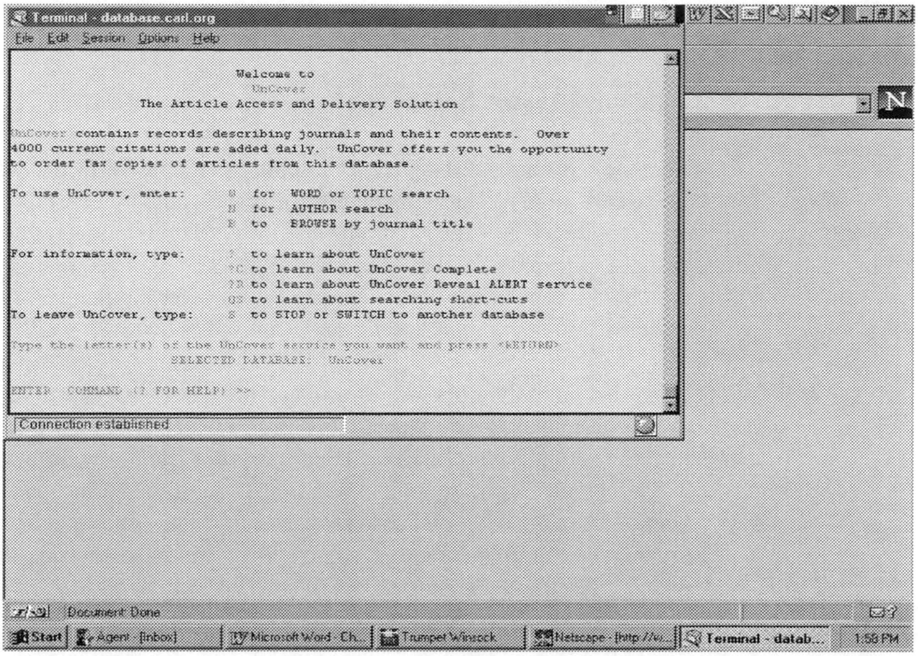

Figure 13 The main search screen. Before this appears, you have to specify which terminal type you are using (VT-100) and choose the no profile, no account public access options. I then chose W for a keyword search.

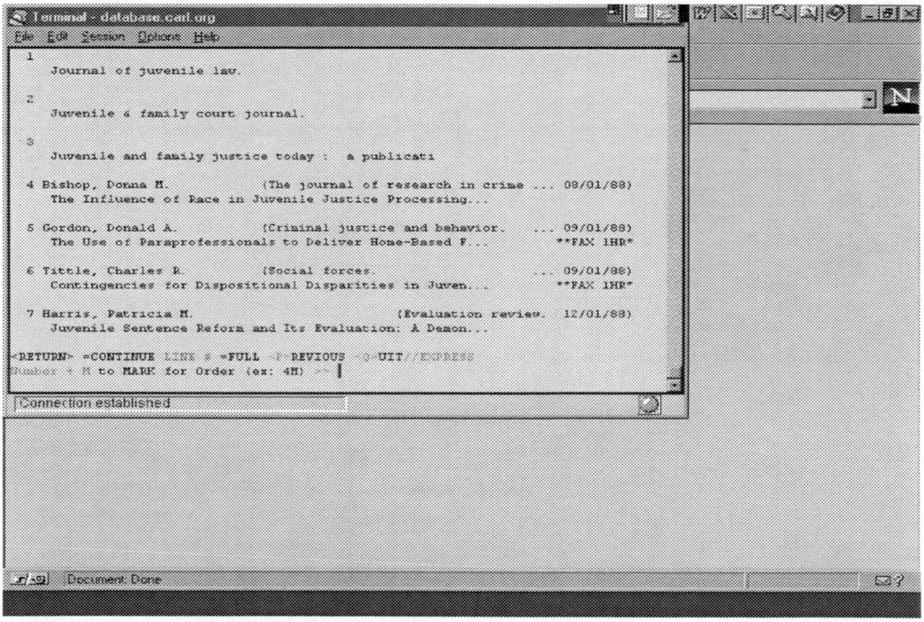

Figure 14 I then specified the search term "juvenile justice". UnCover returned hundreds of references to this topic in the recent literature. Some references have a short abstract but most do not. The next stop is the paper library. Or, I can pay to have a copy of the article faxed to me by the UnCover service.

THE WIDE AREA INFORMATION SERVERS (WAIS)

Near the beginning of this chapter, a screen shot of a WAIS site was shown (Figure 2). There are a large and growing number of WAIS databases available for full-text searching. In order to show the richness of detail available, in this section we will see a text-based rendition of the dialogue with a WAIS site. It is not necessary to do this type of search with text-based tools, though it does offer advantages of clarity in this case since what is being searched for and acquired is text.

The principle behind the WAIS tool is that you as user are given access to the tools to facilitate a search of whole texts within a given area of subject matter looking for references to keyword(s). This is an important step beyond just searching for sites that might have some document you wish to acquire. At this time, a limited amount of whole text material is available for searching. The bases that are available tend to be organized around narrow topics and it is by no means certain that the narrow topic which interests you is the subject of such an organized base of texts.

The best way of approaching this kind of resource is by means of a list of WAIS bases which can be searched to identify a potential source of texts of interest. This search of WAIS bases can be done at several sites. Some of these are:

• the World Wide Web WAIS Gateway at http://www.ncsa.uiuc.edu/SDG/Software/Mosaic/Interfaces/wais/SourceList.html

• the Cern WAIS interface at http://www.w3.org/hypertext/Products/WAIS/Sources/Overview.html

At the latter site, you can consult a directory of WAIS servers, or search by subject, by organization, commercial bases, and through a limited number of USENET newsgroups.

There is also a directory of WAIS servers by topic at http://server.wais.com/directory-of-servers.html; and a list of all WAIS sources at gopher://gopher-gw.micro.umn.edu/11/WAISes/Everything. A sample of the big catalogue of WAIS databases follows; the list represents the first 10 entries of a list which numbers in the hundreds of WAIS databases. Each is keyword searchable:

WAIS SOURCES

The original catalogue

1 Book_of_Mormon.src
   Source

2 CM-applications.src
   Source

3 CM-fortran-manual.src
   Source

4 CM-images.src
   Source

5 CM-paris-manual.src
   Source

6 CM-star-lisp-docs.src
   Source

7 CM-tech-summary.src
   Source

8 CMFS-documentation.src
   Source

9 Connection-Machine.src
   Source

10 EC-enzyme.src
   Source

HOW TO SEARCH A WAIS BASE

Any type of file can be placed in a WAIS database. A WAIS site can include text files, Web documents, GIF image files and audio files if necessary. Indeed you can start one yourself if you acquire the software necessary to do so. It is available free of charge. Most likely though, you will want so search other sites' WAIS bases in search of documents and textual passages on topics of interest to you.

To search a WAIS database, you must first connect to a WAIS gateway such as those listed above. Though the preferable method of doing this now is to use a Web browser, you can also use the *Gopher* tool. The first step in the process is to search the list of bases looking for a database which might have material you could use.

Here is an example of what a page which searches for appropriate WAIS databases at a WAIS gateway looks like:

Getting http://server.wais.com/directory-of-servers.html*
Directory of Servers (p1 of 27)

Directory of Servers

_____

[About Wais Inc] [Wais Home] [Send Mail to Wais] [Help]
_____

YOU CAN SEARCH THE DATABASES BELOW BY SELECTING THEIR NAME.
IF YOU DO NOT KNOW WHICH DATABASE(S) TO SEARCH, ENTER KEY-
WORDS BELOW. FOR INSTANCE IF YOU ENTER THE WORD JOBS, THE
SEARCH WILL BRING A LIST OF DATABASES THAT HAVE INFORMATION
RELATING TO THIS SUBJECT.

_____

   Find: volcanoes_____rn a maximum of [10_]ti-
tles.
   Clear Search

_____

```
            * AAS_jobs
            * AAS_meeting
            * ANU-ACT-Stat-L...
            * ANU-Aboriginal-EconPo...
            * ANU-Aboriginal-Studies...
            * ANU-Aboriginal-Studies...
            * ANU-Ancient-DNA-L..
            * ANU-Ancient-DNA-Studies...
            * ANU-Asia-Pacific-Security
            * ANU-Asia-WWW-Gopher-N...
            * ANU-Asian-Computing...
            * ANU-Asian-Religions...
            * ANU-Asian-Settlements...
            * ANU-AustPhilosophy For...
            * ANU-Austral-SocPol...
            * ANU-Australia-NZ-Hist...
            * ANU-Australian-Econom...
    Data transfer complete*
                    Wais search results (p1 of 2)
```

Once you have found a likely-looking base, focus in on that base by clicking on it or pushing the Enter key while highlighting its title. Then type a word ("volcano"), a question ("What is a volcano"), or a phrase ("volcano causes crisis") in the search field. Then you click on Search, and a list of titles linked to articles will appear. Boolean operators may be used in either type of search. The Boolean operators are AND, OR, NOT, ADJ. Here are some examples of their use:

Volcano OR Hurricane finds articles containing either word.

Volcano NOT Hurricane finds articles containing the first word but not the second.

Volcano ADJ Hurricane ADJ March finds articles containing "Volcano" followed immediately by "Hurricane", followed immediately by "March".

Volcano AND (Hurricane OR Tornado) finds articles containing the first term in combination with the second or third term.

Search queries should be entered in lowercase letters. WAIS ignores common words such as "the" and "on" (known as "stopwords"), along with punctuation (such as question marks and periods), and checks the remaining words against its index of articles. The program then returns a list of articles ranked according to their relevance to the search term(s). The listing also reports on how your request was interpreted.

A WAIS database can be used with plain English language questions. The software doesn't understand the question, it just takes the words and phrases in the question and finds documents that have those words and phrases in them. A specific kind of search asks for documents that contain one or more exact phrases by enclosing them in quotation marks. For example, the query "search volcano" looks specifically for documents that contain this exact phrase. You can also mix English language questions with Boolean operators too such as in "Tell me about volcanoes NOT hurricanes". Since the search engine does not speak any natural language, non-English words or phrases can be used too.

For data sets whose documents have data fields, you can limit the search to those documents containing a value of a particular field, such as a date for instance. If you know the field name (for instance "date"), the syntax would be date > 6-6-95 where the operator may be one of > (greater than), < (less than), >= (greater than or equal to), <= (less than or equal to), or = (equal to). Dates with the following formats are supported: m-d-yy, m-d-yyyy, mm-dd-yy, m/d/yy, mm/dd/yy, m.d.yy, today, and yesterday. Another example would be: date = 7/15/96 TO 7/20/96.

A number of other more complicated questioning structures are also supported. They are documented in the help files at WAIS sites.

Example of Wais search:

Directory of Servers (p2 of 27)
   Find: zoology_____ and return a maximum of [80_]titles.

Clear Search

_____

  * AAS_jobs
  * AAS_meeting
  * ANU-ACT-Stat-L...
  * ANU-Aboriginal-EconPo...
  * ANU-Aboriginal-Studies...
  * ANU-Aboriginal-Studies...
  * ANU-Ancient-DNA-L..
  * ANU-Ancient-DNA-Studies...
  * ANU-Asia-Pacific-Security
  * ANU-Asia-WWW-Gopher-N...
  * ANU-Asian-Computing...

```
        * ANU-Asian-Religions...
        * ANU-Asian-Settlements...
        * ANU-AustPhilosophy For...
        * ANU-Austral-SocPol...
        * ANU-Australia-NZ-Hist...
Data transfer complete*
                            Wais search results  (p1 of 2)
```

WAIS SEARCH RESULTS

[About Wais Inc] [Wais Home] [Send Mail to Wais] [Help]

Results for query: zoology

Search of ANU-Theses-Abstracts
    Score: 1000 , Date: May 23, 1995 , Size: 5668

Search of ANU-Pacific-Archaeology
    Score: 767 , Date: May 23, 1995 , Size: 4384

Search of ANU-Tropical-Archaeobotany
    Score: 755 , Date: May 23, 1995 , Size: 4916

Search of ANU-Radiocarbon-Abstracts
    Score: 736 , Date: May 23, 1995 , Size: 6005

Search of ANU-Ancient-DNA-Studies
    Score: 735 , Date: May 23, 1995 , Size: 5655

Search of ANU-Ancient-DNA-L
    Score: 733 , Date: May 23, 1995 , Size: 6155

Search of com-books
    Score: 712 , Date: May 23, 1995 , Size: 7248

Query Report for this Search
    Score: 1 , Date: Jul 24, 1995 , Size: 674

You may then proceed to read the documents which the search has turned up. To do this, you highlight and click on the document which interests you and it will be retrieved in its entirety for you to read, copy, and send to a colleague or student. The great merit of the WAIS system is that you actually get a complete copy of the source document to work with. Unfortunately, the amount of published material in the WAIS format is as yet quite limited in comparison to conventional publishing on paper. However, in the future, more and more material will be published this way.

In order to have some sense of what a WAIS database catalogue looks like, here is a listing of the first ten items in one particular base. Note the heterogeneity of the contents:

```
Catalog for database: ./com-books
Date: May 31 11:34:01 1994
561 total documents

Document # 1 Type: TEXT
Headline: No Title
DocID: 0 0 /LUMINY/PROGRAMMES/WAIS/com-books.wais

Document # 2 Type: TEXT
Headline: Effets des hydrocarbures sur le ... GUILLAUME J-R.(com-books)
DocID: 0 358 /LUMINY/PROGRAMMES/WAIS/com-books.wais

Document # 3 Type: TEXT
Headline: Etude de la zone de dilution ... DEMARCQ H.(com-books)
DocID: 358 679 /LUMINY/PROGRAMMES/WAIS/com-books.wais

Document # 4 Type: TEXT
Headline: Numerical recipes : the art of ... PRESS W.H. ; FLANNER(com-books)
DocID: 679 897 /LUMINY/PROGRAMMES/WAIS/com-books.wais

Document # 5 Type: TEXT
Headline: L'analyse des ... BOUROCHE J.M.; SAPOR(com-books)
DocID: 897 1093 /LUMINY/PROGRAMMES/WAIS/com-books.wais

Document # 6 Type: TEXT
Headline: Analyses factorielles simples et ... ESCOFIER B.; PAJES J(com-books)
DocID: 1093 1334 /LUMINY/PROGRAMMES/WAIS/com-books.wais
Document # 7 Type: TEXT
Headline: Comment interpreter les resultats d'une ... PALM R.(com-books)
```

```
DocID: 1334 1547 /LUMINY/PROGRAMMES/WAIS/com-books.wais

Document # 8  Type: TEXT
Headline: The analysis of time series : an ... CHATFIELD C.(com-books)
DocID: 1547 1740 /LUMINY/PROGRAMMES/WAIS/com-books.wais

Document # 9  Type: TEXT
Headline: Abstracts ... STATISTICAL THEORY A(com-books)
-- press space for more, use arrow keys to move, '?' for help, 'q' to quit*
Search produced no result. Here's the Catalog for database: com-boo (p3 of
107)
DocID: 1740 1924 /LUMINY/PROGRAMMES/WAIS/com-books.wais

Document # 10  Type: TEXT
Headline: Statistical methods : the geometric ... SAVILLE D.J.. WOOD
G(com-book
s)
DocID: 1924 2142 /LUMINY/PROGRAMMES/WAIS/com-books.wais
```

AFTERWARD

We have seen in this chapter a sampling of the searching and acquiring software and information services available to all users of the Web for research purposes. In a sense, the examples are common to all academic disciplines — they are generic. Beginning in Chapter Nine, we will see a generalized mockup of a research project which utilizes all of the search and use utilities. Then in Chapter Twelve, we will see some discipline-specific examples.

SITES SHOWN IN THIS CHAPTER...

WAIS search form	http://sunsite.unc.edu/cgi-bin/fwais.pl
CANSIM	http://datacentre.epas.utoronto.ca:5680/cansim/cansim.html
Gallup polls search	http://www.carleton.ca/~ssdata/text/gallup.html
Champlain search engine	http://champlain.gns.ca/champlain.html
Aggressive pattern searchers	http://www.carleton.ca/~cmckie/research.html in section 4
Inktomi	http://inktomi.berkeley.edu/query.html
AltaVista	http://www.altavista.digital.com/
Lycos	http://www.lycos.com/
UnCover	http://www.carl.org/uncover/
UnCover (Telnet version)	telnet://database.carl.org

NOTES:

[1] http://www.microsoft.com

[2] They have a "frequently asked questions" file at http://www.apa.org/journals/faq.html. There is also a general APA e-mail address psychinfo@apa.org

[3] A plainer version of this page is available at http://www.carleton.ca/~cmckie/research2.html. It doesn't have coloured backgrounds or Javascript effects and works best with some forms of browsers.

CHAPTER

SEVEN

Elementary Information Dispensing: Web Sites, USENET, Listservs

"Bill Gates, billionaire founder of Microsoft, recently bought one of Leonardo's notebooks...Outbidding the world's great museums and libraries, Gates got himself a piece of the Renaissance. What Bill Gates doesn't realize is that his purchase is in the very best Renaissance tradition. Buying priceless and desirable art objects was the classic Renaissance way of transforming yourself from successful entrepreneur into respected toff."

Lisa Jardine, "Gates: new Renaissance man." **Shiftcontrol**, Issue 3, 18-24, October 1996.

Although at first blush, the Web is the star of current Internet service, there are several other aspects of Internet activity worthy of mention here. Clearly, the World Wide Web is growing exponentially in volume and importance. There is every reason to believe that this situation will continue well on into the future. Web sites can deliver focused material in a highly superior manner in very large volume. However, the Web lacks the human interactive aspect for the most part. For this reason, interactive forums on USENET and listservs are likely to persist and grow as supporting and complementary services available on the Internet.

In addition to supporting e-mail and the USENET newsgroups (which are themselves becoming micro-marketplaces for commerce and the exchange of news, views and opinions), a new set of Internet tools is coming into view which, although Internet-based, offers a new set of utilities. These new capacities include long distance telephoning, video-conferences, co-writing facilities, and direct-to-desktop delivery of news service products. These tools lower the cost of activities previously confined to the well-heeled. For the moment, these new tools are little more than toys; however they do have the potential to grow into something worthwhile in the future. The lesson for users is that although the Web is the current star, the Internet can deliver much more and it is likely that it in fact will do so.

When you can combine standard research tactics with innovative yet timeless ones, such as direct conversations with researchers in remote locations at little or no additional cost, the notion of research takes on a new and much more adventurous tone. The full potential of these new ways of exchanging and sharing cannot now be foreseen. It would not be out of place, though, to suggest that they hold revolutionary potential in all senses of that word. Whether or not this potential will ever be realized is anybody's guess. One aspect is the leveling operation of the tools. Given the low cost barriers to access, it may well be assumed that virtually everyone engaged in the social science research enterprise will have access to everyone else, minimally by e-mail but perhaps much more. More efficient use of resources, much greater timeliness of conversations and of peer review (now recast in a different light[1]), much more innovative uses of scattered human ingenuity are all possible given the right set of conditions. They offer the prospect of easy collaboration between strangers; and the development of non-stranger relationships between colleagues who will never meet face to face. Teaching from a remote location is one obvious outcome; teaching without physical class size limitations is another.

Some of the tools for collaborative writing already exist outside of the Internet environment. Lotus Notes for instance allows co-writing of documents in the intranet (closed corporate network) context. The class of this "groupware" is bound to expand onto the Internet. Already, Microsoft NetMeeting is available for Internet use and more programs will follow. Voice communication software called CoolTalk is already bundled in the Netscape package. And video-conferencing can already be done inexpensively if a high-volume Internet feed is available. For instance, the programs *VDOPhone* and *CUSeeMe* already allow 'face-to-face' conversations.

LISTSERVS

One of the useful features of electronic mail is that you may send the same message to a predefined set of recipients. To do this you use a feature of the mailer program called aliases. You may define a group of electronic mail addresses and give the list a simple alias. Thus, the alias "group" could be defined as encompassing bill@smith.edu, bob@jones.edu, and alice@nowhere.com. The *Elm* mailer has a specific alias function built in to it for setting up alias groups. Other mailers make similar provisions.

After setting up an alias "group", you could send a message to all the members of 'group' by designating "group" as the recipient of your message. The message would only be composed once yet copies are sent to each member of "group". You need not resend the message at all; each member would receive his or her own copy of the e-mail message. This utility is particular useful if you want to send the same message to all members of a group of persons which you will wish to send messages to many times, for example, a particular classroom group. This is a simple technique that takes little time and can be utilized over and over again, there being no limit on the number of times you can use a list, nor how many lists you maintain, nor indeed how many individuals may be on any list. You can control admission to a "group" or allow anybody on it who wants to be; that decision is entirely up to you.

What has tended to happen is that aliases (or standard list mailers), begun initially to reach a small group, eventually grow to contact hundreds of people, something that alias lists were not initially designed to do. The person who maintains a very large alias list becomes in some sense the arbiter of what gets distributed and what does not. But on the other hand, that person must also assume responsibility for changing the membership list of the alias periodically. This can take a lot of time and energy. Maintaining a very large alias list and especially making the editorial judgments about what gets mailed out can come to be a very large job.

To address these difficulties, *listserv* software was developed which automated the process. The software which supports a listserv operation is free of charge and may be easily acquired. Installing it, however, may require the permission of your service host operator, since lists generate large amounts of e-mail traffic and are subject to attack by mass posting by unhelpful persons intent on destroying your list. This is called a *denial of service attack* since routine use of the list has to be shut off as a result. The administrator of your service provider is the person to talk to concerning setting up a new listserv. They can be set up by the administrator relatively easily; watchfulness on the list dynamics may be the price of his or her cooperation.

If you as a member of the Internet community wish to receive posts from such a list (and there are literally thousands of such listservs on topics of every type available), you send a special e-mail message to the automated remailing software of that particular list asking that your name be added to the redistribution list. Remember that what you receive is a stream of e-mail messages some of which will not correspond at all to your interests. The message would take the following form:

```
To: major-domo@beatles.list.smith.edu
Subject: [left blank]
Message: subscribe beatles rluxembe@smith.edu  [your e-mail address]
```

The new name (your e-mail address) will then be added to the list for receiving the posts. To unsubscribe, the process is essentially the same except the word *unsubscribe* replaces the word *subscribe*. Major-domo listserv software operates without human intervention. For this reason, it is susceptible to spoofing. It would be possible to sign up for a list in some notorious celebrity's name, for instance, if you found out what his/her e-mail account address is. This is the electronic equivalent of a malicious unwanted pizza delivery attack.

Today, there are thousands of such lists. Some are moderated (i.e. they are still edited - censored if you will) but most are unmoderated and every message sent to the list (in this example, a message to listserv@beatles.list.smith.edu) will be sent out indiscriminately to the hundreds or thousands of people who have subscribed without further human intervention. Not surprisingly, the volume which such lists can generate can be enormous. And some listservs have little redeeming social content; one carries a single short message, David Letterman's top ten list from the previous evening for instance, to thousands of members of a list. Others may generate hundreds of messages a day to your account. You may well decide that a particular list is not for you for this reason alone. Another concern is the so-called message-to-noise ratio. Some lists carry a lot of extraneous chatter and the occasional bit of substance. You must be prepared as a subscriber to deal with the chatter in a peremptory manner (i.e. delete unread).

SOME EXAMPLES OF LISTSERVS RELEVANT TO EDUCATION....

CNEDUC-L — for discussion of computer networks in education, with an emphasis on online resources *<cneduc-l@tamvm1.tamu.edu>*
COSNDISC — a public discussion group of the Consortium for School Networking *<cosndisc@list.cren.net>*
EDTECH — broad discussions of educational technology *<edtech@msu.edu>*

Another powerful tool, though not a listserv, is AskERIC which provides interactive educational information to educators by Gopher, FTP, Telnet, WAIS, and the World Wide Web including lesson plans and full-text materials such as the archives of postings to EDTECH and LM_NET listservs. AskERIC runs on the SUNSITE servers supported by Sun Microsystems around the United States. The Web version of askERIC can be found at the following address: http://ericir.syr.edu/.

HOW TO FIND OUT ABOUT DISCUSSION GROUPS

Some valiant souls maintain lists of listservs for the general mapping of the Internet. With these lists, you can browse what's available and obtain information on how to subscribe to each. One example is the following:

Diane Kovacs Electronic Conference Lists
http://n2h2.com/KOVACS/whatis.html

An example of what you would see there follows:

Select one of:

(DIR) Anthropology, Cross Cultural Studies, and Archaeology
(DIR) Communication Studies
(DIR) Geography and Miscellaneous Regional and Individual Country Stud-
ies
(DIR) Journalism
(DIR) Latin American Studies
(DIR) Law, Criminology, Justice
(DIR) Political Science and Politics
(DIR) Popular Culture
(DIR) Psychology and Psychiatry
(DIR) Social Activism
(DIR) Sociology and Demography
(DIR) Women's Studies/Gender Studies

[selecting Geography and Miscellaneous Regional and Individual Country
Studies]

.

Transferred 3143 bytes*
  Geography and Miscellaneous Regional and Individual Country Studies (p1
of 3)

      GEOGRAPHY AND MISCELLANEOUS REGIONAL AND INDIVIDUAL
COUNTRY STUDIES

(FILE) ALGERIA-NET
(FILE) alt.culture.alaska
(FILE) alt.culture.hawaii
(FILE) alt.culture.indonesia
(FILE) alt.culture.karnataka
(FILE) alt.culture.kersia

```
(FILE) alt.culture.ny-upstate
(FILE) alt.culture.oregon
(FILE) alt.culture.tuva
(FILE) alt.culture.us.asian-indian
(FILE) alt.culture.us.southwest
(FILE) AMERICAN-STUDIES
(FILE) AMERSTDY
(FILE) BASQUE-L
(FILE) CERRO-L
(FILE) CHINA
(FILE) COASTNET
(FILE) CPS-L


[Selecting CHINA]


Data transfer complete*
                                    CHINA
LN: CHINA
TI: Electronic Discussion Group for Chinese Studies Discussion of
any issue in Chinese Studies is welcomed in this forum. This
includes but is not limited to the fields of anthropology, art
history, economics, history, literature, linguistics, politics,
religion, and sociology. The discussion is handled with regular
electronic mail. For those who subscribe, each submission to the
discussion will be sent to their electronic mail box.
SU: (B) LISTSERV@PUCC (I) LISTSERV@PUCC.PRINCETON.EDU
ED: Yes
AR: Yes, Monthly
MO:  Tom Nimick (B) Q4356@PUCC (I) Q4356@PUCC.PRINCETON.EDU
SA: (B) CHINA@PUCC (I) CHINA@PUCC.PRINCETON.EDU
KE: China - Chinese Culture
PK: Geography and Miscellaneous Regional and Individual Country
Studies= compiled by Gladys Smiley Bell - GBELL@kentvm.kent.edu


Commands: Use arrow keys to move, '?' for help, 'q' to quit, '<-' to go back
```

This minimal chunk of information alerts you to the existence of the China listserv. It also tells you that it is available to everybody and that if you wish to join, you must send a message to *listserv@pucc.princeton.edu* or to the moderator by e-mail. You may post to the list by sending your message to *china@pucc.princeton.edu*. You would use this Kovacs list of lists with either the gopher tool or the Web tools.

There is no way of adequately conveying the number of lists or scope of the listserv universe because it is changing all the time. The content ranges from the highly specific (e.g. growing orchids) to the highly general (e.g. American politics). Even on very specialized lists however, the volume of posts can be formidable. Lists are good places to find highly technical advice on narrow specialties and topics. In general, the experts on any given topic may be found on such a specialty list.

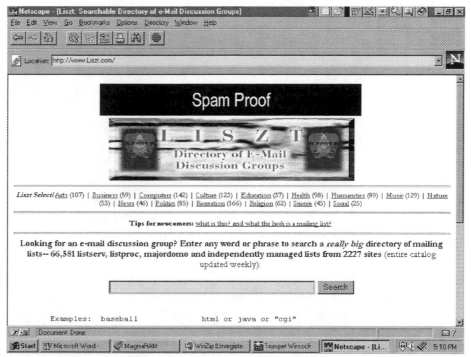

Figure 1 The Liszt site which tracks listservs and makes the database accessible to searching.

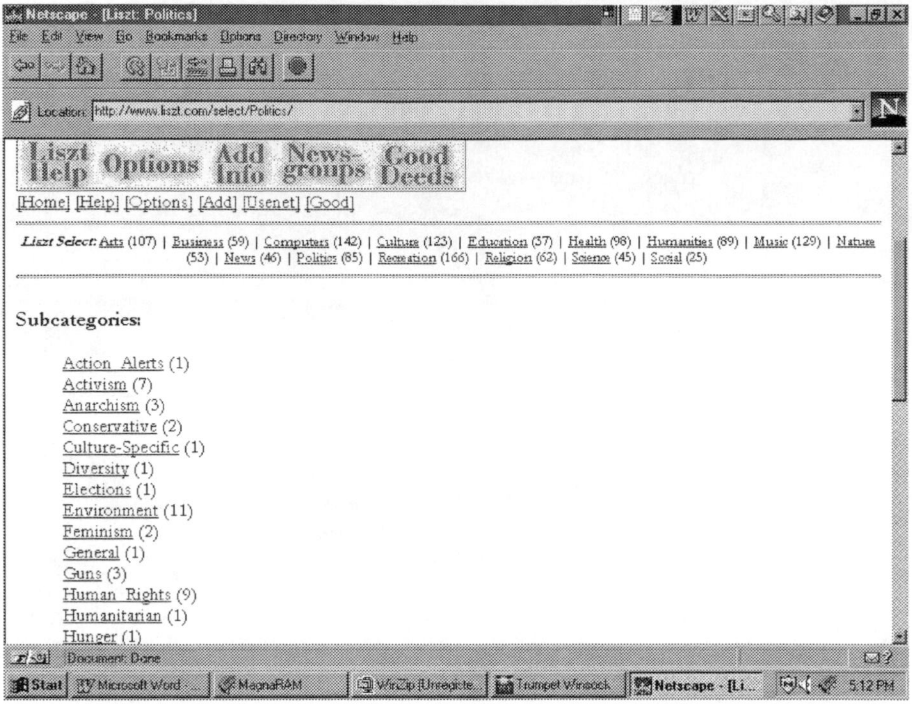

Figure 2 Displaying the breakdown of sub-headings under the general heading of "politics" at the Liszt Web site narrows the search for listservs you might be interested in subscribing to.

Lists are thus a very valuable learning resource if one can find the appropriate list or lists to subscribe to. Really active lists are often the first place new information or findings appear. Listservs may in fact be in the process of becoming **the** primary distribution channel for new information and research findings in certain disciplines and narrow fields already. This is because listservs are virtually instantaneous and are not paper-dependent. In some disciplines (and especially in the physical and biological sciences), participation in specific lists has become mandatory if one has any hope at all of keeping up with new developments, particularly where participants are spread thinly around the world. Because of the volume involved, some listservs now offer a digest format in which each day's message traffic is bundled and e-mailed to you once every day with the postings organized by subject matter.

USENET NEWSGROUPS

Once listservs get very large (in terms of number of subscribers) and/or very popular or influential, they are often moved to USENET. This is a separate Network channel devoted to distributing personal and informational notices, some of which look like e-mail. USENET is a collection of several thousand newsgroups, each of which has a topic focus. To read any USENET newsgroup, your site must have access to the feed of postings (NNTP or the network news transport protocol) or alternatively your personal computer must have its own access at some site. There are numerous public access NNTP servers around the world which can be used by anyone with the reader software. This aspect of the USENET service (multiple sources) is one of its strengths. Attempts by any service provider or any country to stifle any one or any group of USENET newsgroups are bound to fail because of multiple sourcing of postings.

Most sites or hosts on the Internet do not take the full newsgroups feed. There are a couple of reasons for this. First, the volume is staggering - in the range of tens of megabytes per day for the full feed (1 megabyte = a million text characters). Were a site to accept the full feed, temporary storage of staggering proportions would have to be provided and most operators don't want to make this sort of investment in storage hardware. One site which does take the full feed needs 4 gigabytes of online storage (or 4 billion text character storage capacity) to control the flow at its present levels and keep the messages around for a few days so that clients have a chance to read them before they are deleted as stale.

Rather, most sites take and provide to their users only a subset of all available newsgroups, and then only keep the items for a few days. The second reason for selectivity has to do with content. Many of the most popular newsgroups handle a torrent of pornographic material of greater or lesser offence and illegality. Many system operators do not carry the high-volume *alt.binaries* hierarchy both for the reason of propriety and because of the high volumes involved. Digitized pictures make large files and digitized movies make even larger files. The path of discretion usually is to avoid these groups. Nevertheless, they are extremely popular high volume newsgroups. Other examples of high-volume newsgroups are concerned with telephone hacking tips (e.g. alt.2600) and software distribution newsgroups (e.g. alt.binaries.uilities).

There are other very narrowly defined USENET newsgroups which cater to a variety of focused interests (e.g. how to grow tropical vegetables). The appeal of newsgroups in this context is that the small group of the interested is dispersed over the world and members are unlikely to know each other personally therefore making a listserv impractical since there is no prior pattern of information exchange, a necessity for a listserv. Indeed, many people who read a particular newsgroup **never** post a message to it. They are referred to as "lurkers" who just absorb information and do not contribute at all.

With a newsgroup, someone somewhere starts it with a (hopefully) descriptive title and then it is either used or not used based solely on its merits. Such a person need not know of any other persons who share the newsgroup's interest; it is a much more speculative activity than starting a listserv. In principle, if you are intent on starting a new newsgroup, and are persistent in your wish and can demonstrate sufficient potential user interest, you may well be permitted to do so.

Reading of newsgroups is done with a reader program (for example, Tin, Rn or Nn — three common UNIX shell account newsreaders). *Netscape*, the World Wide Web browser of choice, has its own reader built in and there are several freeware products available as well (such as Free Agent, the freeware version of Agent) if you can select either a public NNTP feed site you can use as a source, or the service provided by your own provider. Strictly local newsgroups, such as the newsgroup I run for students in one of my courses, can generally only be obtained through your local service provider, such as your university or college.

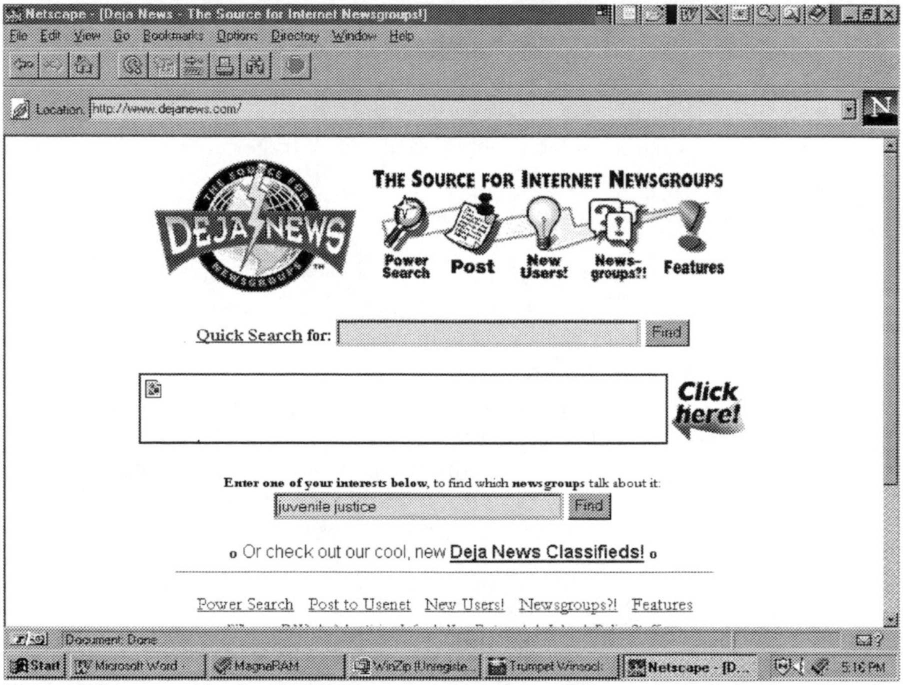

Figure 3 One way of finding USENET newsgroups to follow is to search the Deja News Web site. It also contains archives of past postings you may wish to scan. In this example, we ask which newsgroups might have submissions on "juvenile justice".

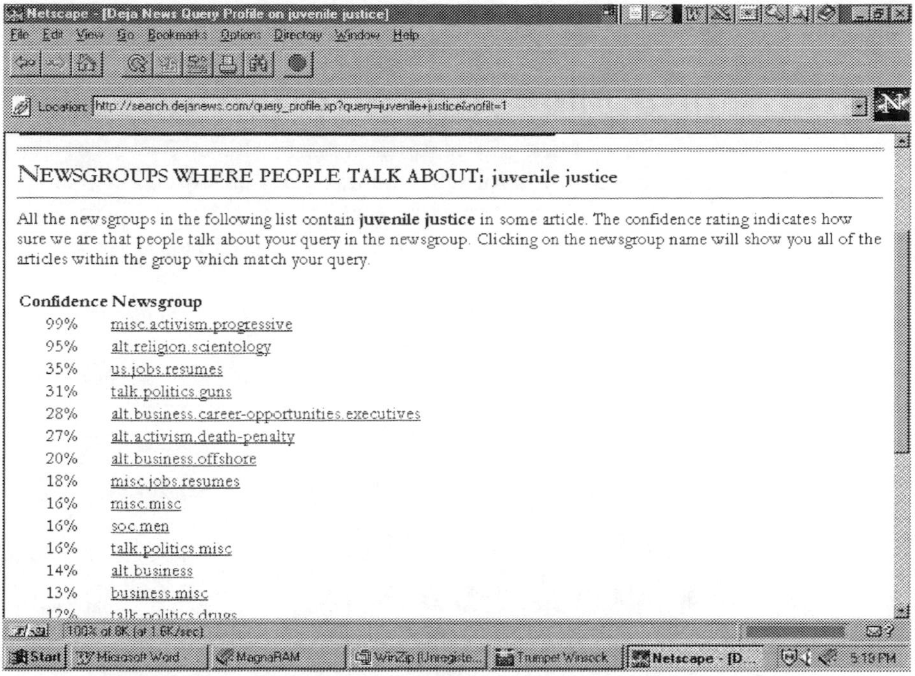

Figure 4 Deja News suggests some potentially interesting USENET newsgroups to look at. Routine access to any of them however is dependent on your service provider accepting the feed for that particular group.

Since the overall volume of postings tends to be extraordinary, it is useful to have a reader that can "thread" the postings. By this we mean the ability to sort the postings by subject and by order of submission so that you can see the logic of post and response in chronological order, more or less. Without threading, a heavy-volume group is very hard to understand since you may well read a response to a question, and comments on the comments, before you are presented with the original posted question. Threading is a response to volume and cross-talk. It also allows you to delete (or mark as read) an entire thread which does not interest you.

When you first start up a newsgroup reader such as *Tin* in UNIX shell mode, Netscape or Agent in TCP/IP mode, you are not "subscribed" to any groups at all. You sub-scribe from the local availability list. In tin, this is done with the **y** (for yank) command which will present you with the complete (yanked in) list of newsgroups available at your site. In TCP/IP mode, you ask your software to secure a full list of newsgroups on offer at your site and then subscribe to the ones you want to monitor. Since this list is itself quite lengthy, you can use a searching tool to keyword search for groups which have your chosen word in their titles. For example in Tin, you might search (the command is the forward slash **/**) for the word education in the title. Tin will find these sequentially and you can browse the contents of each newsgroup it finds, and de-cide whether you wish to subscribe or not. If you do, subscription is done with the **s** (for subscribe) command.

Once you have subscribed to as many or as few groups as you wish to routinely look at, you **y** (for yank) out the rest, leaving only your selections. These selections are then recorded in a file usually called *.newsrc* (or just *newsrc* in Netscape). This file will keep track of what messages your have seen. Newly created groups will be submitted to you for subscription as they are created thereafter; and you can go back and subscribe to other existing older newsgroups at any time. One group of particular use to the new users is *alt.internet.services*. Much of the new content on the Internet is announced in this newsgroup.

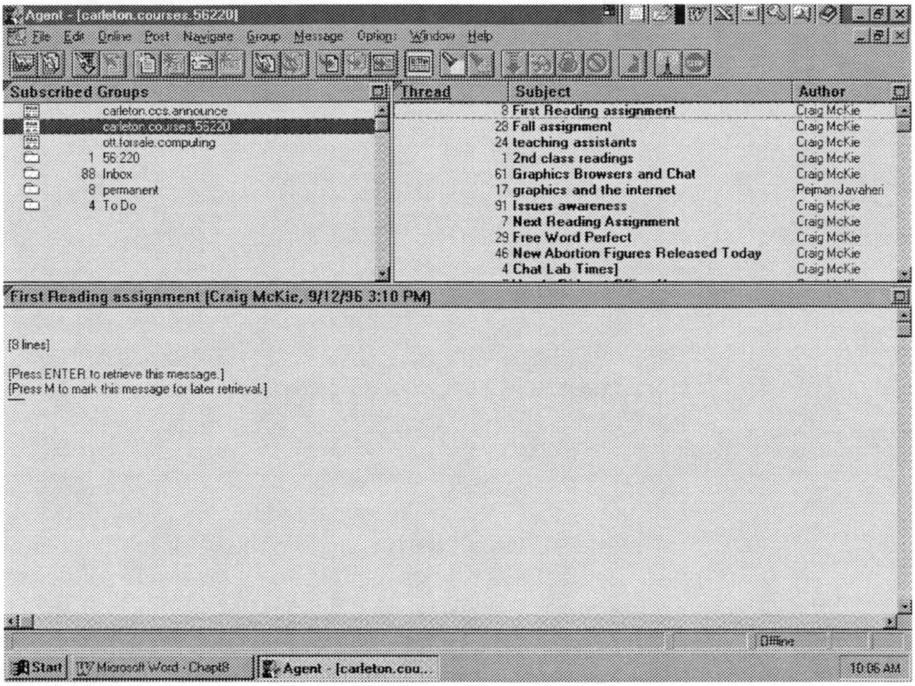

Figure 5 Here is what the USENET newsgroups look like when viewed in a modern TCP/IP new and e-mail reader, in this case Agent.

In Figure 5, you can see an example of the flow of messages in one newsgroup, in this example, my postings to a class newsgroup at Carleton University. Using a reader like Agent allows me to subscribe to as many or as few newsgroups as I wish. Once subscribed, I can ask the program to download the message headings from sub-scribed newsgroups, then select any I wish to look at, then download the message bodies of those I have selected. The process is painless and efficient. Note that I can also construct filters to automatically delete postings from people whom I have iden-tified as persons whose posts can be ignored. I can post new messages to the newsgroup just as easily as I can send e-mail messages; the process is essentially the same.

In addition, you and I can scan virtually the entire USENET information flow for the previous few days using special sites at the following address. Finding a useful article may be frustrating, however, if your site doesn't carry that particular newsgroup. You can try reference.com at http://reference.com/. This service is particularly useful if your local newsfeed is small, restricted or even nonexistent. The service will e-mail postings to you according to the user profile you leave with it on record.

You can post a new message to any newsgroup through your newsreader, either as a new contribution, or as a follow-up to somebody else's comments. You can also post to newsgroups using the UNIX shell *Pnews* program available on many service provider sites, and if you have no newsgroup feed at all, you can still post through an e-mail-to-newsgroup gateway, or *Telnet* to another site which does offer USENET services free of charge, such as your local freenet or some other freenet in the world to which you have subscribed. To use the *Telnet* tool to reach a freenet in a UNIX shell account, the syntax is as follows. From the prompt, type *telnet telnet.ncf.carleton.ca* and then press the Return key (for example) and login as "guest" when you receive a response. If you are using a graphics browser, you open the Goto panel and enter the counterpart line telnet://telnet.ncf.carleton.ca. Information about permanent user accounts can be found in the information menus you will find there. This will work if you have a Telnet client installed on your computer (such as NetTerm). If you do not currently have a telnet client installed, your browser will ask you to obtain one. A simple Telnet client is available free of charge in the Winsock install archive for instance as *trmptel.exe*. It is extremely limited in capability (lacking the ability to download and upload, for instance) but it will do until you get a better one.

There is no reason why you cannot start your own newsgroup or listserv on any research topic of continuing interest to you. To start a newsgroup or a listserv, you need only apply to your service provider for permission to do so. Provided your choice of focus offers no legal liability to the provider, you are likely to obtain approval. There is some overhead effort in maintaining the list and newsgroup software but it is likely to have been undertaken anyway, so your request need not pose a problem to the operator in terms of labour costs.

THE E-LIBRARY: A SPECIAL CASE

There is wide agreement that in the future the world's supply of printed documents currently held in libraries will be digitized and made available in a sort of worldwide electronic library. It is not clear who will pay for and carry out the scanning of these resources which are truly massive in proportion. Technical difficulties abound in trying to scan old printed documents. Old paper becomes transparent or changes colour, type faces are irregular or slightly crooked, and pages can be physically missing. Nevertheless, the grand digitization project is underway, but with limited results so far. The process of course has a legal copyright aspect as well, so it is to be expected that digitized books, for instance, will first appear when their copyrights expire. Another issue is what to do with diagrams and illustrations. If conversion of text only occurs, important graphical elements will be left out. Notwithstanding all these difficulties there are modest initial examples of what is to come. We will look at one here, the E-Library, a commercial service.

If you find that the literature material you are searching for is contemporary, and occurs in trade publications, then it might be wise to investigate the E-Library (http://www.elibrary.com). This is a commercial service but it does offer two week free trial periods, and probably a sequence of them if you handle your accounts properly.

The E-library deals with contemporary literature (mostly from magazines and trade publications) plus a selection of newspaper and television transcript sources. It can be useful in locating commentary and extremely recent material to add to your document. Since it searches the bodies of its text files and not just the titles, it can find obscure references that other searchers cannot. The sequence of figures below shows how to use this service.

In the first of the sequence, we have visited the E-library main page and have entered a name in the search box, Phil Agre, the philosopher of the Web who teaches in the Department of Communications at the University of California in San Diego. Since Phil is a loquacious soul who holds forth at public gatherings frequently, we can expect to find his name scattered through the text files at the E-Library.

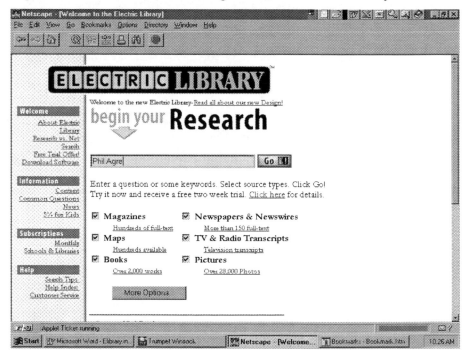

Figure 6 The E-library entry screen.

In the second frame, we see the results of the search. Indeed it is the case that Phil's name is embedded in a large number of text files. For the sake of this example, we will ask for the whole text of the first article found. Note that the resources found are ranked by a score which reflects the closeness of fit to the pattern being searched for. This is important because partial matches can often lead the researcher onto unanticipated and fruitful side trips into related matters.

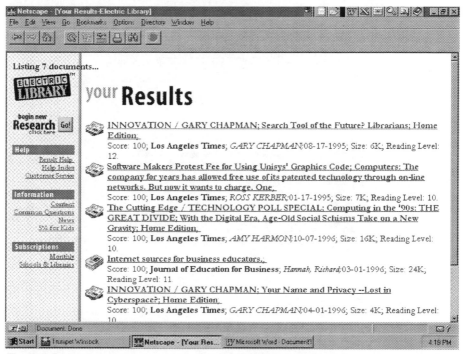

Figure 7 E-Library presents the results of the information request.

In the third frame, we are asked for our account name and password. Normally this would incur charges, but again there is a two-week free trial available to everyone who visits. On this frame, we enter the user name and password. Note that if you were a fees-paying customer, you could click on the box which requests this information be saved. Clicking on this box will create a cookie on your computer so that you do not have to enter the account and password on subsequent visits.

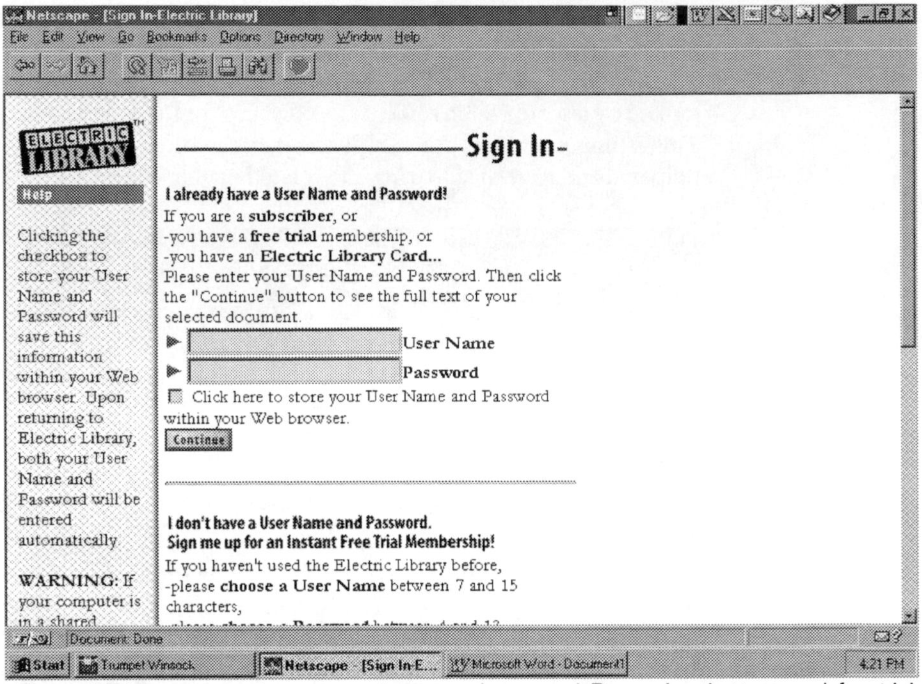

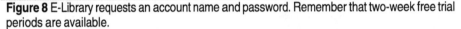

Figure 8 E-Library requests an account name and password. Remember that two-week free trial periods are available.

Finally, in the fourth frame in this sequence, the whole text of the article we have requested is presented. You can save it, use parts of it to paste into your own document as a quote, or send copies to your friends. The only difficulty with the attribution of your quote is that since you have left the paper copy behind, there is generally no way to tell which page your quotation appeared on in the original paper copy. In the absence of this, give the source as an electronic copy retrieved from the E-Library and give as much other detail as you can.

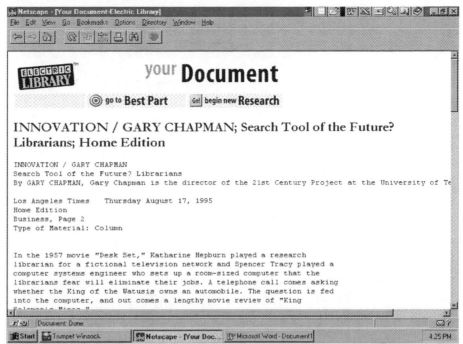

Figure 9 Finally, E-library sends you the whole text you requested. Note that some whole books are available where the copyright has expired.

SITES SHOWN IN THIS CHAPTER...

Diane Kovacs Conference List	http:// n2h2.com/KOVACS/whatis.html
Liszt	http://www.Liszt.com/
Deja News	http://www.dejanews.com/
E-Library	http://www.elibrary.com/

NOTES:

[1] Consider the following item, for example, which appeared in Edupage in the February 27, 1997 edition: "An editor at The Journal of the American Medical Association and an adjunct professor of medicine at the University of California at San Francisco have recommended an electronic peer-review system that would allow researchers to have ready access to all comments related to a particular paper through a consolidated database. Editors could review readers' comments, request responses from authors, and update the database on a quarterly basis."

PART
THREE

SKILLS FOR EVERYDAY WEB USE IN RESEARCH

We now move on to the core material of this book. All of the technical detail, the software, the hardware and the preparation are all preparatory and peripheral to the task at hand, that of successfully carrying out social science research projects. In this section, we will show in a detailed fashion how the tools of the Web interact with and enhance traditional skills and knowledge to form a more potent and dynamic mix of tools, skills and human insight with the depth of the emergent digital research community in the world.

In Chapters Nine through Eleven, we will work step by step through the social science research process, first in a generic case involving a generalized program of work according to a generalized process of steps from inception to the completion of a social science research project. Then, in Chapter Twelve, the process will be reproduced in abbreviated discipline-specific form.

Other aspects of the Web form the subjects of the remainder of this section. Specifically, the question of how to become an active information provider on the Web through mounting your own Web pages will be discussed.

CHAPTER

EIGHT

The World Wide Web: Basics

"I've done many [horoscope] readings on Bill Gates, mostly in an attempt to figure out how to deal with him and his effect on the world. He is the focal point for the computer industry. It is the inappropriate marketing and use of computers that is largely responsible for the destruction on this planet. Most really hard core people in this industry understand this, but due to non-disclosure agreements and threats, can say nothing about it."

Joan L. Brewer, one of the few true female kooks on the net; her specialty is paranoia about BillGates.
She blames him for most of the world's evils including the destruction of her health and family.
The source of this posting was: redrose@chinook.halcyon.com (Joan L. Brewer),
Newsgroups:alt.fan.bill-gates, Subject: Bills Numerology future, Date: 13 Mar 1995 01:09:16 GMT.

We have briefly discussed the nature and structure of the World Wide Web in previous chapters but let us first review the concept. The Web was designed for easy automatic distribution of public information files, initially to scientists running experiments at the CERN facility in Switzerland. The basic elements of the information transaction were that non-sensitive material would be placed in a public area on a public server and that thereafter anyone could request and immediately receive a perfect literal copy of anything in that public area. The nature of the transaction was to be automated by removing most security controls and reducing the transaction to a barebones you-want-you-get basis. Very simple text-oriented software was written for UNIX computers in order that the information requests could be complied with without human intervention; no controls of any kind were implemented on who could take what files away, nor how many copies they could take.

In practice, the early browser client (called WWW) would send a brief request for a file and the server software would transmit the requested resource without further ado, authentication or encryption precautions. No records would be kept outside of a routine transaction event log, and if the transaction was anonymized the log would not reflect the true recipient of the files transmitted in any case.

Today, the process works in much the same fashion except the number of active servers and the number of files on offer has increased immeasurably. In all probability there are now hundreds of thousands of such servers, each of which may have dozens or hundreds of Web sites on offer. The number of documents and files on all Web sites at any given time is unknowable, but certainly the total is now in the multiple millions and is increasing at a very high rate as commerce comes to the Web to stay.

While very many of the documents and files on offer are of no intrinsic interest to the social science researcher, there are many that are. We can break the process of using these resources into some basic elements, together with an indication of where these electronic research activities fit into the age-old analytic process:

• learning how to use a Web browser and relevant search engines, archives, and catalogues of library literature resources;
• locating whatever resources are of potential use by active searching, e-mail queries, and listserv postings;
• locating relevant literature in your area by means of CARL UnCover and similar literature searching sites (some local to your library such as scanning Current Contents and Sociofile);
• prioritizing the importance of documents and resources you have found and obtaining the actual analytic resources, in electronic form if possible, or on paper or magnetic media if necessary;
• the classic cerebral analytic exercise of writing, examining, analyzing and reflection;
• remote computing on remote data sets if required;
• communicating with scholars interested in your material by e-mail and listservs for advice and analytic assistance;
• composing draft analyses and commentary;
• posting your drafts to valued reviewers for comments;
• starting a Web site to make your finished materials available to the public coincident with traditional publication efforts;
• maintaining a unique compendium of resources in your particular disciplinary specialty on your own Web page, which would grow as your career as a student or professional elaborates over time.

The material now available on the Web is a blend of fact and fancy, scholarship and nonsense, subversion and orthodoxy, books with expired copyright, sports scores, news, and advertisements. Since no one is in charge (by design), and since there is no real regulation of the Web, an agreeable chaos confronts the scholar. While nonsense abounds, the effects of censorship do not. That is the basic information anarchy trade-off. A symptom of this fact is the appearance of academic essay archives available to anyone anywhere for browsing and appropriation. Indolent students can pick up an essay, for instance one originally written 10 years ago in Texas, and submit it to an unwitting instructor in Ottawa. Realistically, the chances of getting caught are small, provided the subject matter does not make grandiloquent claims of intimate personal observation in the barrios, for instance. You may browse one such archive at http://www.schoolsucks.com.

If you have a UNIX shell account, or if you have access to a Web server running Windows95, or NT with which you can construct Web pages with Microsoft FrontPage or other similar products, or if your service provider mounts Web sites for you, you too can participate as an information provider on the Web. You must, however, explicitly ask for procedures to follow, naming conventions to use, and what file locations and permissions are required so that you know where to put your HTML files. HTML is the lingua franca of the Web. It is a system of marking up functional elements in a file so that the browser that acquires your file knows what to do with the elements you have included.

LEARNING HOW TO USE YOUR WEB BROWSER

In order to fully utilize the research potential of the Web, you must become comfortable with the use of your Web browser. For most people now, this will mean learning how to use a graphical Web browser such as Netscape. The following figure shows its screen as it would appear to you when you start it up.

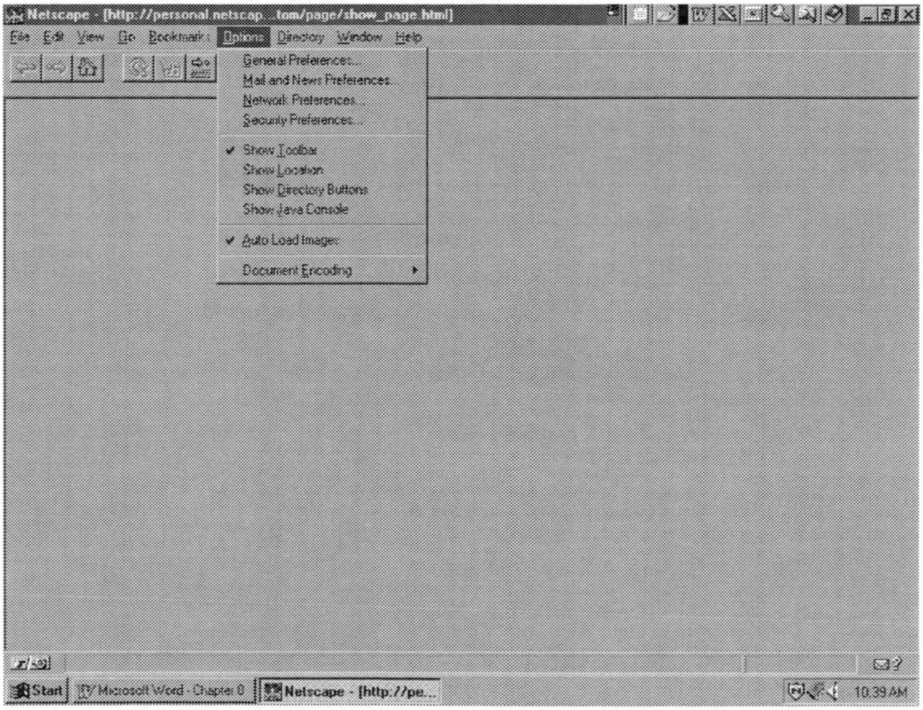

Figure 1 The Netscape screen on startup with the options menu pulled down.

The Netscape screen is configured in the standard fashion that all versions of Windows want to show you a screen. A series of functional categories is listed across the top, each of which when clicked reveals a menu of choices, in the case of the menu shown in Figure 1, options relating to how the Netscape control and command function choices can be arranged. Below this line of text choices is a button bar with the main commands you will need. These functions tend to be presented as pictographs. For example, the little drawing of a house, if clicked on, will load the Web page you have designated as your overall starting off page (if any). Another button shows a right pointing arrow with a series of dots underneath. This is the button you push to go to a new site; a panel opens when you click on this button and you write the address you want to visit in the panel and then press return. Note that in current versions of graphical Web browsers the first part of the URL address can be omitted (i.e. leave out the http:// if you want). The left facing arrow returns you to the page you visited immediately previously (if any). If you are using the program in a lab, the preferences section will already be set up for your use, but if you install Netscape on a home computer you will have to supply information in the preferences section in order that the program works properly.

If you can get comfortable with the steps listed above you can use the help files to learn everything else you need to know. Alternatively you can press every button and see what is revealed; the options tend to be self-explanatory. One further word of advice concerns bookmarks. "Bookmarks" appears on the text line of menus. When you visit a valuable site, always try to click on this word, then choose the "add" option. This will allow you to return easily to this site later on. Its location will be stored permanently in your bookmarks file.

For some people who lack access to a graphical browser, use of the Web may mean using *Lynx* (the text-only browser in use if you just have a UNIX shell account or if your computer equipment cannot use a graphics browser, or if your service provider does not provide TCP/IP service). It is often said that the large majority of Web users in the world still use *Lynx*; this is no longer true in Canada but it is wise to keep in mind that in other parts of the world, technological advancement has not proceeded at as brisk a pace as it has here. You use the Lynx client with a series of simple commands and the arrow keys.

Lynx can do quite an acceptable job of presenting the text content of Web pages, provided the Web page operator makes provisions for Lynx users. Occasionally you will load a page on which no such provisions have been made. It will appear essentially as blank to the Lynx user. This is an important consideration when it comes time to prepare your own Web pages. Always provide text content which mirrors the graphical content of the page, or else provide a separate page for text-only users.

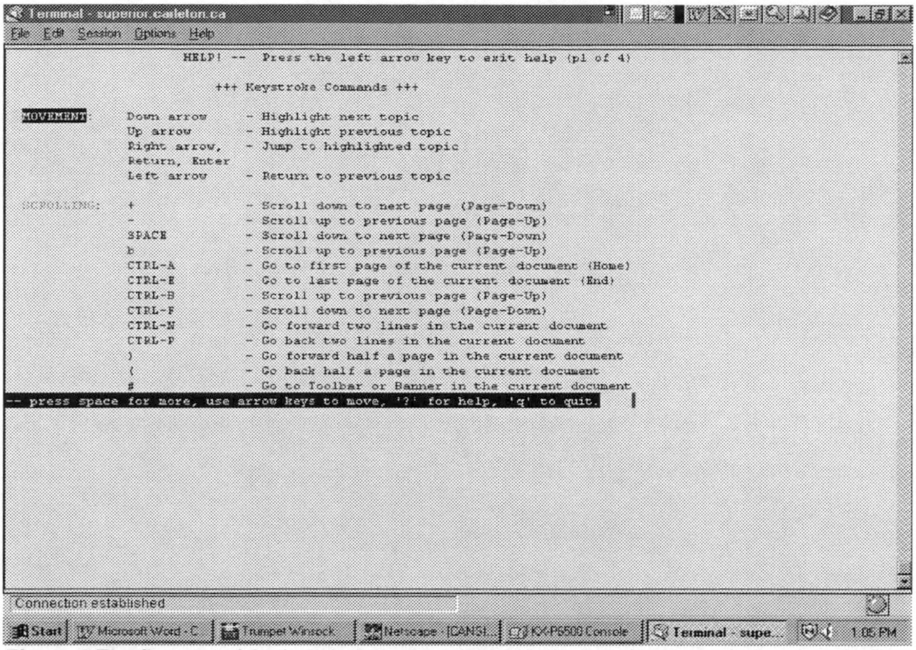

Figure 2 The first part of the Lynx help screen viewed in the Lynx browser window. Lynx is the browser you use for basic text service of Web pages

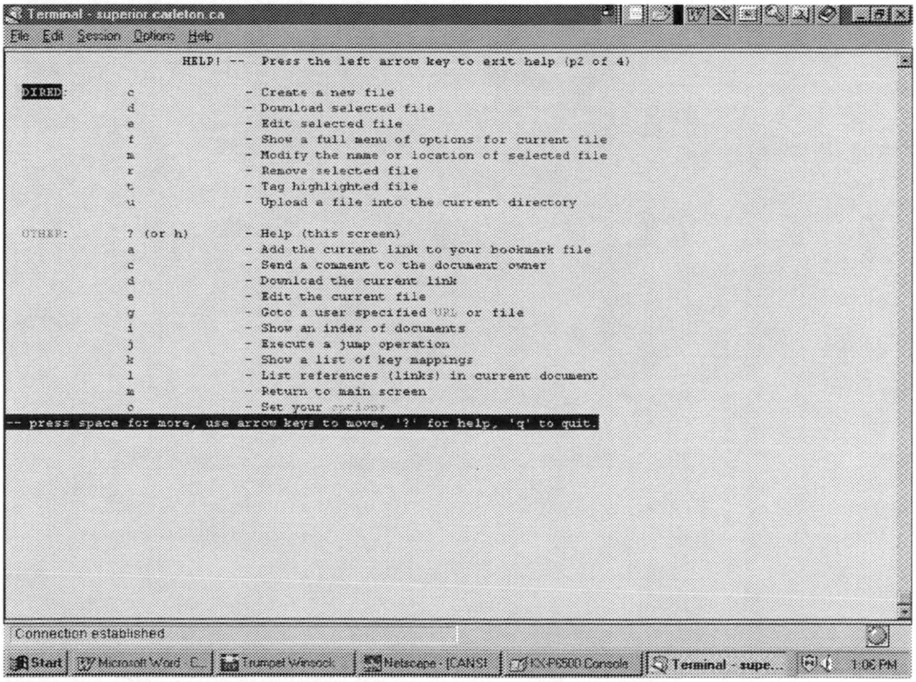

Figure 3 More Lynx commands from the help screens of the Lynx client.

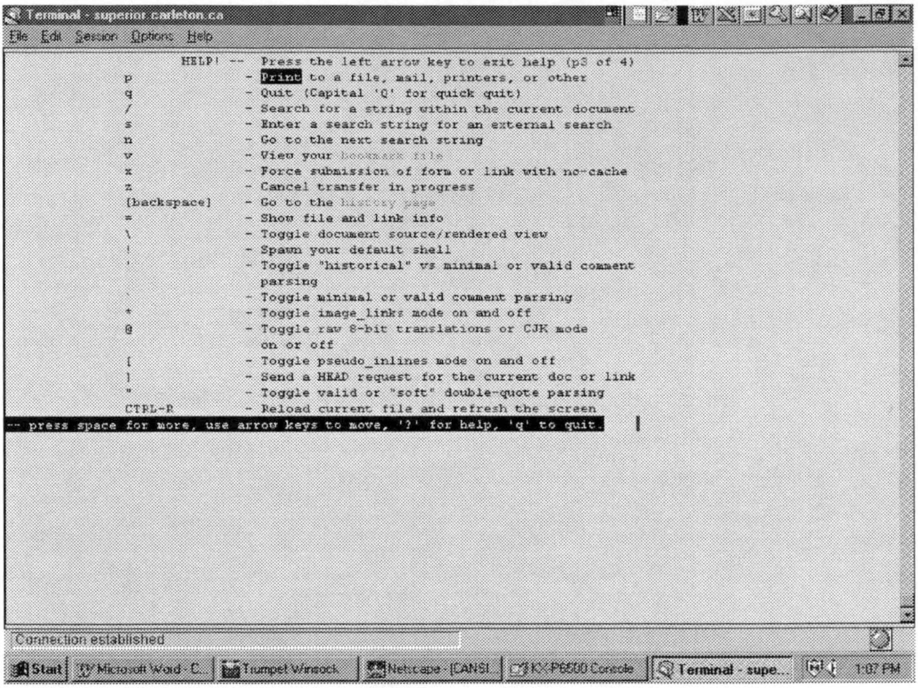

Figure 4 The balance of the Lynx commands help page.

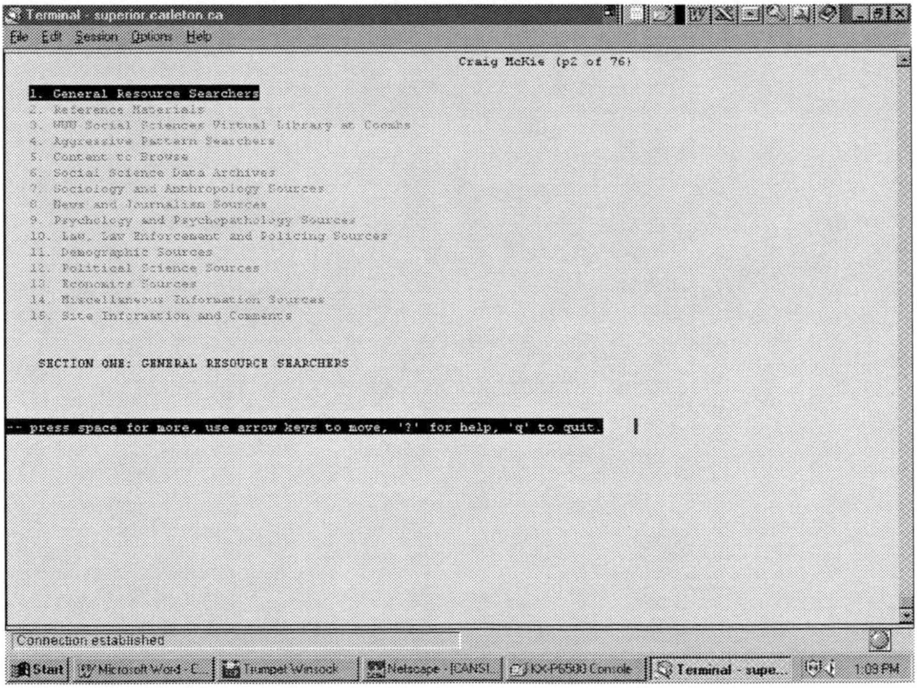

Figure 5 My research links page as seen in the Lynx viewer.

A PLACE TO STAND

For most of the examples which follow in the balance of this book, the research activity begins from what I have been referring to in this text as my research page. Its address is:

http://www.carleton.ca/~cmckie/research.html

Briefly put, it is a large collection of links to resources (Web pages) that are of use to social science researchers. It is classified by discipline, with the addition of sections of general use links. One of the great problems with the Web in its early days was that no one knew where to start off a research activity. As time went by, the search engines were added as general starting points. As subject matter materials were added, it became possible to subdivide the resources by discipline and by purpose. My research page has mirrored this development. It started in the fall of 1995 with a few useful links for my students. In the interim, the list has expanded to several hundred links which I update and add to regularly. Often, new sites are brought to my attention by their originators as well.

The page can be used by either the Lynx browser or the graphical browsers such as Netscape or Explorer. While it is best used with a graphics browser it functions well in the text-only mode. I recommend that you start your research activity at this page, returning to it each after each search to pick up a fresh way of searching, or new materials to look at. Beginning in the next chapter you will be shown in some detail how such a process works and what it is likely to turn up.

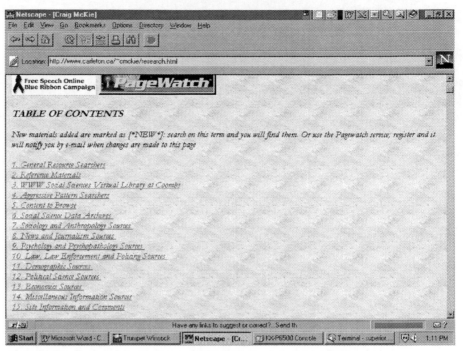

Figure 6 The Research page as seen in the Netscape browser's window.

Following any one of the major headings on the research page leads you to a set of resources. Choosing one of the specific resources from section 1 of the research page leads you, for example, to the University of Michigan Documents Center where there are in turn many onward links to resources of various sorts. Once you have exhausted this line of inquiry, you can click on the "Go" heading in the top line of menu options and return to the research page to start another thread of inquiry. Cycling from and back to the research page will keep you from the "lost in space" feeling of losing your bearings, something which can occur if you do not have a base to return to.

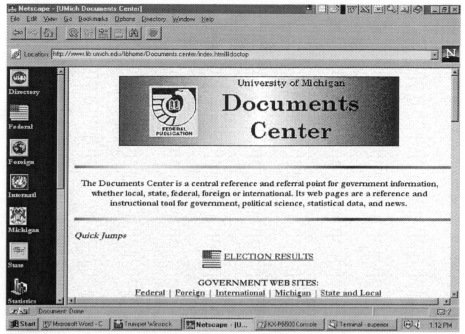

Figure 7 A specific resource located using the research page, first general section.

WHEN ALL YOU HAVE IS E-MAIL

In some circumstances, you will find that the only tool which is working for you is e-mail. This situation is infrequent now but there may still be isolated students who still only have access to e-mail and no direct Web access at all. This would be the case when your Internet connection is indirect, for example in geographically remote communities where there is only a local electronic bulletin board system which bundles, ships and receives e-mail several times a day and not continuously, as would be the case on a full Internet service provider. If this is the circumstance, you can still avail yourself of some of the more advanced services of the Internet, including Web pages, by forming and placing your requests for information via e-mail.

You may do this by e-mailing your information requests to a special gateway machine which fetches the information you require and then e-mails it to you automatically. You would do this if you knew there was a file called *info.txt* sitting on a machine called *ajax.edu*. Leaving aside the question of how you might know the information is there for the time being, this is how you proceed. In this example, you would send an e-mail to one of these special addresses *ftpmail@decwrl.dec.com*. The body of the e-mail message would look as follows:

```
reply    youraddress@somewhere.edu  insert your e-mail address
connect  ajax.edu                    insert the machine you want
                                      something from
binary                                standard setting
chdir  /pub                           change to the directory in which
                                      the file you want is located
uuencode                              standard setting
chunksize  48000                      standard setting
get  info.txt                         get and the name of the file you
                                      want
quit                                  last line
```

At this stage, it is not necessary to pay too close attention to how these utilities work, only to the fact that it is possible to obtain such resources entirely by e-mail. The body of your e-mail message is really just the commands you might use if you were obtaining a copy of the file yourself using the *FTP* (file transfer protocol) utility, a standard Internet utility discussed previously which can be used by itself at any time. However, since in this example you cannot use the Web or FTP directly, the machine *decwrl.dec.com* executes the commands for you, gets the product, breaks up the file into e-mailable chunks (many sites will not accept e-mail messages which are larger than 60,000 bytes), and *uuencodes* the chunks. *Uuencoding*, discussed previously, allows the file contents to pass undamaged through the e-mail system. This is necessary because some documents contain special characters (such as are used in WordPerfect or Word files) which are damaged in transit otherwise as has been pointed out repeatedly.

Once the chunks arrive in your e-mail, you have to delete the e-mail shells with an editor, paste the chunks together and unpack the resulting file using the special free utility called *uudecode*. If you have a UNIX shell account, this utility may be available to you on the service host machine. Alternatively, you may download the file (using the transfer protocols like *zmodem* of this chapter) to your personal computer and *uudecode* it there. Once *uudecoded*, it is an exact letter-for-letter replica of the original file *info.txt* on *ajax.edu*.

This process is cumbersome and fraught with the possibility of error. Nevertheless it will work and give access to Web resources to persons whose only contact with the Internet is sporadic e-mail service. Other public service options along these same lines are available as well. At the time of writing the remailer at mixmaster@kether.alias.net had the capability to handle WWW requests by e-mail as well. Note that you can view any HTML file which resides on your computer (perhaps having got there by this circuitous route) with Netscape by clicking on the "File" heading and then choosing "Open File" and supplying its name and location on your computer.

Here's how to use that facility. The remailer will get a formatted text WWW page (or Gopher menu/file or FTP file, but ONLY TEXT at this time, and not binary files) if it gets a **Get-URL:** header with the URL following the space. This will retrieve the page the way it would appear as a text file. It will also get the HTML source (the codes which produce a Web page on your personal computer) of a URL if it gets a **Get-HTML-Source:** header with the URL following the space.

If you send a message with just one of those two headers, the page will be returned to you via e-mail. In the example, the e-mail message goes to mixmaster@kether.alias.net. The sample message body to retrieve my research page is as follows:

::

Get-HTML-Source: http://www.carleton.ca/~cmckie/research.html/

The source code for my page will be returned to you by e-mail if all goes well and that particular remailer is still in operation (they tend to come and go from time to time). There are specific provisions for retrieving files anonymously should you wish to acquire the page in complete anonymity, a topic beyond the scope here. With the source code on your machine, your Web browsing software can create the page without further necessity for contacting the site. Examples of such pages are to be found in previous chapters. Graphic images, a common characteristic of Web Pages, will be omitted, however, when the page is retrieved in this fashion by e-mail.

Again, for those who lack routine access to the Internet, it is also possible to access resources available to the *Finger* tool with e-mail. *Finger* is a UNIX tool. (If you have TCP/IP service, there is usually a copy of the finger tool included in your software and you may want to try it out). *Finger* is a means of triggering a response of information from a remote logon account. Originally, it was intended merely to check on the status of a person's e-mail account, perhaps to see when the individual last logged in and whether any new e-mail was in the account. However, it was later augmented to transmit a *plan file* containing text to anyone who sent a finger request to the account. These plan files now report on various forms of information. In the example that follows, an account at Caltech in Pasadena reports on any earthquakes which have recently occurred in Southern California.

The regular means of finding out this information would be interactive. You would execute the following command from the prompt: **finger quake@scec.caltech.edu.** You would soon receive a report back.

If you do not have the finger tool available to you, you can still get the information by sending an e-mail message to a special location which will get the information on your behalf and e-mail it back to you. Send your message to *mg5n+finger@andrew.cmu.edu*, with no subject heading. In the body of the message, you place the address of the finger information you want, in this case

quake@scec.caltech.edu. That's all you have to do. The information will be sent to you though there may be a delay for processing. Here is an example of what you get back:

```
From mg5n+@andrew.cmu.edu  Wed Jul  5 20:56:02 1996
Return-Path: <mg5n+@andrew.cmu.edu>
Received: via switchmail; Wed,  5 Jul 1996 20:55:25 -0400 (EDT)
Message-Id: <Added.IjynG8e00Ui3Q=UU4e@andrew.cmu.edu>
Received: from unix7.andrew.cmu.edu via qmail
                 ID  </afs/andrew.cmu.edu/service/mailqs/q002/
QF.MjynF6:00WB84Fn049>;
      Wed,  5 Jul 1996 20:54:34 -0400 (EDT)
From: mg5n+finger@andrew.cmu.edu
Apparently-To: nobody@smith.edu
Status: OR

>>> finger quake@scec.caltech.edu
[scec.gps.caltech.edu]
Login name: quake              In real life: SCSN Data Access
Directory: /export/scec/user1/quake      Shell: /bin/csh
Last login Sun Mar 20, 1994 on ttyp1 from bombay.gps.calte
New mail received Wed Jul  5 16:29:04 1996;
  unread since Wed Jul  5 13:39:36 1996
Plan:
     WELCOME TO THE SOUTHERN CALIFORNIA EARTHQUAKE DATA
CENTER (SCEC_DC)
 AUTOMATED LOCATIONS OF THE CALTECH/USGS SOUTHERN CALI-
FORNIA SEISMIC NETWORK


  DATE  UTC TIME  LAT.  LON. DEPTH  MAG. Q      COMMENT
yy-mm-dd hh:mm:ss (deg.) (deg.) (km)  typ
_____ _____  _____ ___ _____ - _____

_____
96/06/28 17:17:37  34.40N 118.66W  10.8 2.7MLG A   7 mi. SSW of CASTAIC
96/06/28 21:29:09  34.35N 116.91W   5.1 3.0MLG A   7 mi. N  of BIG BEAR
LAKE
96/06/30 00:35:26  37.56N 118.78W   0.1 2.7MGN C*  12 mi. ESE of MAM-
MOTH LAKES
96/07/02 04:49:33  37.63N 118.86W   0.1 3.2MGN C*   6 mi. ESE of MAM-
MOTH LAKES
96/07/02 04:49:50  36.80N 118.54W   0.1 2.7MGN C*  19 mi. W  of INDE-
PENDENCE
```

```
96/07/02 10:41:10  34.98N 116.96W  6.3 2.5MGN A*  6 mi. NE of BARSTOW
96/07/03 03:02:13  34.62N 117.45W   7.1 2.5MGN B*  11 mi. NW of
VICTORVILLE
96/07/03 20:53:40  36.88N 117.68W   9.3 2.7MGN C*  21 mi. WSW of
SCOTTY'S CASTLE
96/07/05 06:37:08 35.00N 116.97W  6.6 2.6MGN A*  7 mi. NNE of BARSTOW
96/07/05 10:37:33  34.12N 116.41W   0.0 2.6MC A   2 mi. ESE of YUCCA
VALLEY
96/07/05 12:36:54 37.07N 117.39W  6.0 2.6MGN C*  3 mi. NW of SCOTTY'S
CASTLE
96/07/05 15:23:57 32.38N 115.28W  6.0 2.8MGN C* 23 mi. SSE of MEXICALI
96/07/05 15:25:54 32.37N 115.28W  6.0 2.6MGN C* 23 mi. SSE of MEXICALI
```

---

 * Last update was at 5-JUL-1996 15:29 gmt
   (List is updated when a new event occurs, not at regular intervals)

-> Entries marked with a "*" are PRELIMINARY and have NOT BEEN HUMAN
REVIEWED <-
   Entries may contain ERRORS and may be UPDATED or DELETED at any
time.
   Entries with origin times within 30 seconds may represent a single event.

   This is a list of automated locations for magnitude 2.5 or greater
    earthquakes recorded by the CALTECH/USGS Southern California Seis-
mic
   Network in the past 72 hours. All times are Greenwich Mean Time.
   Subtract 8 hours for Pacific Standard time, and 7 hours for Pacific
   Daylight time. Depths are in km.

   MAGNITUDE TYPES:
    MGN = empirically calibrated ML based on readings from high-gain com-
ponents
     MLG = ML based on synthetic Wood-Anderson response from low-gain
components
     ML = ML based on synthetic Wood-Anderson response from TerraScope
stations

   The SCEC_DC is a member of the Council of the National Seismic System.

Finger is often now used to supply the reports of automated measuring equipment such as that which measures seismic activity as in the above example. It is ideal for this purpose and allows anyone anywhere in the world to check on seismic activity for unattended arrays of sensors at any time. Though giving the appearances of a toy, and having origins in a somewhat trivial activity, it now performs an important service to the world.

We will now move on to a generic research strategy for locating, acquiring and using Web resources in the social science research process. The next three chapters are devoted to such a generic research strategy continuing example. Then, in Chapter Twelve, we will see discipline-specific abbreviated examples of what concretely a researcher should do to use these resources.

Sites shown in this Chapter...

Research Engines page   http://www.carleton.ca/~cmckie/research.html
University of Michigan Documents Center
                               http://www.lib.umich.edu/libhome/Documents.center/
                                  index#doctop

Finding and Using Information for Research: Defining Your Needs

"Last year Microsoft made profits of $2.2 billion on revenues of $8.6 billion. That dwarfs the profits of even the best media companies. The biggest of them, the Disney empire, earned $1.4 billion last year, while Rupert Murdoch's fearsome News Corp made just under $1 billion. Even the richest newspaper empires make less than half that. At best, media firms achieve margins of less than 12% and enjoy 15% annual growth; most live with single digits for both. By comparison, Microsoft has been growing by over 30% a year, and consistently enjoys net margins of over 25%."

From "Citizen Gates," in the electronic edition of **The Economist**, 23-11-96.

The purpose of this and the following two chapters is to demonstrate, in a generic manner in which the particulars of disciplinary approaches do not figure actively, how a social science student would search the Web for useful research material, capture it, manipulate it and finally prepare a research report.

With this in mind, it might be helpful therefore to start with the reduction of the research process to a programmatic set of steps which might capture the essence of the routine you might find undertake in preparing an academic assignment, a research paper, or a piece of research assigned in the employment context. This approach is an obvious oversimplification, but it is helpful in understanding the various stages at which the Web tools can be employed.

SOCIAL RESEARCH: A GENERIC APPROACH

A TWELVE STEP METHOD:

1. Specify your research problem as best you can; this will help you identify what it is that you need to find. Without this requirement specified in advance you might not recognize value if you find it. This step typically also includes selecting a theoretical perspective within which to frame your problem. You need not be firmly committed to a "theory"; it is just a helpful device to channel your questioning.

2. Select keywords which best typify the major elements of your research problem. You will need these words in several contexts. Try to find several ways of expressing the core idea of your research; have short one word options and also longer multi-word phrases you can use.

3. Do exploratory work with the aggressive Web searchers such as AltaVista. Capture and retain references so that you can make return visits and document your work. Use your bookmarks file to good advantage and save documents which seem likely to be valuable resources for your work. You may print them if you wish.

4. Do a literature search with CARL UnCover, and Current Contents if you have local access to it at your library.

5. Review the material that your searches have turned up. This typically involves a visit to the library to locate resources in the paper periodical literature which does not as yet have an electronic publishing counterpart.

6. Search the world's social science data archives for data sets, maps, and other electronic resources which might be available to you for secondary statistical analysis. Do CANSIM retrievals to understand the basic time series nature of the phenomenon you are studying if it is at all pertinent to your chosen research problem.

7. Retrieve the best available data sets for secondary statistical analysis if any are found to be potentially useful. If there are many such data sets located, try to pick the best two or three since secondary analysis is labour intensive. The step is often not called for in the work of junior undergraduates, though learning how to do secondary analysis often is.

8. Do local analytical data analysis runs on the retrieved data sets (or remotely on another host computer if this is available to you) using SPSS, SAS, or other statistical packages, or with the use of a spreadsheet and graphing program such as Excel. Again, this type of work is not generally seen to be appropriate for junior undergraduates though it is to be expected in the work of senior undergraduate students and above.

9. Interpret and analyze your results as they pertain to your initial theoretical framework and research question(s).

10. Draft your paper, employing imported graphics from your analysis runs or from the Web. Graphics such as tables, charts and graphs are now a routine and expected feature of research reports and essays. The more professional they appear, the better. Worksheet programs such as Excel can help immeasurably in preparing this sort of graphic. Excel may well be available in you computer lab facility. It also is a Windows program.

11. Obtain private review of your draft paper from trusted colleagues. This review is designed to prevent serious mistakes from becoming a permanent part of your report. Make this a lifelong habit and try not to take the comments personally. Be grateful that a trusted colleague found your errors before they had a chance to do damage to your grade point average and to your reputation. Assume always that more errors remain in your work no matter how many times you have been over it.

12. Submit of your paper, possibly employing a short verbal presentation with support from Powerpoint screens which organize and present the main points of your paper. Verbal reports now routinely involve a visual component, either with overhead transparencies or with electronic "slides" prepared in your computer with programs like Powerpoint and presented via an LCD (Liquid Crystal Display panel) connected to your computer and illuminated with an ordinary overhead projector. Visuals convey the aura of organized thought and preparation; both are valued intellectual commodities.

Step 1. Specifying the requirements

When you start any social science research project, it is helpful to know what the end product will include and what it will look like. Asking for some concrete examples of comparable work would be useful. As well, some measure of the depth of the analysis required is necessary (whether this is expressed in number of finished pages, words, topics covered or another measure). It is obvious that a short research report will require much less finished work than a book length project. While you should try to meet or exceed expectations, additional length in submitted pages is not normally an effective strategy.

In the case of each new piece of research, exploratory searches for the work of other scholars are required in order that you do not inadvertently attempt to duplicate work others have already done, and that you give full weight and credit to the findings of others in framing your problem. In order to do this, you must initially do a search of the relevant literature. This will help you further specify your research objectives and indicate avenues of exploration for the future.

You should remain mindful of the requirements of the intended audience. Professors do not in general want 150 page term papers (though undoubtedly there are occasional exceptions to this rule). If you know roughly the length and depth required, if you have narrowed the proposed topic to a manageable degree (always keeping in mind that you cannot get "there" if you do not know where "there" is), you can assess for yourself how much time, effort, and monetary resources you are prepared to devote to bringing your project to completion. Cost must be mentioned because primary data collection is now so expensive that you are often forced through circumstance into the secondary analysis of data, for instance. Primary data collection also takes a tremendous amount of time to accomplish and if you do not have research assistance, this factor alone may rule out attempts to collect new data. A full exploration of what data is available for secondary analysis is therefore obligatory, especially for projects undertaken at the senior undergraduate level and above.

You will need a keyword phrase or a set of phrases which you can use for literature and data searches, and for searching for contemporary commentary on your topic. Keep in mind that a theoretical approach to the topic is also usually required and that the theoretical school you choose to use can help you specify your research problem. For the sake of the generic approach in this chapter, we require a continuing example to use. For this chapter, the example will be **juvenile justice**.

Step 2. Select keywords

This step should be easy but sometimes unaccountably becomes difficult. The objective is to land on a short list of keywords which capture the essence of your project topic. These keywords will be used to search for relevant materials. In our continuing example in this chapter, the keyword phrase will be "juvenile + justice". In some search engines this would be expressed as "juvenile justice" while in others it could be "juvenile AND justice" or just "juvenile justice". You will have to look at the examples given at each searching site to determine the correct syntax. You might also wish to think of alternative wordings like "young offenders," the older "juvenile delinquents," or other formulations like "hooligans," "lager louts," or "punks" which, while different in semantic loading, nevertheless capture one aspect of the phenomenon you are researching. To be on the safe side, you should try to think of several variants. Searching on each term successively will reveal a slightly different take on the phenomenon. You will know you have exhausted the topic search when the same materials are returned on searches no matter where or how they are conducted. You may wish to introduce geographical constraints as well, such as adding the word Canada or Canadian to search keyword phrases if you find to many references are being returned and you wish to narrow the scope of your topic.

Step 3. Do exploratory work with the aggressive Web searchers

The object of this stage of the exercise is to beat the bushes of the Web (figuratively of course) to find threads of material which will be of assistance to you in both fleshing out your research topic and also indicating lines of inquiry, "veins" of information, and the work of others which pertains to your own interests.

The place to begin is my research page at **http://www.carleton.ca/~cmckie/ research.html**. This is a place to start your searches; it has been shown before in passing in earlier chapters, but it is at this stage that its power can be utilized to advance your project. It is shown in Figure 1 below:

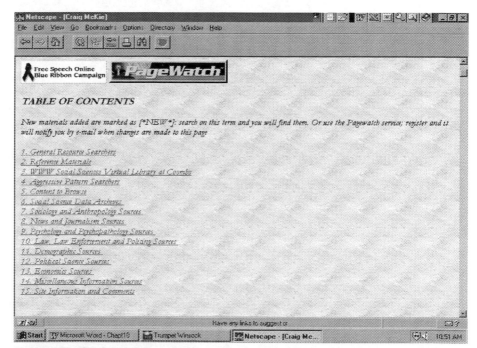

Figure 1 The Research Page as a place to begin your search for resources. In the following examples, it is the anchor page to which the researcher returns time and again to pick up successive searching tools. Its use therefore is the implicit foundation of all succeeding examples.

The question obviously arises as to ***which search engines are the best***. The answer lies in the qualification 'best for what purpose?'. Below are my current choices for various purposes. Links to all of these tools are to be found on my research page shown in Figure 1 above.

FOR GENERAL SEARCH PURPOSES...

AltaVista
Infoseek
Yahoo
Profusion

FOR DATA ARCHIVES...

ICPSR at the University of Michigan
Carleton University Library Data Centre
CANSIM database at the University of Toronto

FOR BACKGROUND MATERIAL...

WWW Virtual Library for the social sciences
NTU Electronic Library for the social sciences

FOR LITERATURE SEARCHES...

Current Contents (not yet available on the Web)
CARL UnCover

*Note: a full review of search engines and what each is best suited for can be found at the WindWeaver site at: http://www.windweaver.com/index.htm.

Starting from the resources of the research page, we first wish to visit some general information sites. There are several such sites listed in the first section of the research page. In the following example, we visit the NTU Electronic Library Resources for the Social Sciences site as an example of the more general type of resources.

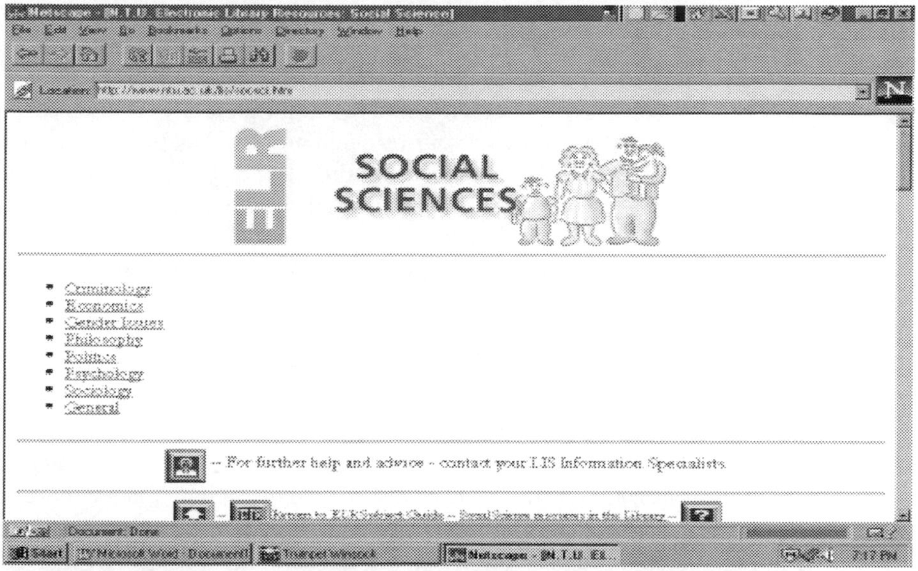

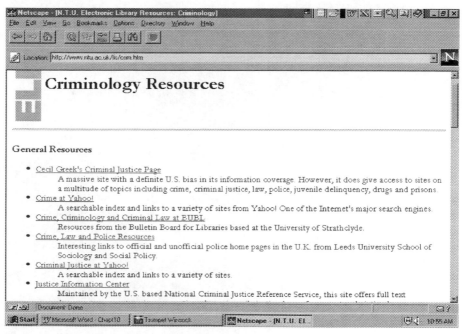

Figure 2 The general electronic library site. One selects the disciplinary heading which seems best to apply. The researcher then follows the onward links looking for material related to one's topic, in this case the example is "juvenile justice", the continuing example in this chapter.

Having selected the criminology heading, we then search in a more particular fashion for sites which are likely to have material related to our example topic. In the following example, we select the first link which happens to lead to Cecil Greek's Criminal Justice page.

Figure 3 Sites located by the electronic library primary site

We now visit the Cecil Greek site for more specific information. Note the nature of the process: you follow links from a single starting point (the research page) through several layers of specification getting (hopefully) ever closer to specific resources you can use to frame your research problem and to provide actual material to use in your paper. The sequence of addresses of the pages you visit are kept under the "Go" text heading in Netscape. Clicking this heading shows a list of the sites you have visited in the order in which you visited them. However, this list is not saved after a particular Netscape session is over, so be sure to bookmark the especially valuable links.

Here a general note of caution is called for. Assessing the quality of what you find by way of specific resources is a thorny problem. In the print publishing era, one could assume that if a publisher paid to have a book or article published that the content had been vetted and assessed by peer review as being worthwhile. On the Web, none of these constraints are necessarily in operation. You are more responsible than was ever the case before to critically assess the value of what you find. If you search for them, you can find resources which confidently assert that all manner of human problems are the result of alien invasion, bad nutrition, impiety, or any manner of other extraneous and non-obvious causal factors. For this reason, you must never assume that what you find is to be taken literally as evidence. It may just simply be someone's personal expression of views and even the evidence presented may be doctored. A healthy skepticism is necessary. Obtaining confirmation from a second source unrelated to the first is one rule we can usefully borrow from good journalism practice here.

Figure 4 Cecil Greek's Criminal Justice Links site.

Now at Cecil Greek's site, we find a specific listing of resources on the topic of juvenile justice. You would now examine these resources individually in detail, searching for specific material to use, always keeping in mind the necessity to critically assess the validity of what you find.

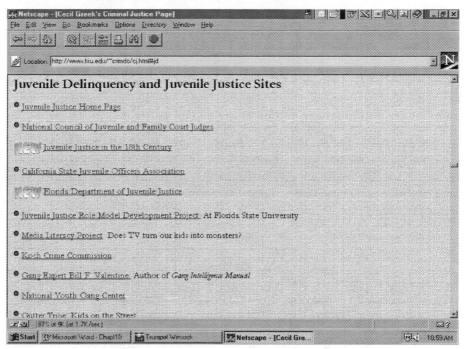

Figure 5 The juvenile justice sub-page at the Cecil Greek site.

To pursue another line of inquiry, we first return to the research page, going then to section four, the portion which contains the aggressive pattern searchers. These are the so-called search engines which search for a word or phrase through the pre-stored selection of resources each has on hand.

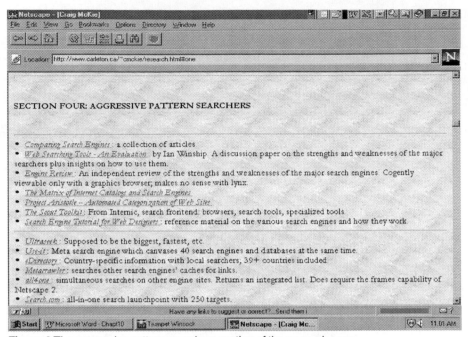

Figure 6 The aggressive pattern searchers section of the research page.

From this section, we will first select the Infoseek search engine. It has a truly enormous selection of pages and sites to draw upon. In addition, it rank orders what it finds in terms of perceived relevance. In this case, as in many other situations, you enter the term you are searching on (in this case "juvenile justice") and then press the search button. A very large amount of information will be returned to you, but in chunks of 20 or 25 citations at a time. In each case, you can follow the link that Infoseek delivers to you to the actual site itself.

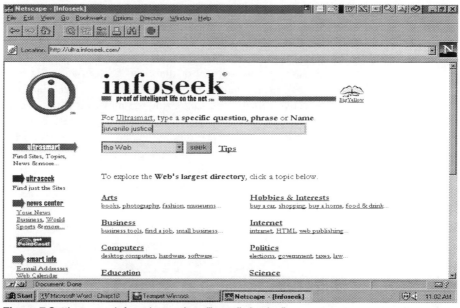

Figure 7 Setting up an Infoseek search on "juvenile justice".

After Infoseek finds resources for you (and in this instance it found a very great many), it will present results of the search to you in groups of 20 links with the most pertinent of these appearing first.

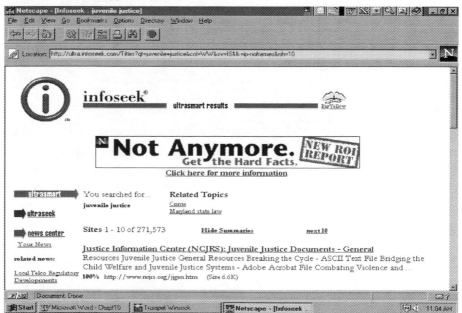

Figure 8 In this example, Infoseek presents the Justice Information Center site as the first and most pertinent link.

Infoseek is only one of the aggressive pattern searchers. There are many others listed on the research page and each searches in a different fashion. Therefore, it makes sense to use several of them. In the following figure, the search page for another aggressive pattern searcher, *Inktomi*, is shown. Each has its peculiarities but the objective remains the same: find the most relevant research resources for your research process, then capture the reference with BioBase and bookmark the location for future return visits. The reason they are different, and produce different search results, lies hidden in the proprietary logic each possesses in the underlying computer code. For especially valuable resources, save them in their entirety to your computer or to a diskette if you are in a lab. You can print them later if you wish, or cut and paste valuable passages right into your report in a word processor program.

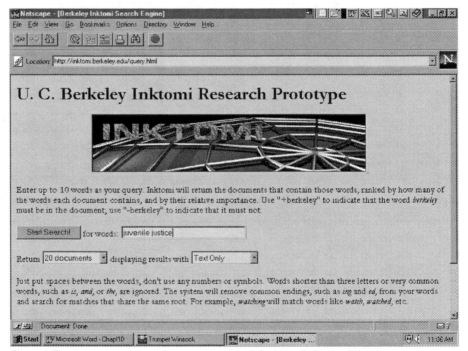

Figure 9 The Inktomi search engine set up to search for juvenile justice links.

Yet another search engine is shown below, AltaVista. It is one of the biggest and fastest of all the Web search engines. It is also somewhat indiscriminate, often returning tens of thousands of links.

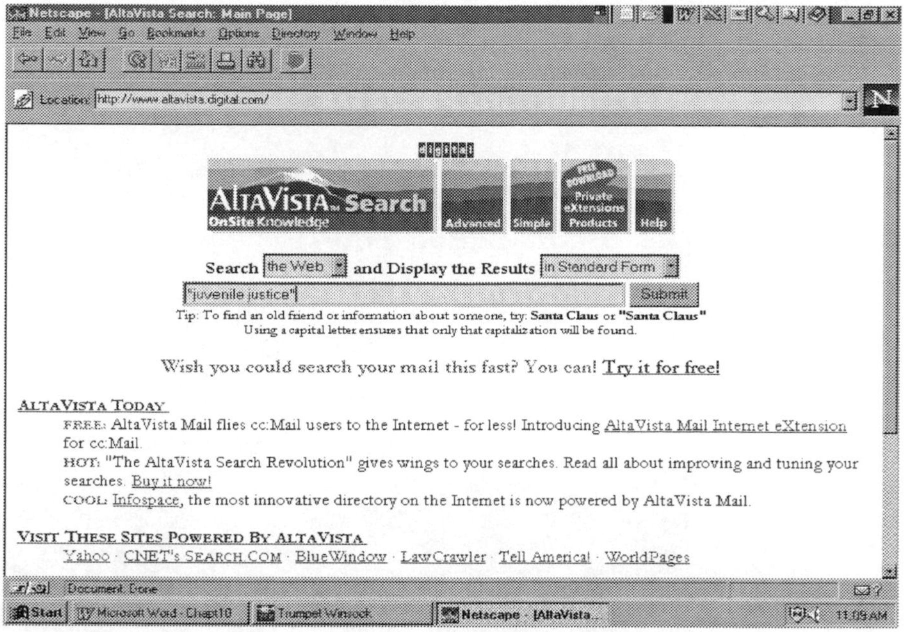

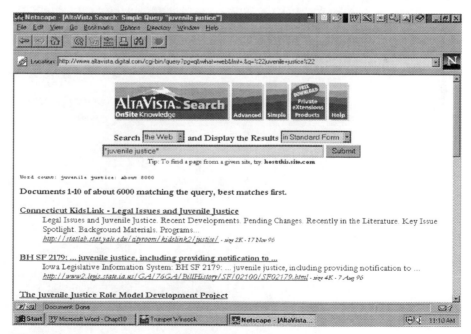

Figure 10 Search on "juvenile justice" on the AltaVista search engine. Note that the compound search term "juvenile justice" must be bounded by double quotes at AltaVista.

In this case, AltaVista returned about 6000 links which you could investigate.

Figure 11 The product of the AltaVista search on "juvenile justice".

Again returning to home base (the research page), we next try the SUNSITE WAIS search site. WAIS is a tool which searches *within* an accumulation of text documents looking for your keyword(s) *inside* the document (as opposed to in its title). Following is a figure which shows how you set up a WAIS search on "juvenile justice".

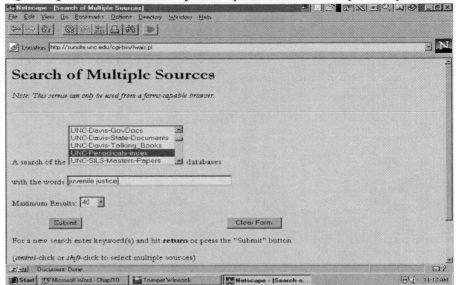

Figure 12 Setting up a WAIS search on "juvenile justice" through a document database at a SUNSITE.

Next we will try the electronic resources of the National Library of Canada. It maintains a Web site of subject-classified files and links. The first step is to go to the main electronic information site of the National Library. Its page is shown in the figure opposite on top.

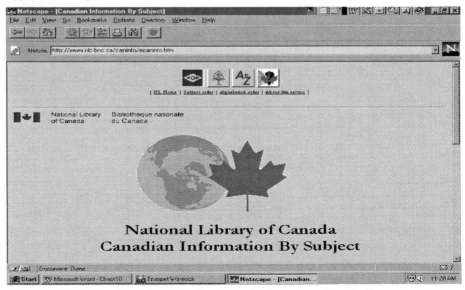

Figure 13 The National Library of Canada electronic information site.

Selecting first the social sciences information section of the National Library site, we then proceed to the section on law. Note the Dewey Decimal library classification numbering which runs down the left side of the page.

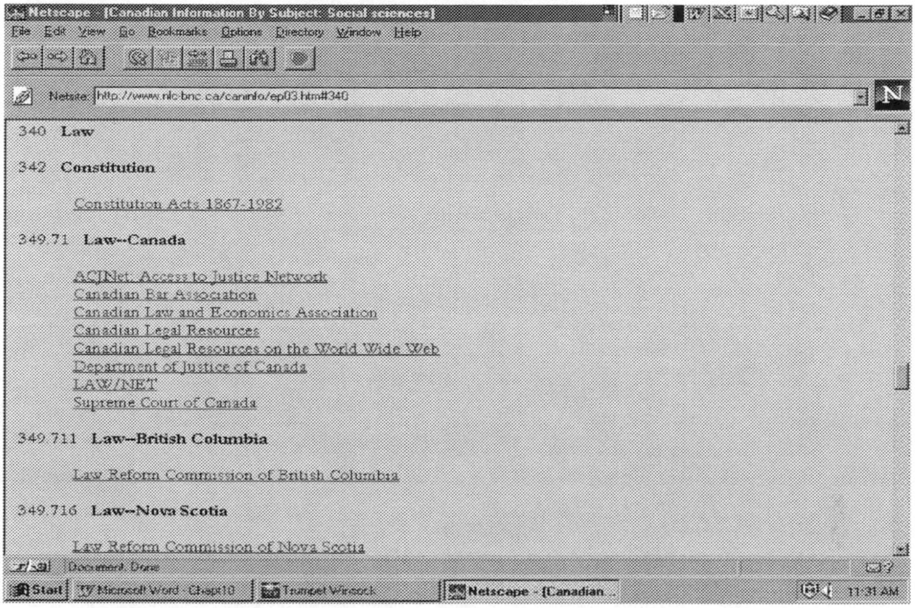

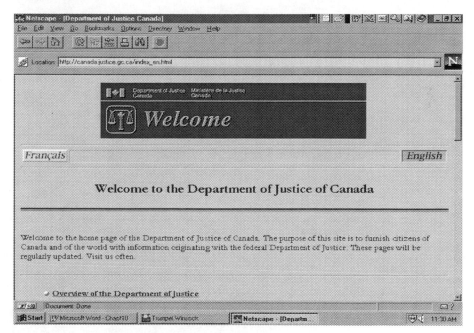

Figure 14 Within the social sciences section, we first select Law—Canada, then the Department of Justice page link.

Figure 15 The Department of Justice page.

There are of course comparable sites in other parts of the world. In the following figure, the central site of the General Printing Office of the United States is shown. It is possible to keyword search the entire resource list at this site.

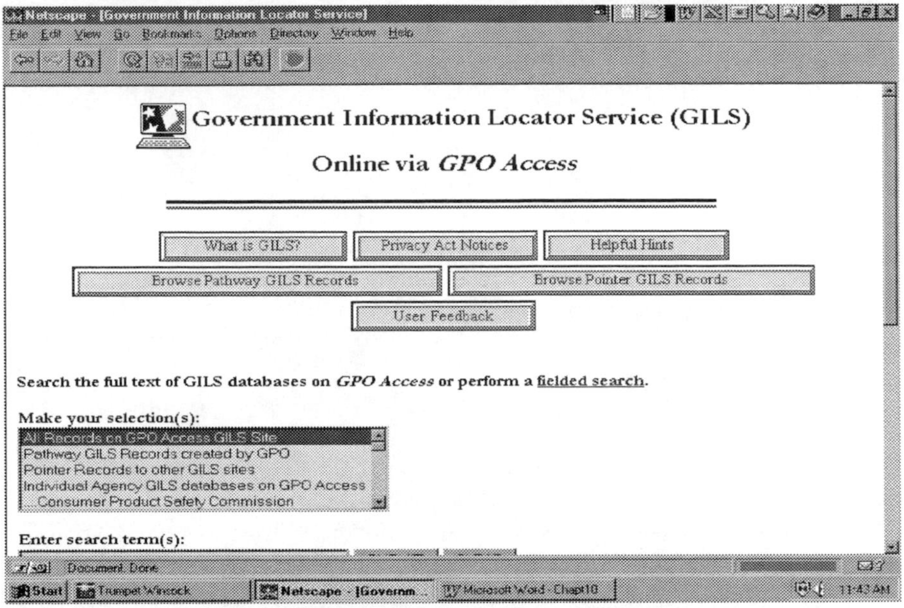

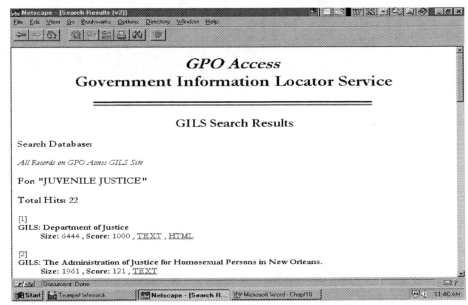

Figure 16 The GPO site, once again searching on the term "juvenile justice."

Figure 17 As a result of the GPO search, 22 documents are presented as potential research resources.

Finally, to close this section of the first of three chapters representing the entire research process in 12 generic steps, we return to one more example of a general site, in this case the Social Sciences Subject-Oriented Bibliographies at the World-Wide Web Virtual Library site for the social sciences. It is quite possible that someone has already developed a research bibliography on your topic of choice. It is worth checking this site against that possibility, since if one has been done, you can avoid a great deal of work. In the case of this example, "juvenile justice", this proves not to be the case. Were you to compile such a bibliography however, you are encouraged to deposit an electronic copy at this site. It is in this way that social scientists acting in a collaborative fashion can further develop the electronic resources available to subsequent generations of scholars.

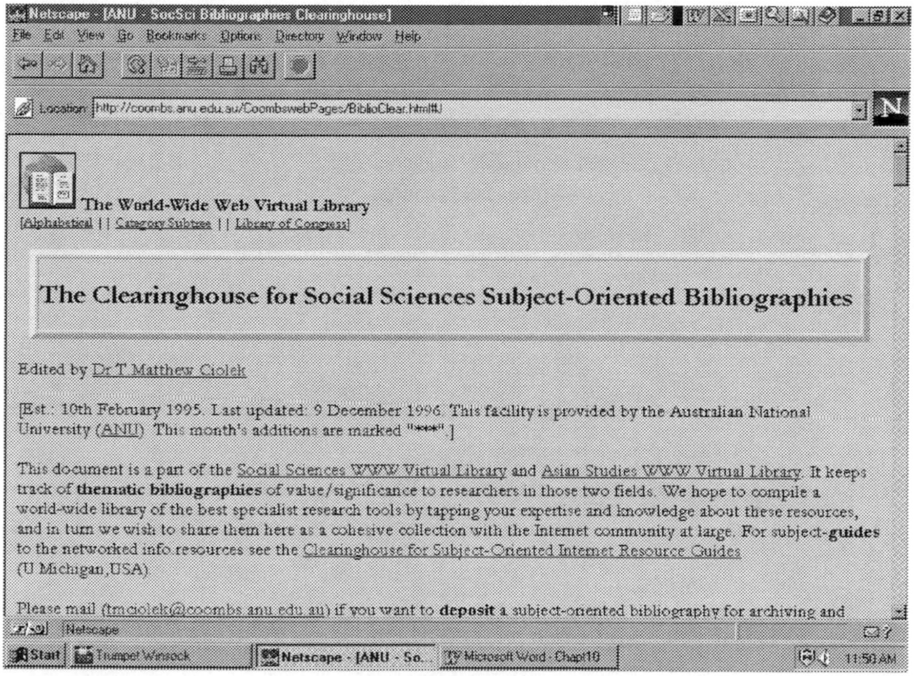

Figure 18 The Clearinghouse site at the WWW Virtual Library for the social sciences at Coombs University in Australia.

Hopefully the material in this third section of the generic model of social science research will help you understand how to use the Web searching tools to set bounds around your project, specify the major variables you can use, provide key definitions, give you a sense of the current state of knowledge concerning this problem, and point you towards sources of secondary data to analyze.

Having been sensitized to the general dimensions of your research topic and gained some sense of the gravity of the problem and the attention devoted to it in the past by others, we then move on to the fourth of the twelve generic steps. It is worth noting again at this stage that the process we are describing here is not unlike either that pursued by professionals in the social sciences or work assignments in the employment context. It may be exaggerating somewhat to suggest that the subject matter here is an occupational skill in the new information economy, but there is a grain of truth in such a remark.

Sites shown in this Chapter

Research engines page	http://www.carleton.ca/~cmckie/research.html
Electronic Library Resources	http://www.ntu.ac.uk/lis/socsci.htm
Cecil Greek's Criminal Justice Page	http://www.fsu.edu/~crimdo/cj.html
Infoseek	http://ultra.infoseek.com/
Inktomi	http://inktomi.berkeley.edu/query.html
AltaVista	http://www.altavista.digital.com/
WAIS form	http://sunsite.unc.edu/cgi-bin/fwais.pl
National Library of Canada	http://www.nlc-bnc.ca/caninfo/ecaninfo.htm
Department of Justice of Canada	http://canada.justice.gc.ca/index_en.html
Government Information Locator	http://www.usgs.gov/gils
Clearinghouse of Social Sciences	http://coombs.anu.edu.au/Coombsweb/ Biblioclear.Html#J

Finding and Using Information for Research: Finding Materials

"The Internet is made of glass. Anyone can see what you're saying or doing with relative ease."

Tom Sleding, President and CEO of PGP Inc., reported in **Business Wire**, 11-15-96, "Pretty Good Privacy Acquires Leading Web Privacy Company, PrivNet."

In this second of a group of three chapters, we will continue on following the generic outline for social science research projects given at the beginning of the previous chapter. By this stage we have identified the topic and linked it to a series of keywords, and then carried out some general searching on the Web looking for resources which relate to our topic and which can help us further specify the research topic and concretely link it to the reports of other investigators.

STEP 4. DO A LITERATURE SEARCH WITH CARL UNCOVER AND CURRENT CONTENTS

Part of the obligation imposed on the scholar is the necessity to review the work of others for relevant research work and commentary on the topic of your choice. For centuries, the literature review was a solitary activity carried out in the stacks of libraries and in the periodicals section of the research library in particular. Often, materials which proved to be pivotal could not be located locally and would have to be ordered from elsewhere, imposing a lengthy time delay on the process.

This situation is now changing rapidly for several reasons. The first is the appearance of electronic whole text editions of the periodical literature. The second is the digitization of existing paper copies, a process only now getting underway. Neither is as yet anywhere near complete in the conversion to digital format. However, indexing of current literature is well advanced and can be relied on.

To search the periodical literature now, you can still resort to the discipline-based paper abstracts, large reference volumes which used to be the mainstay of library research, but which are now being supplanted by electronic sources. Of the electronic aids, two are the most prominent. The first is CARL Uncover, a service of the Consortium of Research Libraries in Colorado, and the second is Current Contents, published on paper and CD-ROM by the ISI Institute in Philadelphia. Your research library may also carry the CD-ROM product called Sociofile or the discipline-based CD-ROM products of the Silverplatter company. They are all well worth using, even if you have to make a physical visit to your library to use them. Often this proves to be the case since single user licenses are much less expensive than licenses for local network use. Access to many of these products is very often limited to students and faculty at a university or college. CARL UnCover is available to anyone with an Internet account.

UnCover is available both over the Web, and in Telnet sessions from your home or lab computer. The Web service tends to be busy all the time, but it is still relatively easy to obtain a Telnet connection from your browser software if you have a Telnet client installed and identified in the browser's preferences section. UnCover offers several for-pay services including the faxing of whole articles to your location for a fee. The service of searching recent literature is, however, still free. And it is invaluable for social science researchers. An example session follows:

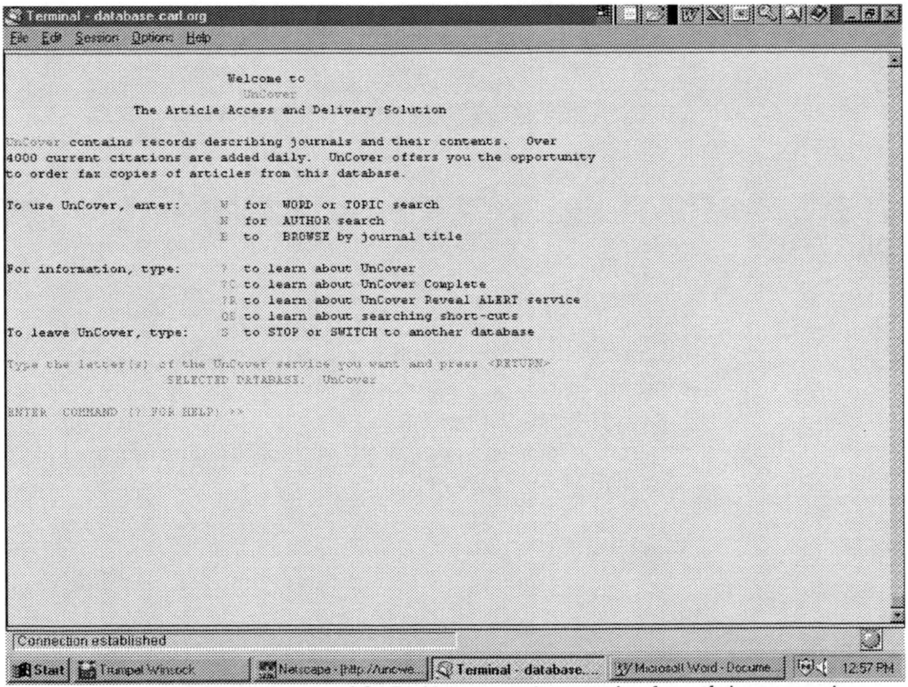

Figure 1 The main search screen of CARL Uncover, telnet version free of charge service.

CARL UnCover scans all periodical literature (a slight overstatement, but only slight) in the English language from about 1990 to the present. In this example, we asked it to search using the term "juvenile justice". It returned 331 items on the initial search. Each of these can be examined to get the complete reference if they look to be likely candidates for your work. Abstracts are seldom included but they can be obtained from Current Contents later on.

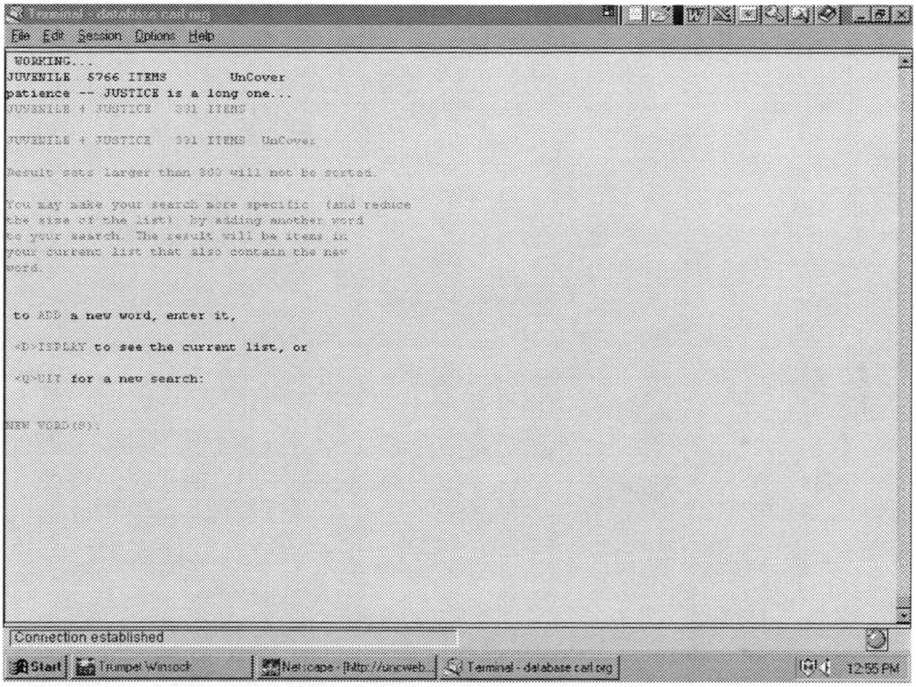

Figure 2 The initial CARL UnCover scan for juvenile justice. Note that you can narrow the search by adding terms. For instance, you could add "Canada" to the search pattern to narrow the collection to only those items which deal with Canadian material. If the term "Canada" does not appear in the title however, you may lose some articles this way. Remember that titles are the search object for the most part.

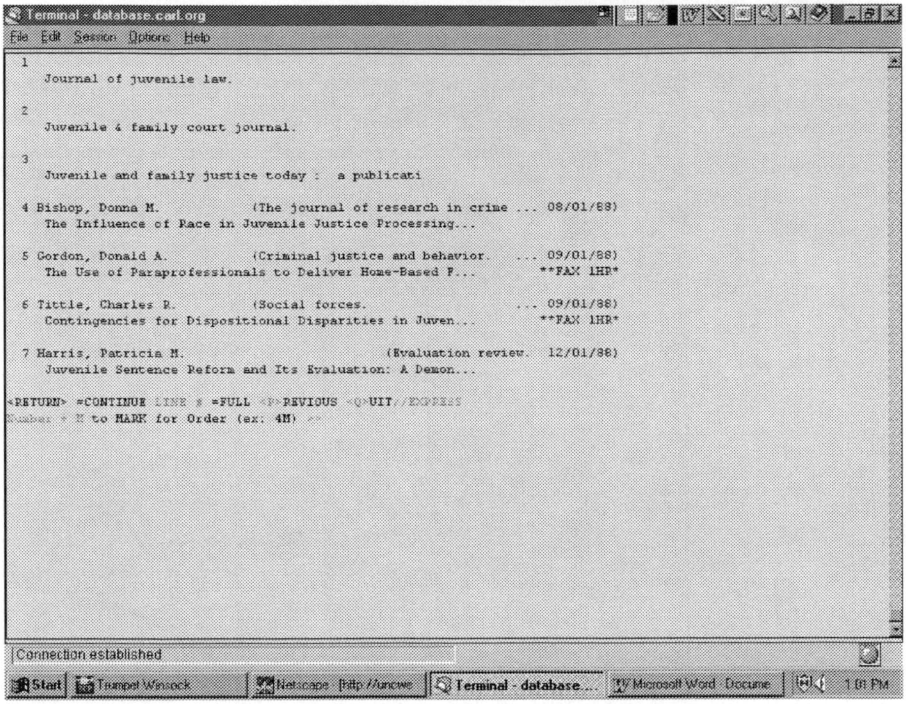

Figure 3 Here are the first few references of the 331 items which UnCover identified in the original search. Note that there is no easy way of recording the references. Copying and pasting to another text file proves the best way.

Turning to Current Contents, this product provides, in addition to article titles, abstracts for many of the articles it covers. Coverage is for the most part directed to the periodical literature and does not include many books. In searching for recent books, your library catalogue, if it is electronic, is probably a better source. Current Contents publishes a set of retrospective CD-ROMs which covers the whole of scholarship in the periodical literature for the last 20 or more years. But since Current Contents is such an expensive service, many university and college libraries provide it only on paper (weekly updates are available) or on recent CD-ROMs covering the last six-month period that can only be used at the library itself. I am fortunate enough to be able to access the latest six-monthly edition over the university network. There follows a figure which shows its operation.

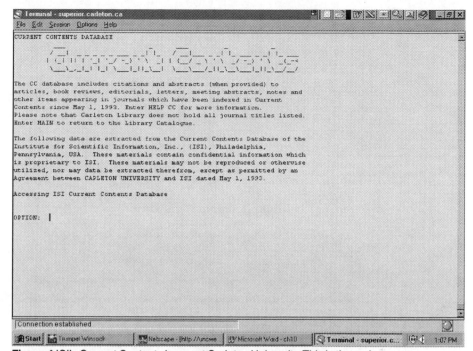

Figure 4 ISI's Current Contents in use at Carleton University. This is the main screen.

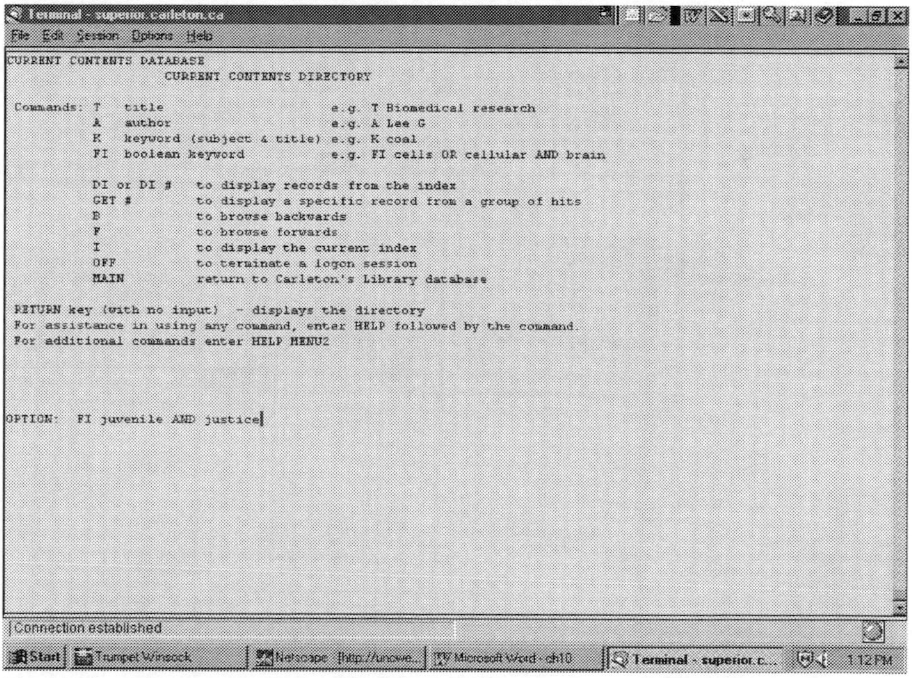

Figure 5 Searching the last six months of Current Contents for juvenile justice articles. Note the Boolean form of search logic: juvenile AND justice

Again, a reminder about other means of electronic literature searching. Many university libraries make their catalogues available over the Net. In addition, the Library of Congress catalogue can be searched over the Web (it was shown in an earlier chapter). These latter sources are good for locating books which have your keywords in the title. Remember that your list should include "near miss" keywords. This is especially important when dealing with books since authors often find their preferred title has already been used and they must come up with a near-miss title themselves.

Some academic journals (but by no means the majority) post their entire editorial content on the Web. You can check whether journal articles you have identified are available in electronic form at the Gopher site at the following address: gopher:// gopher.cic.net:2000/11/e-serials/managed. At this site is a current list of journals published in electronic form.

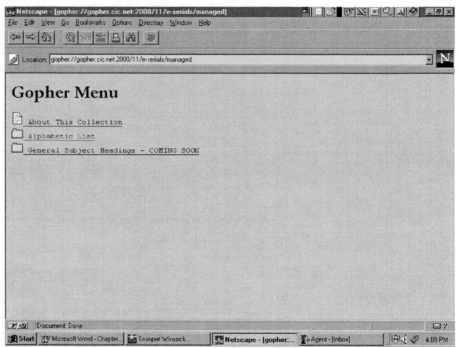

Figure 6 The online list of electronic journals.

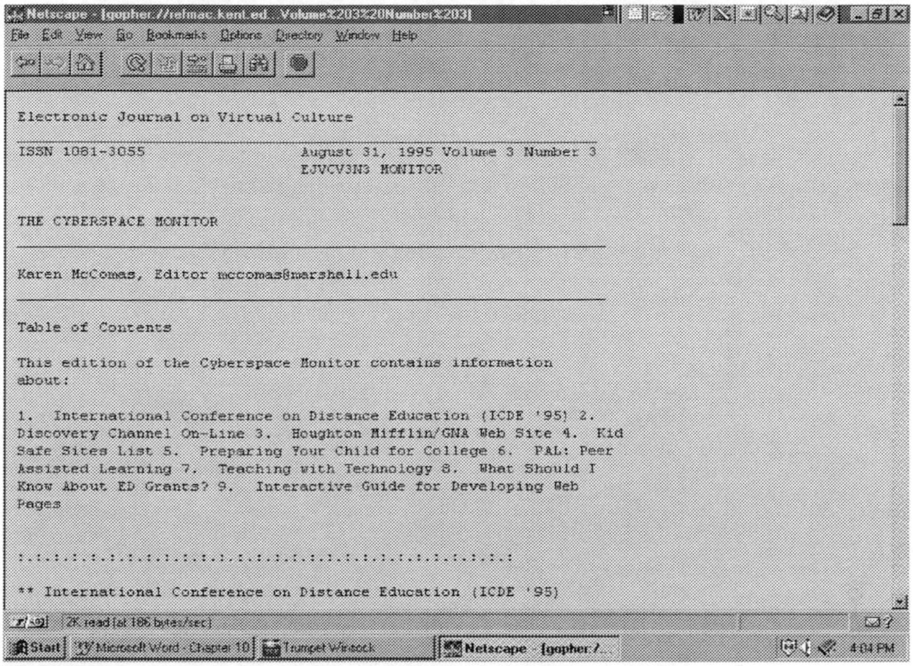

Figure 7 One example of an online version of an academic journal.

STEP 5. REVIEW THE MATERIAL THAT YOUR SEARCHES HAVE TURNED UP.

Now is the time to take stock of all the research materials that you have found, whether from traditional library sources, electronic sources of one sort or another and link them to your theoretical insights and your initial plan of action. You may wish at this stage to recast your problem in light of what you now know to be feasible. It is likely that recasting will take the form of narrowing the topic. Since most searches reveal far more material than can be assimilated, narrowing often takes the form of restricting the time period, the geographical jurisdiction considered, or the target group(s) included. On each of these dimensions it is possible to apply systematic restrictions which have the effect of winnowing the available material which you will use.

Once you have done this reduction, it might be a good idea to return to the searching tools and redo the search process, this time using a new set of keywords that reflect your narrowed focus. If the result of this second pass is a successfully framed and achievable research topic, you can then proceed to the next step which consists of looking for data sets which might be available for secondary analysis. Note that if your project is exclusively literary or qualitative at this stage, there may in fact be no data sets which are applicable to your topic. In the case of our chosen illustrative topic "juvenile justice" however, we might reasonably expect to find such material in the world's data archives.

STEP 6. SEARCH THE WORLD'S DATA ARCHIVES FOR DATA SETS, MAPS, AND OTHER ELECTRONIC RESOURCES WHICH MIGHT BE AVAILABLE TO YOU FOR SECONDARY ANALYSIS.

In the data archives of the world, there now exists a treasure trove of data sets which are catalogued in a highly detailed and eminently searchable fashion, in many cases right down to specific question wording. Starting from my research page at **http://www.carleton.ca/~cmckie/research.html** you can find the major data archives. Pursuing our example of "juvenile justice" here, we will visit a couple of the major archives. The first of these is the ICPSR at the University of Michigan at Ann Arbor.

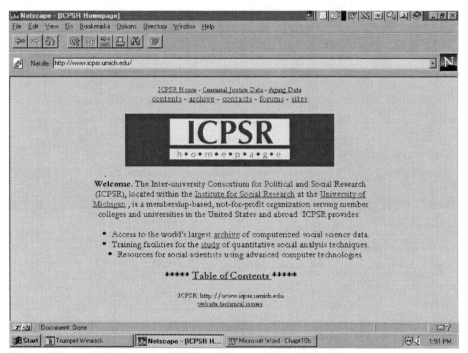

Figure 8 The main Web page at ICPSR, the biggest data archive in the world.

Since the example topic is in the Criminal Justice area, we follow that active link on the ICPSR main page. In the NACJD area, we enter our usual search term.

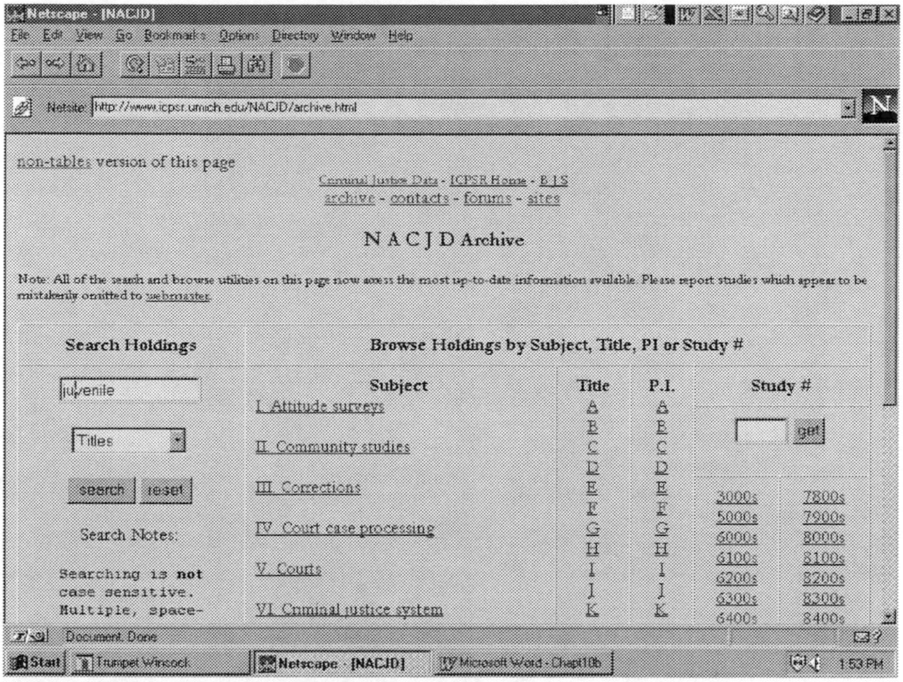

Figure 9 Searching at ICPSR for juvenile justice data sets.

The search results, as shown in Figure 9, reveal a multitude of data sets which contain information on juvenile justice. In general, copies of these data sets complete with codebooks and methodological notes can be obtained by individual researchers. In order to do this however, your educational institution must be a member of the ICPSR directly, or through a regional consortium. Most Canadian universities belong to regional consortia and if this is the case, you may obtain copies of data sets from ICPSR at no charge. You would make your request through your institution's data archive or library data centre. Junior social science students will not generally be required to pursue secondary analysis with such data sets, but learning how to do this is part of the undergraduate program at some stage. Learning how to use a statistical package such as SAS or SPSS is now a recognized part of the desirable skillset for graduates.

Once you obtain your copy of the data set you require to do your secondary analysis (if you have decided to proceed with this aspect), you are responsible for mounting it on a computer and for any subsequent analytical data runs using packages such as SPSS or SAS. Often, you can obtain the data set you want already in SAS or SPSS export file format, so that little coding and labeling work is necessary on your part once the data set arrives. Generally, the datasets are shipped electronically to your institution by means of FTP (file transfer protocol). If as is often the case, the received data set is a very large file, you may have to make special arrangements to have it stored locally at the campus computer centre in such a way that it is accessible to you for analysis purposes. This may well mean that it is stored on the university or college's UNIX mainframe service and you may have to learn to use it (the mainframe's) version of SAS or SPSS. This is all good experience and a credential which will help you in the search for postgraduation employment.

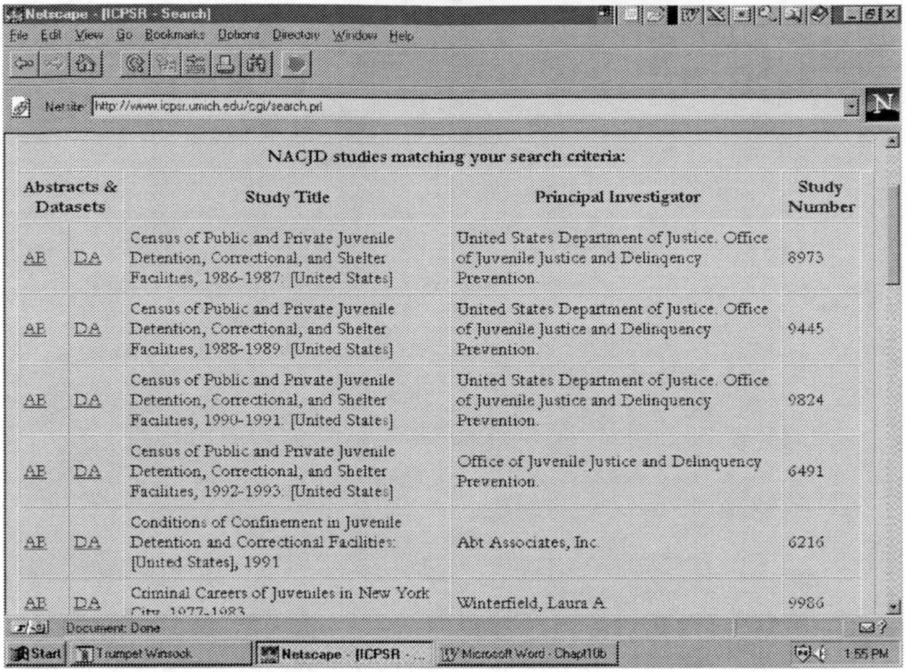

Figure 10 The beginning of a list of ICPSR data set holdings which might be of use to you in your research.

For another example, we will turn to the University of Essex in Colchester England. It houses the British social science data archive. This archive is searchable in great detail using a Web engine known as BIRON. The BIRON search engine is also usable with a Telnet connection if you do not have access to a graphical Web browser.

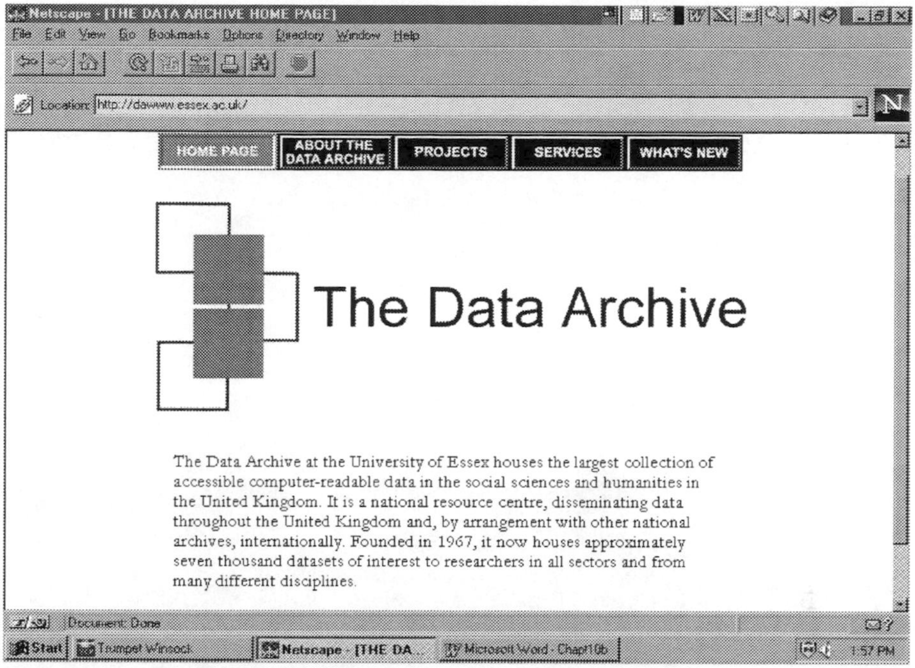

Figure 11 The Essex archive main page.

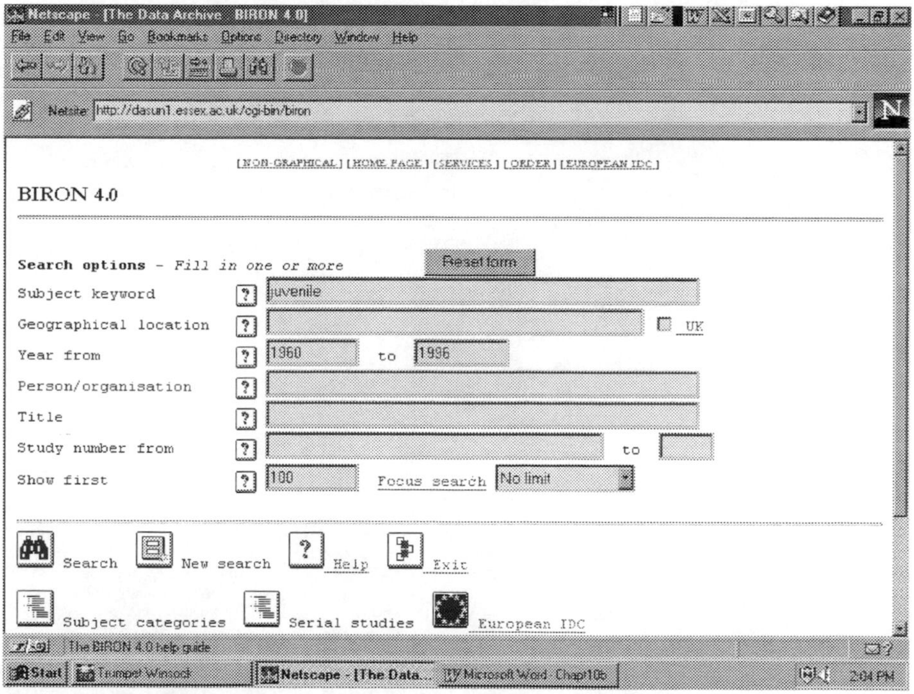

Figure 12 The BIRON search engine set up to search the Essex archive for data sets which have pertinence to our example.

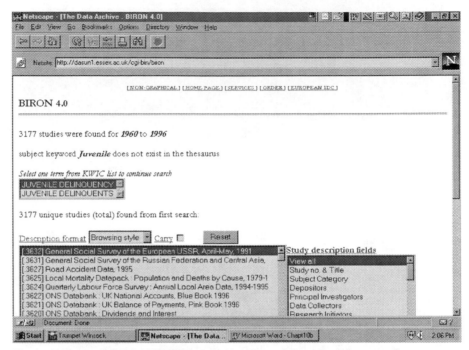

Figure 13 Respecifying the BIRON search using the term "juvenile delinquency."

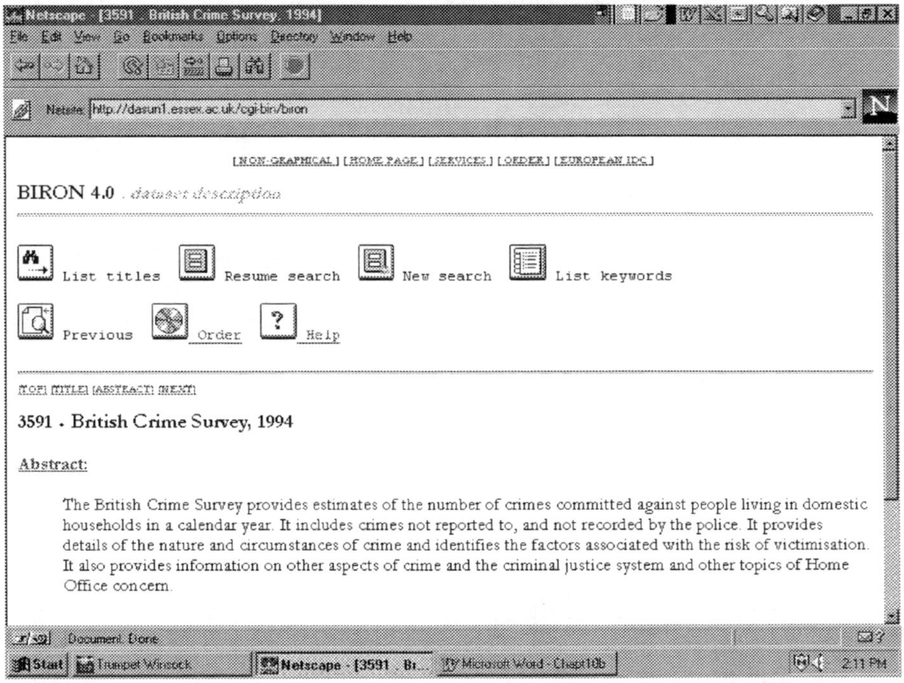

Figure 14 Asking for the abstract of the first data set on the list presented by BIRON.

As with the case of ICPSR, the holdings of the University of Essex archive are available to researchers, though it is an easier process if you are accredited with a British college or university. If you are not, you should approach your own institution's data librarian for assistance in obtaining a copy of the data set you need. In general, a means can be found to obtain the copy for you. And again as with ICPSR, you are responsible for carrying out runs on the data once it arrives.

A third example of a data archive is the one at the Library Data Centre at Carleton University. For example, it hold most of the data from Canadian Gallup polls going back to their inception in this country in 1949. These polls can be keyword searched as well, and basic frequency counts obtained online. Copies of the poll data themselves are available to academic users through the Canadian data library and archive system.

Figure 15 The main page at the Library data Centre at Carleton University in Ottawa.

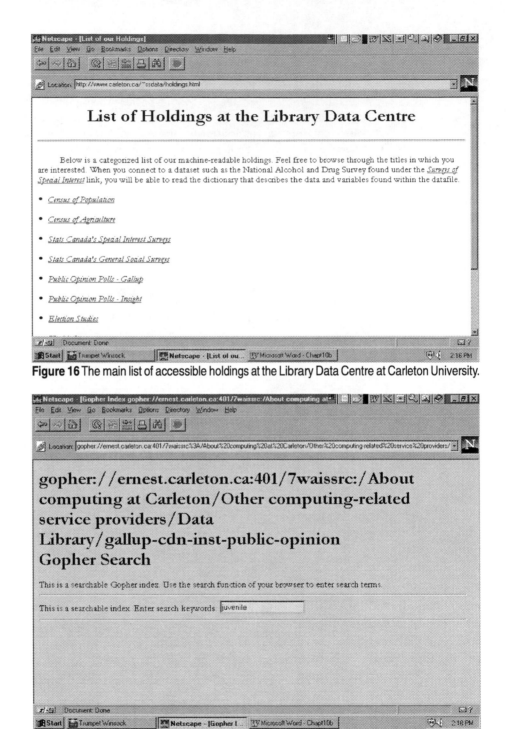

Figure 16 The main list of accessible holdings at the Library Data Centre at Carleton University.

Figure 17 Searching the entire holding of Canadian Gallup polls for instances of the word "juvenile" in question wordings.

STEP 7. RETRIEVE THE BEST AVAILABLE DATA SETS FOR SECONDARY ANALYSIS.

Once you have reviewed the suitability and the availability of data sets, and your particular project's requirement for secondary analysis, and have decided that one or more resources is suitable for secondary analysis in the context of your research topic, you should contact your institution's data archive or library data centre for assistance in obtaining a copy to work with. Once it arrives and is stored in a suitable location, you can then do analytical work on these data in order to augment and enrich your own project. Many books and manuals have been published dealing with the skills and knowledge necessary to carry out secondary analysis of this sort[1]. In addition, the person who obtained the dataset for you should be a resource as well in carrying out this sort of analysis.

STEP 8. DO LOCAL ANALYTICAL DATA ANALYSIS RUNS

Actually carrying out the secondary data analysis is beyond the scope here, there being whole books published on this topic, notably by Earl Babbie in various formats with various colleagues. However, it is possible to show some related examples of work using the Web in which the analysis is actually carried out at a remote location. This is possible because various data archival sites are beginning to make it possible for remote users to submit actual data processing requests remotely and then to receive the results of these requests by means of a Web files delivery of some sort.

Here are some examples of this type of process using the CANSIM database at the University of Toronto data centre:

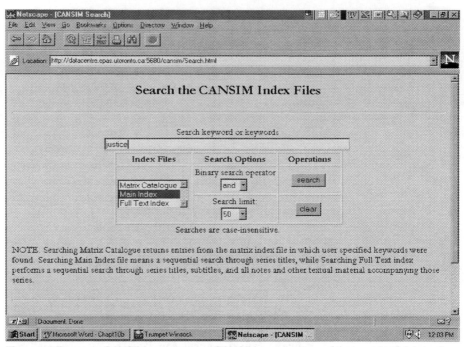

Figure 18 The main CANSIM search page. CANSIM contains tens of thousands of data series from Statistics Canada.

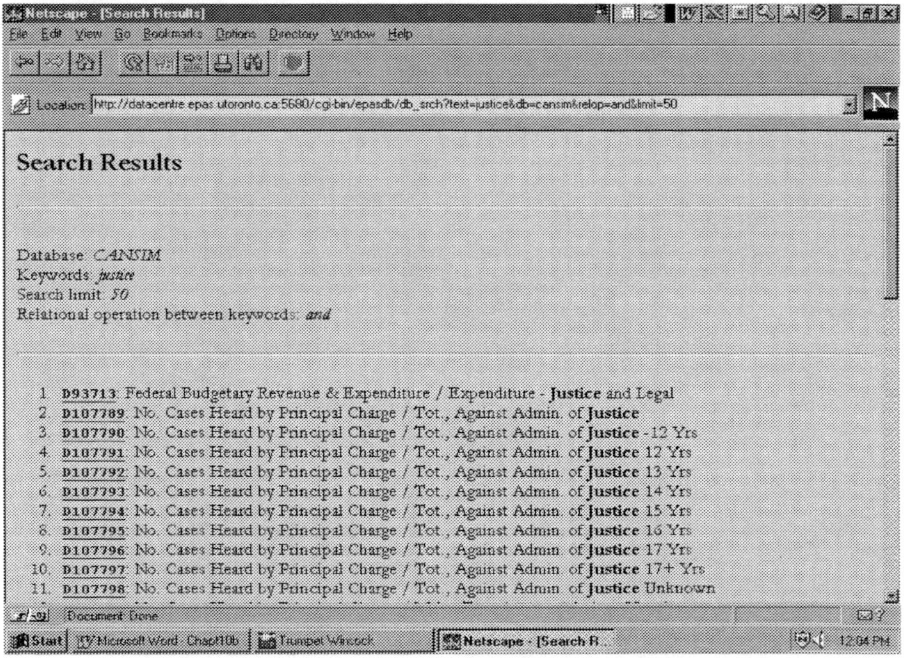

Figure 19 The results of a search on the CANSIM main index for data series on 'justice'.

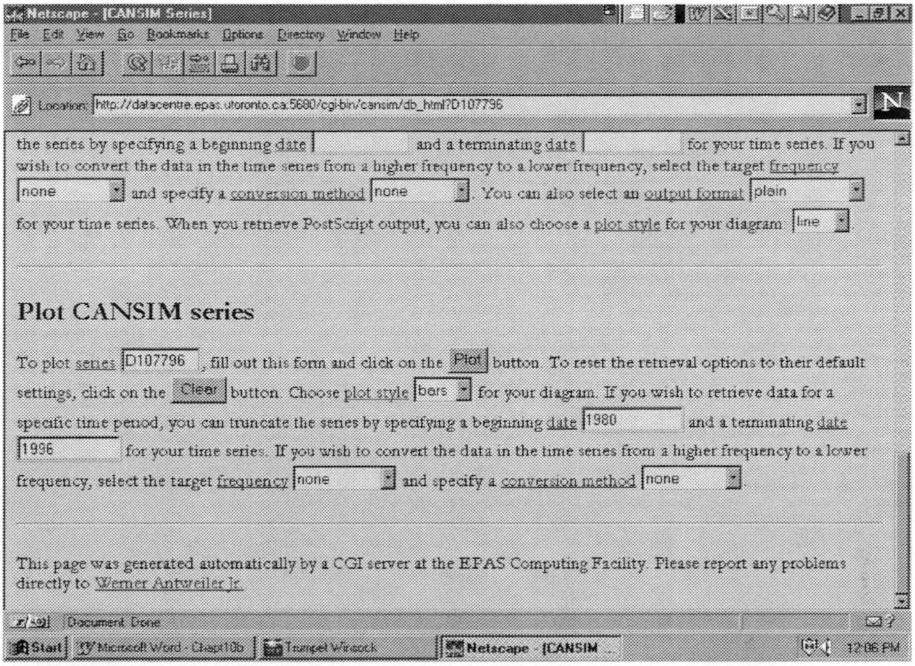

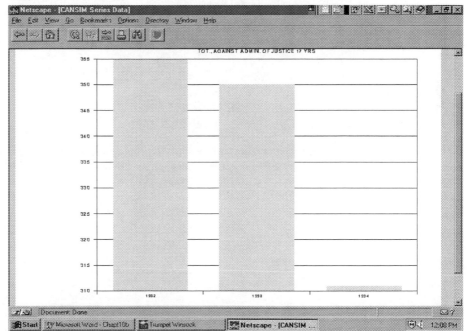

Figure 20 Requesting the retrieval of the data series on 17-year-old male offenders in the form of a plot.

Figure 21 The plot produced by CANSIM. Note that the data series are not always up to date. You can paste this graphic directly in your paper if you wish by copying it to the clipboard and then pasting into your word processor at an appropriate place.

In this chapter we have pursued our quest for useful information into databases stored all over the Web. In most cases it is not necessary to understand where they are located or how the information is stored. The browser acquires and presents the information in a usable fashion. It remains our responsibility to capture bibliographic information along the way, even if the resource cannot easily be accommodated in traditional referencing formats (for example, the graph in the last figure above will change continuously as time passes and additional data points get added to the underlying data series).

We end this chapter in the following condition: we have specified our topic, worked out successful search patterns, captured relevant references, some documents and relevant data sources, plus a few summary graphs and tables acquired over the Web and saved as graphic images or printed on paper. We must now assemble the collected material which together with our analyses and interpretations will form the substance of the finished paper that will in due course be presented, either in person, or on paper, or electronically by e-mail, or all three of the above.

Sites shown in this Chapter...

CARL UnCover	telnet://database.carl.org
Electronic journals list	gopher://gopher.cic.net:2000/e-serials/managed
Electronic Journal of Virtual Culture	gopher://refmac.kent.edu/
ICPSR	http://www.icpsr.umich.edu/
NACJD	http://www.icpsr.umich.edu/NACJD/archive.html
Essex Data Archive	http://dawww.essex.ac.uk/
Carleton University Data Centre	http://www.carleton.ca/~ssdata/
CANSIM	http://datacentre.epas.utoronto.ca:5680/cansim/Search.html

NOTES

[1] One example is Earl Babbie and Fred Halley, **Adventures in Social Research: Data Analysis using SPSS for Windows**. Thousand Oaks, California: Pine Forge Press, 1995.

CHAPTER

ELEVEN

Finding and Using Information for Research: Organizing and Presenting Results

"A network is only as strong as its weakest link."
Hal Varian, Dean of the University of California, Berkeley's School of Information Management and Systems. In the **New York Times**, "No Shortage of Bottlenecks," by Jamie Murphy and Brian Massey, June 29, 1996.

Having gathered whatever resources are available to you from a combination of sources, electronic, intellectual, on paper, from conversation, the exchange of e-mail messages, and whatever other sources you might use, it is time to organize and present your findings.

STEP 9. INTERPRET AND ANALYZE YOUR RESULTS

Interpretation and analysis is the core of social science research activity. Alas, there are no quick fixes and shortcuts for this stage. It remains as it always has been the full intellectual responsibility of the author. While software aids can help you identify, substantiate and then present your principle findings, the greatest weight still falls on the abilities of the author to discern patterns and present evidence. You must always keep in mind the obligation to check the correctness of your results and your conclusions based upon them, to reduce or eliminate redundancy of argument and evidence, to check for consistency with the conclusions of others, and finally, to ensure the reproducibility of your results by others.

In addition to these obvious measures, you should also ask yourself whether your results fit with common sense. And if they do not, provide an explanation as to why this is not the case. Ask yourself whether there are additional aspects of the topic you have not yet considered. Revisit the data and the literature repeatedly to ensure you have not left out important dimensions of the problem. See how well what you have found fits with your chosen theoretical perspective. If it doesn't fit, do you have an alternative explanation? Are there any data gaps which prevent you from making a comprehensive treatment of your problem?

STEP 10. DRAFT YOUR PAPER, EMPLOYING IMPORTED GRAPHICS IF POSSIBLE

The gist of writing a research paper is to organize and present your thoughts and your evidence on a particular topic. Were there to be no evidence, no description of sequences of events or processes, no attempt at analysis, and no organization, then a piece of writing likely doesn't qualify under this heading. In order to prepare and submit a research paper therefore, certain elements are required. Conventionally, these elements are presented in a certain order. While there are no ironclad rules involved, and certainly some rhetorical license is granted, the generic research paper does have a conventional structure. In turn, this structure reflects the presence of habitually occurring items.

The first section of a research paper introduces the objective of the work represented in as clear and focused a fashion as possible. This initial section should ideally tell the reader what the major focus will be, what your major point of view is, and if possible, into which theoretical framework this problem may be fitted. Obscurity and little-used words seldom insure a warm and generous reception. Rather, simple and clear expression is the goal, one which admittedly is often not fully achieved.

The second section contains the major presentation of your findings, broadly construed to include your critical review of the literature which has dealt with your research problem in the past, any new materials you have been able to accumulate, and any other evidence which seems pertinent. And of course you specify your integrated view or interpretation of all of this material, arguing for your own point of view as to what it all means. In a sense, this whole section is advocacy, though there is an obligation to take into account opposing views if only to refute them with your evidence. The net effect of this section is to raise the information level of the reader on your research topic, give the reader a coherent integration of what is known, and lastly, your argument as to what it all means. Especially in the case where you are paid for your efforts you are also obliged to give the reader a sense of confidence that there are no other major counterinterpretations lurking somewhere out there in the weeds waiting to blindside your employer as he or she parrots your views and interpretations in some public venue. The employer has paid in part for protection against this sort of embarrassment; your fee is an insurance policy of sorts.

If you are presenting new data analysis, whether based on newly collected data or on secondary analysis of data someone else collected, there is an obligation to consider the validity of this data as a major part of this second section. This would be done in an initial discussion dealing with methodological questions of data collection, any systematic data errors, flaws in coding, and other related data problems. These dimensions address the question of valid measurement and valid interpretability of your data.

Also, if you are using data analysis as an element in your paper, you will be obliged to show your major findings in some manner, either graphical, in tabular form, or in summary tables of correlations. The researcher cannot argue from hidden evidence; it must be presented, if only in an appendix. In general, all sources must be acknowledged and properly cited. This is required so that the reader could reproduce your results independently if required. Analysis takes your research paper beyond description and into the realm of explanation. As such, your explanation should ideally fit in some fashion into the theoretical framework introduced in the first section, even if only in refutation of that initial set of ideas.

When your analytic material has been presented, there are two sections still to prepare. In the first of these, you are obligated to present a summation of your evidence in which the various threads of your argument are combined to synthesize a unified picture of your research topic, including the highlighting of areas in which little or nothing is known. These should be explicitly acknowledged and not glossed over. It is a good practice to revisit the promises made in your first section and show that the promises have been honoured; or if they have not been, say why you were unable to do so.

Finally, it is also habitual to have a final short section entitled "conclusions." In this section, you can go past the evidence you have presented and speculate on the bigger picture into which your topic fits. You may also suggest areas into which your research work could be expanded to fill in gaps in understanding. Often, this is the section to which the reader pays most attention. Most readers have limited time to spend on your contribution. For this reason, the title of your paper must be attractive, accurate, and summarizing. The same could be said about the conclusions section as well. If an abstract is required, the same remarks apply in spades. You have only a few seconds to attract and retain a prospective reader's interest. Remember as well that indexing programs work from your title. Your principle findings or conclusion *must* be reflected in the title, and to a lesser extent in your abstract if there is one, if your research paper is to receive any detailed attention at all. The torrent of print in the world is now so great that you have to compete for any attention at all.

Stylistically, you should try to be clear in your expression, ignore side issues for the most part, and ensure that the ideas and the data presented flow logically in your rhetoric. Intelligibility is of utmost importance. If your best friend doesn't understand your paper, take whatever steps are necessary to rectify that situation.

As stated before, accurate referencing is a scholarly obligation. This means following the referencing style of your discipline, whether that involves footnotes, endnotes, or embedded reference cues. There are many different discipline-based style sheets and some of them are on the Web. Search for the one you need; you may only be able to find it in the library, however.

Design considerations surface in respect to font size, line spacing, the nature and size of graphics exhibits and other related matters. These considerations were seldom an issue in the long-past era of typewriters; however contemporary researchers have much more control over design parameters and the decisions taken do have an impact on the production values of the finished paper as a physical thing. Researchers now, for instance, have many typefaces in many sizes available to them. In general, double-spacing of manuscripts and size 12 fonts are appropriate, with one inch margins all around. There will be exceptions to these guidelines, however. The insertion of graphics, for instance requires judgment and good sense. Any opportunity to present graphs and charts in a pleasing manner as drop-in graphic images should be considered positively. However, this practice can be overdone. Whole page graphics with simple two variable bar charts for instance may be seen as space filling by some. Spell checkers and grammar checkers should be used routinely. They will not detect words used incorrectly or in a misleading manner however; your best friend should check the whole paper for sense and elegance one more time after you are all finished. It can save you from embarrassment or worse.

STEP 11. PRIVATE REVIEW OF YOUR DRAFT PAPER WITH TRUSTED COLLEAGUES

Have your paper reviewed for sensibility, spelling, and for any gaps or discrepancies in logic. The more trusted the colleagues that review the paper the better. Try to get in the habit of distributing drafts well in advance to give your reviewers adequate time for a thorough assessment. Your informants may have a better view of the likely reaction of your audience to the paper than you do. Gamesmanship in presentation of research is also a factor to be considered. The packaging of arguments is often a critical aspect of your paper. You do not have to agree with reviewers' comments, and you may choose not to follow suggestions. Nevertheless, you may be made aware of potentially weak points you hadn't previously considered by virtue of this preliminary review process.

STEP 12. SUBMISSION OF YOUR PAPER, POSSIBLY EMPLOYING A SHORT VERBAL PRESENTATION WITH SUPPORT FROM POWERPOINT SCREENS TO ORGANIZE AND PRESENT THE MAIN POINTS OF YOUR PAPER.

In the case of straight submission of your paper, nothing further need be done except printing and/or reproduction. You may find that you will subsequently be given the opportunity to revise your paper in light of comments. Take the opportunity if offered.

Increasingly it is the case that papers are accompanied by some form of oral presentation. This type of presentation can occur in a classroom, at a conference, or in support of the paper at the time of submission. For such events it is extremely advantageous to reduce your main points to a series of pages with a program such as Powerpoint which is part of the MS Office suite of software. If you have a notebook computer and can borrow a LCD projection tablet to use with your computer and an overhead projector, you can flash these screens of information on the wall as you speak. You can also show data graphics, charts, etc. to make your points. Audio visual aids are of considerable value in improving a verbal presentation. In the same fashion, printing a physical copy of your finished paper on a high quality laser printer is a definite asset as well. In general, presentation values matter in the assessment process. The reader often reacts to the form of presentation as well as the content and this dynamic can work in your favour.

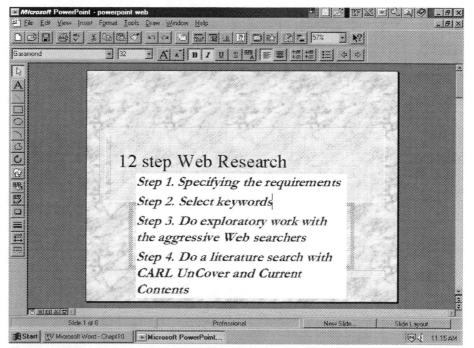

Figure 1 Making a Powerpoint page with your main points for use in support of a verbal presentation. A graphical element such as this greatly strengthens the impact of your paper.

AFTERWARD

Up to this point in this Part of the book, we have been dealing with social science research in a generic sense. We recognize that the methods and procedures in the various social science disciplines differ noticeably. Therefore, in the next chapter we will briefly point to some discipline-specific starting points for Web resource searching to offset the generality of the Part of the book to this point.

CHAPTER

TWELVE

Discipline-Specific Research Examples

"BELGRADE, Serbia — When President Slobodan Milosevic, faced with large anti-government demonstrations, tried to shut down the last vestiges of an independent news media last week he unwittingly spawned a technological revolt he may soon regret. Tens of thousands of students, professors, professionals and journalists immediately connected their computers to Internet web sites across the globe".

Chris Hedges, "Serbian Response to Tyranny: Take the Movement to the Web,"
New York Times, December 8, 1996

In the previous chapter, we pursued a generic example of a complete research project from inception to completion through the various stages in which research activity normally takes place. For this example, we used the topic of "juvenile justice" though any other example would have done. In so doing, we avoided the issue of social science disciplines and their own particular approaches to the subject matter.

Disciplinary boundaries reflect occupational roles, theoretical views, and methodological choices made long ago. Specialization in any knowledge area such as social science occurs for many reasons not the least of which is the increasing inability of any human being to absorb the breadth of the social sciences *in toto* and simultaneously. For this reason we have to recognize for our purposes here that the individual social science disciplines have taken divergent paths and that subject matter and approach can now differ in a quite striking fashion from one to the other. For each discipline there is a "pathway" to suitable Web resources and one must find a gateway to this path. As always, a good place to start and return to is my research page at **http://www.carleton.ca/~cmckie/research.html**; that is what it is designed for.

In order to show these disciplinary gateways, in this chapter we will provide a series of brief forays into the disciplinary areas to indicate where specialized starting points lie and what one is likely to find there. Again, for the purposes of having an example to work with, we will persist with the youth in conflict with the law example, modified as required in the various disciplinary areas where it has no direct applicability. It is not possible to pursue the full plan of research action outlined in the previous chapter for each discipline. This course of action would add much in length and the greater part of the added material would be of no interest to the specialized reader. Therefore the sections will be brief indications of how to begin in the discipline-specific context.

With respect to the availability of Web resources, there is considerable variability discipline to discipline in the social sciences. Some disciplines appeared relatively early on the Web, with separate disciplinary sections on the WWW Virtual Library (for example demography), while others such as geography have been relative late-comers. To some extent, this must reflect the nature of the knowledge they propound and the ease of its reduction to digital form. But notwithstanding the staggered start, all disciplines are now represented. As yet, none is as fully developed as say, the medical diagnostic literature which is freely and fully available to anyone on the Web. It is not overly optimistic though to expect that in the fullness of time, most if not all materials in all academic disciplines will be fully available in digital form over the Web. It is only a matter of time.

SOCIOLOGY

The amount of material in sociology is moderate, but there are several very good starting places. Choosing any one of them will result in the revelation of much material. Sociology has benefited greatly from the provision of data sets for secondary analysis by the various social science data archives discussed in the previous chapters. For instance, the availability of reputable public opinion surveys by a number of sites is a large positive factor for students seeking thesis projects which can be carried out with minimal expenditure of scarce money. Shown below are some pivotal primary sites. As always, starting at a prominent discipline-specific site found on my research page is the best way to start off in search of specific materials for your project.

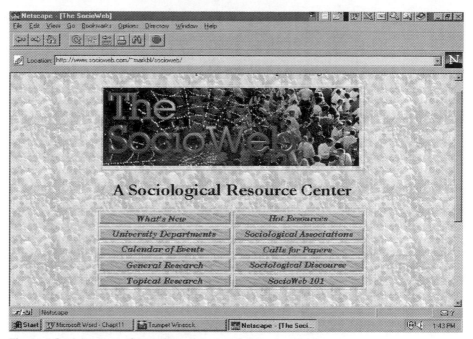

Figure 1 Sociology-specific starting point, one of several available.

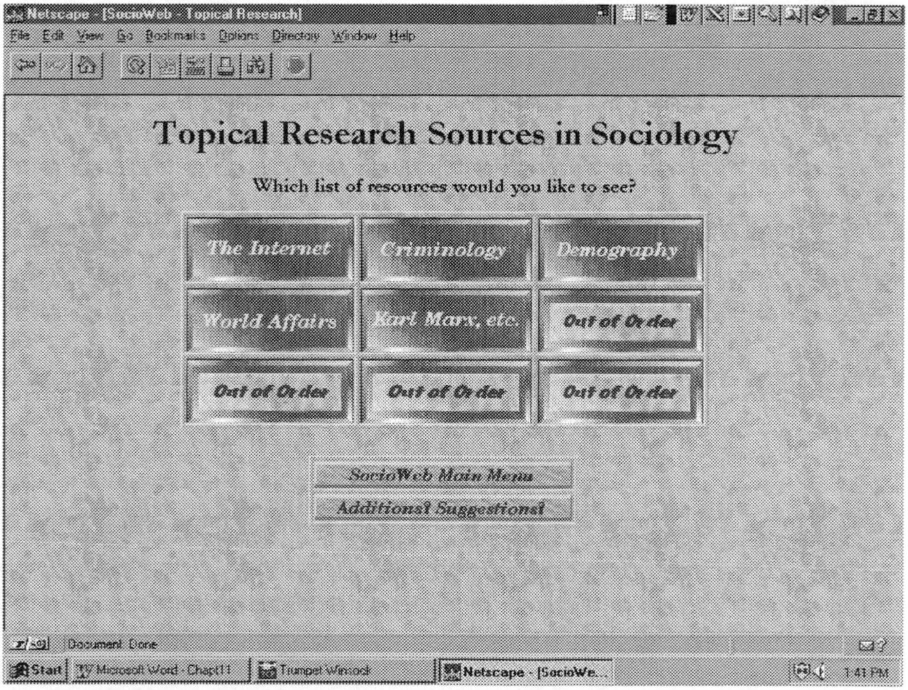

Figure 2 One level down at Socioweb we encounter specific materials to retrieve.

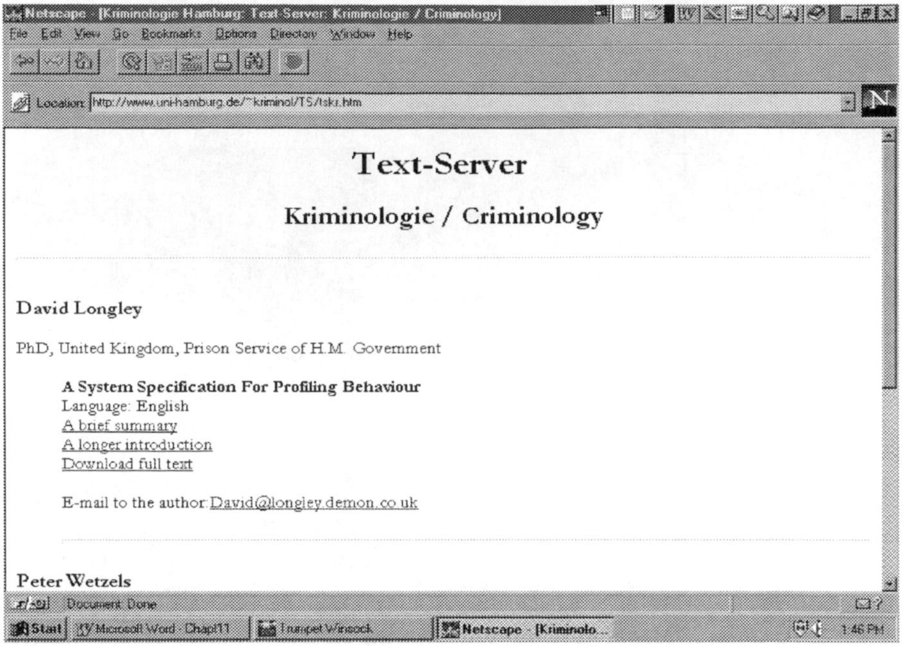

Figure 3 An example of a specific crime-related text to download if desired. It is located on a server in Germany.

ANTHROPOLOGY

Anthropology materials were quite late in arriving on the Web. There are still not that many primary sites devoted to dispensing anthropological information. Shown below is one particularly nicely designed primary site and following it, some more specific materials that are available.

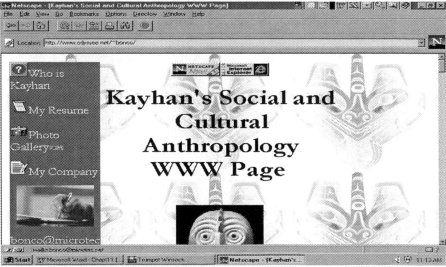

Figure 4 A primary anthropology Web site.

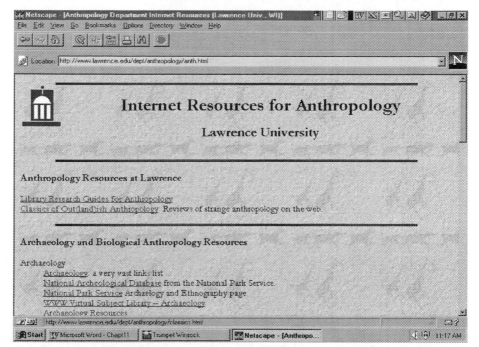

Figure 5 A secondary anthropology site located with the primary site shown in the previous figure.

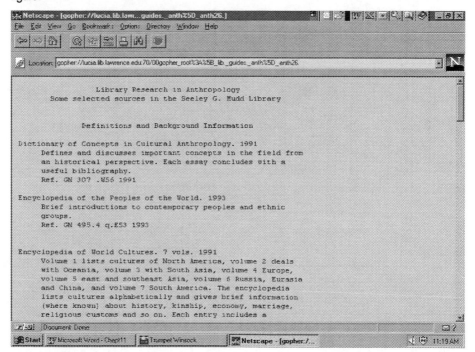

Figure 6 A very specific set of useful resources located using the site shown in the previous figure.

PSYCHOLOGY

By now, an extensive range of materials in psychology and related medico-legal disciplines are available in digital form on the Web. In part this is so because of the proximity of clinical psychology to the fully digital medical realm. Starting at one of the prominent primary sites in psychology, it is relatively easy to uncover a wealth of information and other materials.

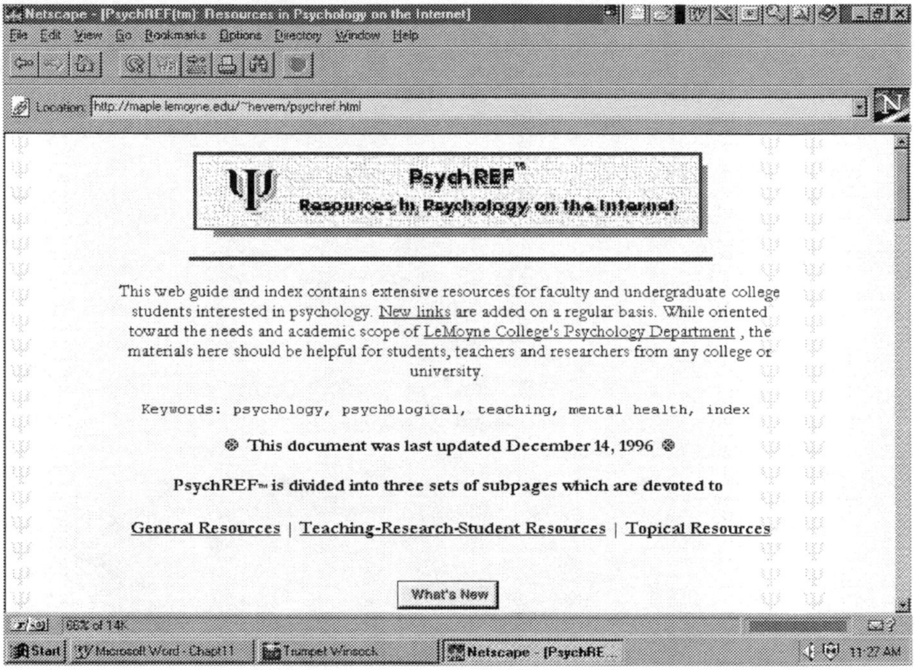

Figure 7 A primary psychology site. Note the availability of teaching materials as an integral feature. In some disciplines there is a rigid boundary between professional and pedagogical materials. This is not the case in psychology.

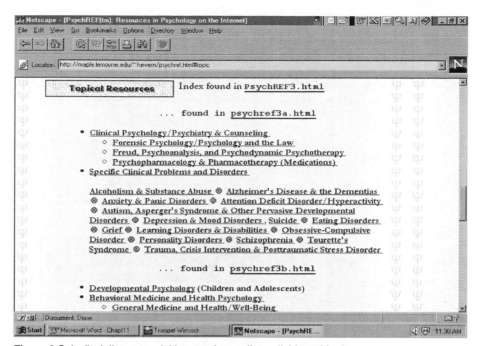

Figure 8 Sub-disciplinary specialties are also easily available at this site.

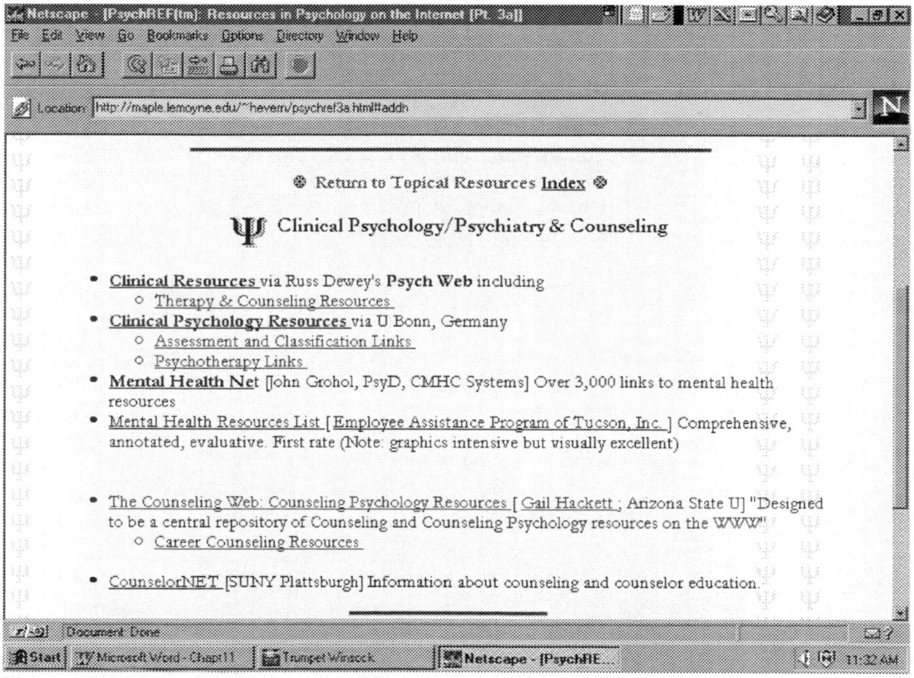

Figure 9 Well-labeled specific materials are located only two levels down.

GEOGRAPHY

Geography materials were relatively late in arriving on the Web for reasons unknown, possibly having to do with the nature of the materials themselves. Even today, the resources presented tend to be "borrowed" from other specialties or at least have overlapping relevance. No doubt this situation will not continue. The growing availability of geographic boundary files and automatic mapping facilities on the Web would seem to hold much promise for the future.

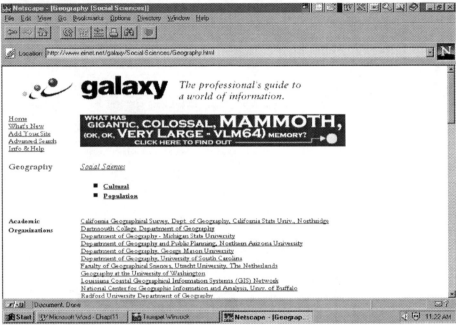

Figure 10 A primary geography site; note that this one carries advertising, an increasingly prevalent phenomenon as sites move from the aegis of one interested individual to a more institutional and thus a more costly basis.

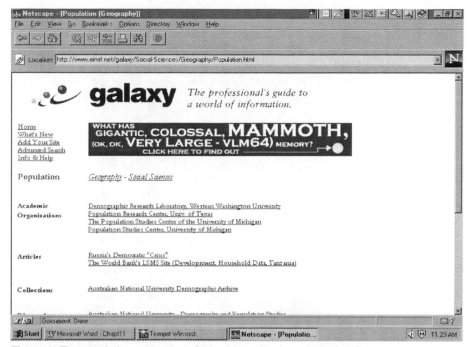

Figure 11 The population subsection of the primary site shown in the last figure.

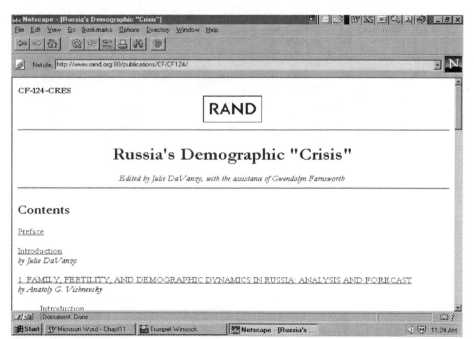

Figure 12 A specific textual resource downloadable from the RAND site, located through the auspices of the primary site shown in the previous figures.

POLITICAL SCIENCE

There are many useful political science primary sites. They are augmented by very substantial government sites oriented to international relations, particularly the military staff colleges' series of working papers. In addition, journals such as *Foreign Affairs* are published in electronic form in full text (see http://foreignaffairs.org/).

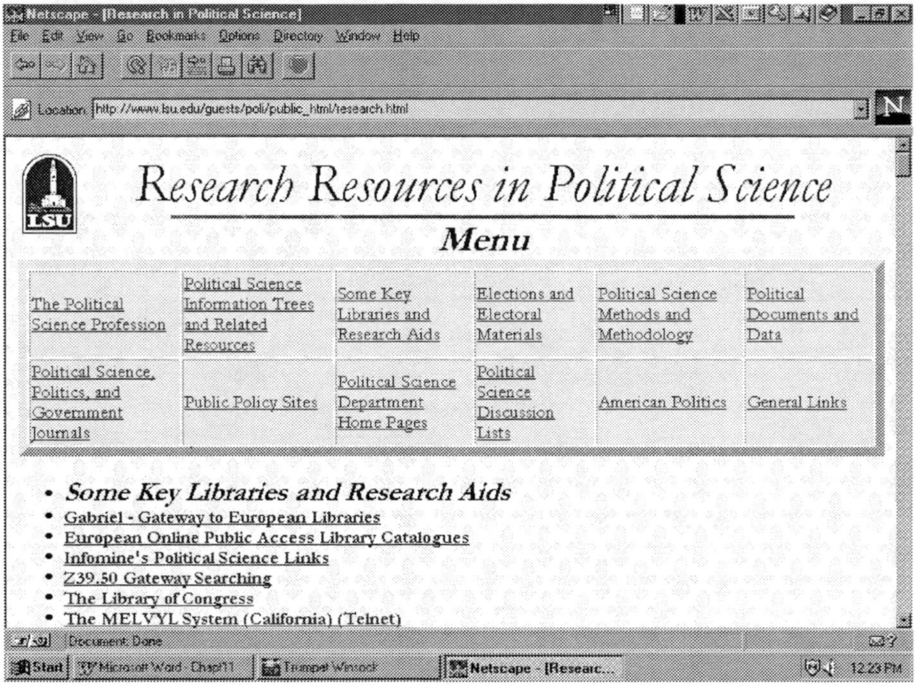

Figure 13 A secondary site with very specific and useful resources in political science.

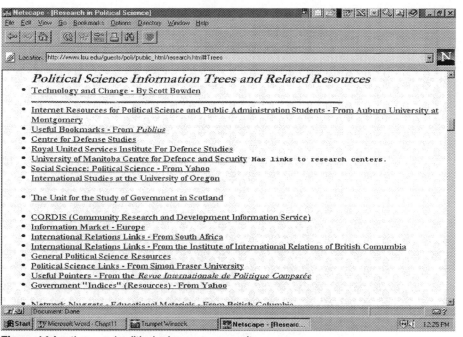

Figure 14 Another good political science resource site.

Figure 15 A military staff college site; there are many others in other countries.

WOMEN'S STUDIES

Women's studies is another relevant recent and underdeveloped disciplinary area of the Web. There are few primary sites. However, some of these are very well constructed and contain a wealth of materials to review. There follow some specific examples:

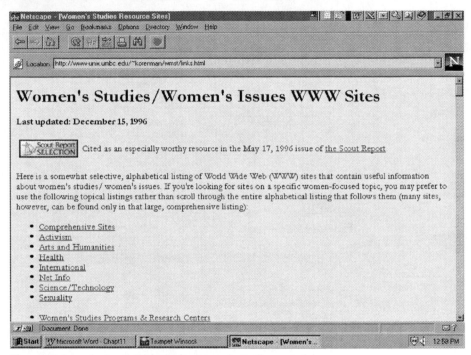

Figure 16 A good primary Web site for women's studies materials.

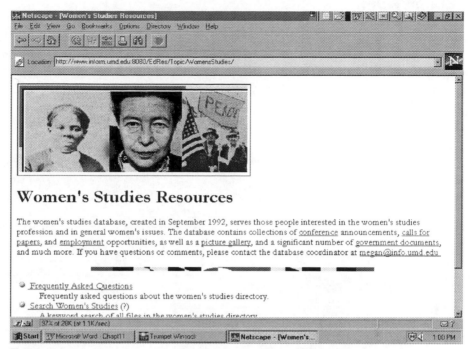

Figure 17 A secondary women's studies Web page located with the use of the primary site shown in the previous figure.

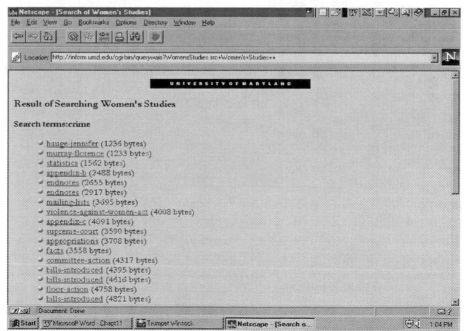

Figure 18 Some specific materials located using a materials searcher at a women's studies Web page.

SOCIAL WORK

There seem to be a large number of resources available in the field of social work. These have appeared largely in the last year, suggesting an accelerated development in this area. There are several good primary sites, one of which is shown in the figure below.

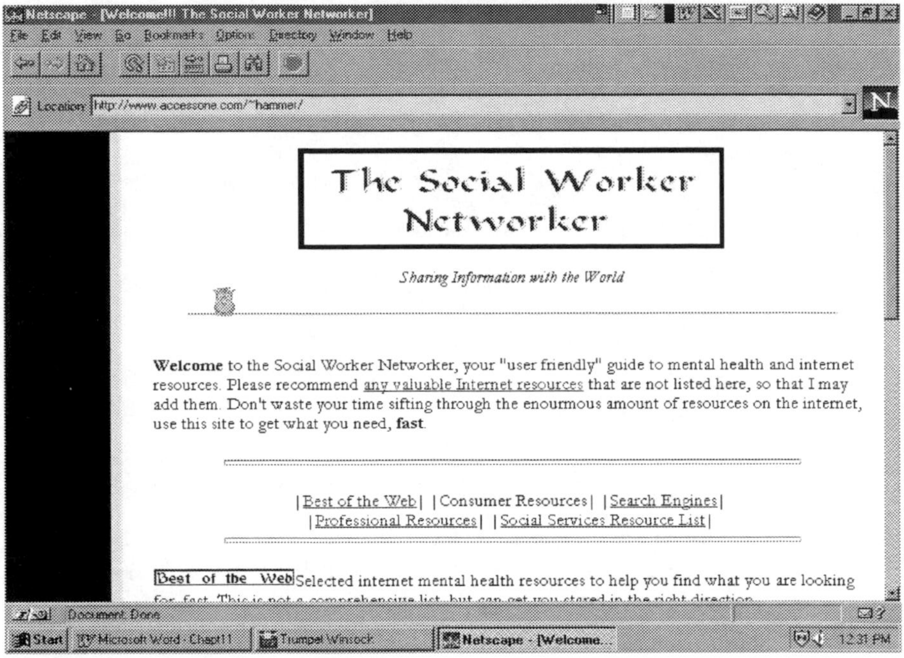

Figure 19 A primary social work Web site.

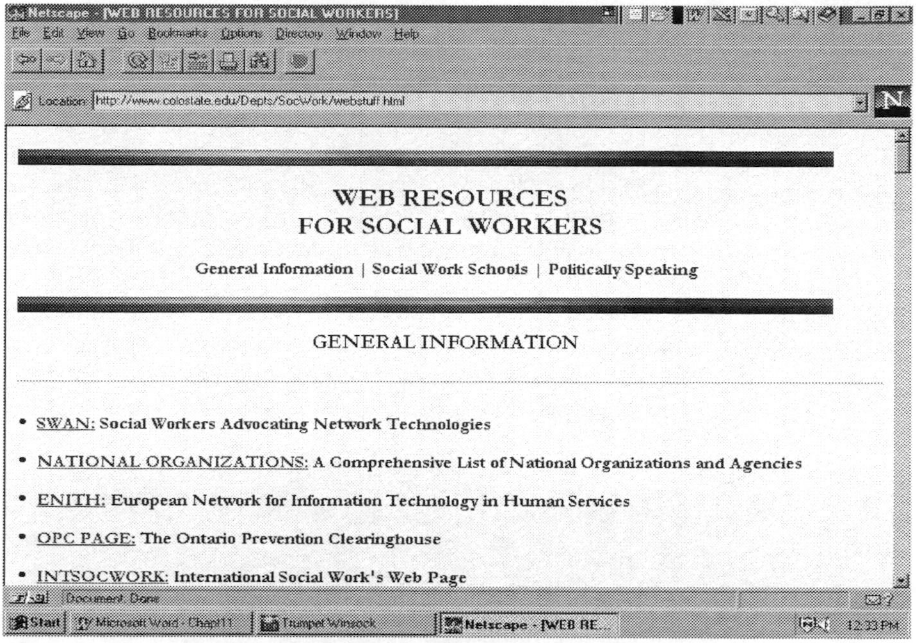

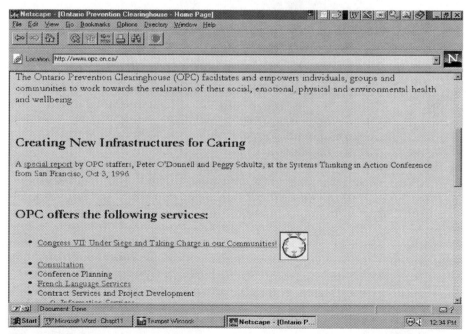

Figure 20 A secondary social work Web site showing specific resources that are available to visitors.

Figure 21 A fairly specific set of materials for social work located by means of the pages in the previous two figures.

MASS COMMUNICATIONS AND JOURNALISM

There is an extraordinarily rich selection of materials on well-designed Web pages available to students of mass communications and of journalism. This is so because the world's print media are rapidly converting to a digital production basis. Most of the world's great newspapers and periodicals now appear in electronic form. While these are available to all Web users, they are especially pertinent resources for those professionally concerned with the practice of journalism today.

In addition to the digital media themselves, there are a large number of sites having to do with academic reflection on the meaning of the rapid conversion to digital media by the previously print and television-directed organs of information, commentary, entertainment, and of course advertising. Shown below is one excellent primary site.

Figure 22 One excellent primary Web site in mass communication and journalism resources.

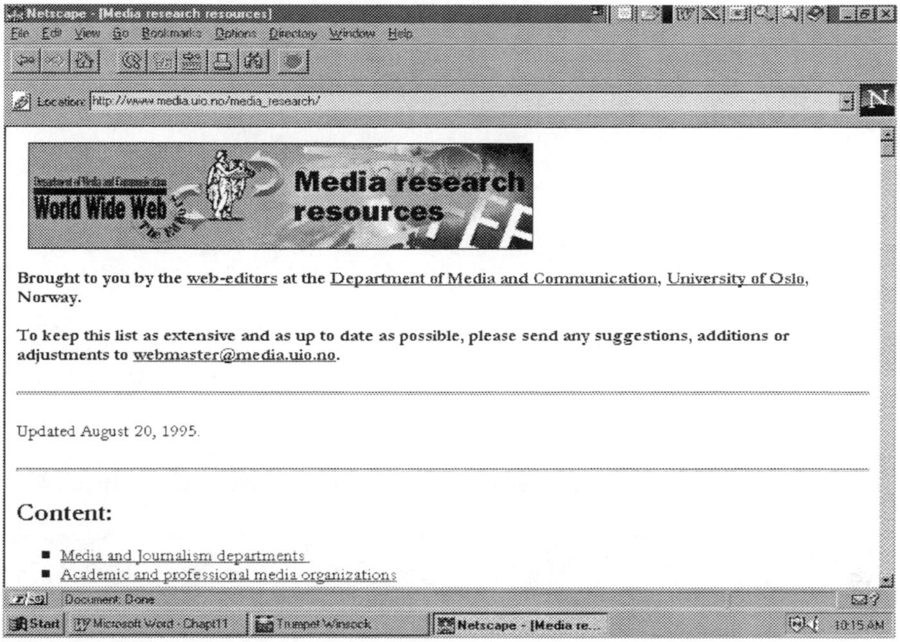

Figure 23 A secondary mass communications and journalism site.

In this chapter, I have tried to show some of the entrance ways to disciplinary materials on the Web. Once you find a primary site that is relevant to your discipline, you can bookmark it and return to it as a starting place for successive searches.

As a general rule, employing these burgeoning electronic resources in your routine research activities will become a standard feature of social science research in the future. The sooner you integrate it into your routine activities, possibly in the manner indicated in the previous chapter, the better off you will be.

Sites shown in this Chapter...

Socioweb	http://www.socioweb.com/~markbl/socioweb/
Text-Server Criminology	http://www.uni-hamburg.de/~kriminol/TS/tskr.htm
Kayhan's Social and Cultural Anthropology WWW Page	
	http://www.microtec.net/~bonco
Internet Resources for Anthropology	http://www.laurence.edu/dept/anthropology/ anth.html
Resources in Psychology	http://maple.lemoyne.edu/~hevern/psychref.html
Geography	http://www.einet.net/galaxy/Social-Sciences/
Geography.html	
RAND Corporation	http://www.rand.corp:80/publications/
Research Resources in Political Science	http://www.lsu.edu/guests/poli/public_html/ research.html
Canadian Forces College	http://www.cfcsc.dnd.ca/links/index.html
Women's Studies	http://www-unix.umbc.edu/~korenman/wmst/ links.html
Women's Studies Resources	http://www.inform.umd.edu:8080/EdRes/Topic/ WomensStudies/
The Social Worker Network	http://www.accessone.com/~hammer/
Web Resources for Social Workers	http://www.colostate.edu/Depts/SocWork/ webstuff.html
Ontario Prevention Clearinghouse	http://www.opc.on.ca/
Mediapolis	http://www.partal.com/mediapolis/ANG/ index.html
Media research resources	http://www.media.uio.no/media_research/

CHAPTER THIRTEEN

Providing Services: HTML and your Web Site

"You spin it, I'll jump in it."

Bob Uecker, speaking about the Web on ESPN coverage of the first game
of the American League Baseball Championship, October 1, 1996.

Part of the charm of the World Wide Web as it develops in fascinating and unexpected ways is its ability to turn anyone into a publisher. With very little study and minimal skills acquisition, you can become an information provider on the Web. Assuming you have the kind of service account needed for this purpose, you can proceed to make your own Web page content available to the world. No one's permission is needed, nor are you likely to encounter censorship, assuming you stay away from two kinds of content: hate and pornography, both of which are likely to cause you trouble. The only other possible sources of trouble are that your public files area occupies too much storage space (a function of your service provider's rules and guidelines) or that your site is too successful and attracts too many visitors, thus degrading the service for others. Otherwise, it's up to you. You can place draft papers on your pages for comments, any resources you may have found, or any other non-corrosive materials you want to present.

DESIGN CONSIDERATIONS

Designing a Web site is a relatively recent art. There are few rules, but here are some style guidelines:

• Try not to have too many levels of information: a site should never be more than three levels from "top" to "bottom". Otherwise, visitors become confused as to where to find resources they know are there but can't find.

• Try not to have too many large graphics which take a long time to load.

• Be sparing in the use of animation and dancing doodads on your page. These tend to irritate rather than engage.

• Copy the features of sites that you admire. You can look at how they are constructed by looking at their source code with the "view source" command in your browser. Even the text-only browser *Lynx* has a view source command, the "\."

• Remember that many visitors will look at your site with Lynx. Include either a text-only version of your site as a side path from your main site, or put text equivalents for each graphic image you use employing the ALT= tag.

- Avoid huge files, especially for the main page. Break up the material into sub-pages and load them only when the visitor requests them.
- Include an e-mail back tag or an e-mail address on your page so that visitors can get in touch with you easily. Ask as well for suggestions and tips.

Designing Web pages is a newly created occupational role. There are many manuals and tip sheets available on the Web to help you get started and learn more sophisticated techniques such as Javascript and Java applets which are now included in complex Web sites. You can learn a great deal from looking at other people's pages, and at the Java code they involve; look both at the finished product and at the HTML and Java code that creates them in the viewer's browser.

THE LANGUAGE OF THE WEB: HYPERTEXT MARKUP LANGUAGE (HTML)

In order to create Web documents and present them in a pleasing manner at your Web site, you will need at the very least an effective text editor. The editors that come as part of the Windows packages are not sufficiently featured to serve this purpose. It is better to acquire a copy of the shareware text editor called Programmers' Favourite Editor (or PFE). It comes in separate versions for Windows 3.1 and Windows95. In essence, the two versions are identical in capability. PFE has the singularly useful feature that it is able to write files in either DOS or UNIX format. And since in all likelihood your HTML files will reside on a server running the UNIX files system, this is a useful feature indeed. HTML files created and debugged on your computer must be uploaded to your public files area on your Internet host in order to be available to Web users. This host is likely to be a UNIX computer of some sort, though it sometimes is now a powerful Windows-based server.

Other editors specifically designed for writing HTML in some senses automate the creation of Web pages by allowing you to construct the appearance you want without any detailed knowledge of HTML at all. The Web editor package takes care of actually producing the code to give the desired effect you have indicated on the screen of your computer. Some such packages of Web creation tools are Claris Homepage, Microsoft's FrontPage, PageMill, Corel Webmaster, and a number of others. If you use this sort of program, however, you may find you lack the level of knowledge necessary to make small but important alterations in the file by hand. The latest version of FrontPage, for instance, is a very impressive integrated page creation and maintenance package. It is fully integrated with other aspects of the Office97 suite and allows you to move files from other Microsoft programs right on to a Web page with no difficulty (a Word document for instance). It also allows you to insert Powerpoint slide shows directly into your Web page with no alteration which should make giving Web courses easier for instructors in years to come. But using FrontPage routinely, you will not understand what is going on at the level of the HTML code. Once the files are perfected to your satisfaction on your computer, the files are shipped up to your service provider's server for implementation, with either FTP or the package itself. On the other hand, if you design pages completely on your own with a simple text editor, you may lack the knowledge as to how to create the effects you want. In either case, some time spent learning basic HTML is well spent.

Another similar approach to constructing Web pages is to use the Internet Assistant augmentation for Microsoft Word versions 6 and 7 (separate packages for each). The Internet Assistant is a free package of code available from the Microsoft FTP site. Once it is installed, the user creates the Web page in Word and then instructs the Internet Assistant to create a set of HTML code designed to produce the identical page in HTML. Sometimes, though, the fit is not that good and you may even end up with a page which is quite a bit different than the one you created in Word itself. For simple text Web pages however, the Internet Assistant works passably well and is definitely worth having. Be prepared to do considerable editing on the HTML version after it is produced. A somewhat similar utility is included with version 7 of the WordPerfect software from Corel. It works well. You compose your document in WordPerfect and merely save it in HTML format when you are finished. You must have some sort of browser to view your pages under construction. Netscape, for instance, allows you to open local HTML files. You can bounce between your text editor and Netscape, reloading the altered document to view the results of an experimental change in the code. Note however that there is no guarantee that your page will look the same in another browser. For more detail on constructing your own Web page, look at "Constructing your Web page" in the Technical Appendix. Some concrete examples of HTML code for pages may be found there.

HELPER SOFTWARE FOR WEB PAGES

Other software which can be of great assistance in preparing a well-designed and executed Web page falls into several general categories: a graphics editor, animated GIF code, and image map code. Since images form such an important part of impressive Web pages, these can be of considerable value.

1. *Graphics editors*. In terms of resizing images and changing storage formats, by far the best program to acquire is the shareware *Lviewpro*, which comes in several operating system variants. For creating images, there are many alternatives, some of them quite expensive, especially if a scanner of physical images is required. Photoshop, for instance works with a scanner to digitize physical artwork. For creating images from scratch, the Corel Draw line of products is likely the best overall product. Another digital editing product called Truespace allows you to create images with the illusion of depth and shading.

2. *Animation*. With a combination of these products, quite stunning visuals can be created for your Web site. Additionally, animation and movement can be introduced with the Shockwave line of products and separate animated GIF image files (which loop in the browser causing the illusion of movement). *Lviewpro*, discussed above, also allows you to create *interlaced* GIF files that load and are viewable immediately as they resolve to their ultimate crispness (rather than waiting for the whole image to load and then display). Transparency of backgrounds in GIF files is also a standard feature. This allows ragged-edge images rather than the standard rectangular GIF image. Lviewpro will also give you the pixel dimensions of images you intend to use on your Web pages. This is important because if you specify the width and height of your images, the visitor's browser doesn't have to wait to load the entire image from

your site. It can leave a space for them and load them later. This speeds up the loading process. In HTML language, the inclusion of an image is indicated with a line such as this piece of code we have seen before:

<IMG SRC="sitelogo.gif" alt="Site Logo" HEIGHT=55 WIDTH=62>

3. *Image maps*. Image maps are the transected property space which underlie large graphical images you now encounter regularly on the Web. Parts or sections of the image have been mapped off to indicate particular onward links. You can imagine a simple rectangular image map as a space in which the words Yes and No appear. When you place the browser pointer over Yes, a little hand with a pointing index finger appears indicating the presence of an onward link to the Yes resource. Similarly, when the pointer is positioned over the No part of the image, the pointing index finger indicates the presence of an onward link to the No resource. Image maps can be constructed to accommodate many onward links, each of which has a visible prompt to cue the user. As a concrete example, you could present a map of North America in which clicking in the Canadian landmass would take you to a Canadian government site, while clicking in the U.S. landmass would take you to a United States government site, and so on. There are two types of image maps, those which exist on the client side and those which exist on the server side. Making the latter type requires high level access to your Internet server's software, something which is not routinely given users. Should you wish to pursue the topic of server side image maps, consult the Image Map Tutorial at the NSCA site. Client side maps are much easier to construct. The actual details about how to construct image maps are beyond the scope here but good tutorial materials exist in abundance on this topic, and on the topic of animated GIF files on the Web. Use a search engine such as Infoseek Ultra to find them.

One last word of advice: start simple. Once you have absorbed the principles of simple formatting then you can move on to more complex effects. Good design does draw favourable comment and more visitors; however, unique content is the main way to attract visitors. In order to determine which elements of your pages are attracting attention, you will need some form of logging program which notes who has visited what element. Probably your service provider can provide you with advice and assistance on how to do this. There is much more detailed learning involved in starting and maintaining a sophisticated and attractive Web site. For instance, active links which you list on your pages must be checked periodically. Links have a disconcerting way of going bad over time as other Web site operators move their files around, rename them, or move service providers. It is not possible in this volume to go into more detail about all the special skills and technical knowledge that is needed over the long run though some more detail is included in the Technical Appendix. When learning this new skill, the documentation available on the Web can be most helpful in providing the needed information. Simply use one of the better search engines like Infoseek to find the assistance you are looking for. Finding a knowledgeable coach at your physical location can be of immense benefit as well.

CHAPTER
FOURTEEN

Communicating: Other ways of gathering and dispensing information

"Here we are crawling all the cracks between the walls of church state school & factory, all the paranoid monoliths. Cut off from the tribe by feral nostalgia we tunnel after lost words, imaginary bombs."

Hakim Bey, **The Temporary Autonomous Zone**. Brooklyn: Autonomedia. 1991, p.4.

The Web now has a host of new ways of communicating, person to person, person to mass audience, computer to person, and so on. Many of these new ventures are in their infancy and it is not yet possible to determine how these tools might be employed in the future or by whom. Notwithstanding the newness of these novel avenues of communication, some clearly do offer the prospect of delivering research information in very effective ways. In this brief chapter, we will look at just a few of them in hopes that they may suggest new ways of collecting, analyzing, discussing and presenting information.

REAL-TIME MEASUREMENT AND AUTOMATIC PRESENTATION

Data can be gathered, collated and disseminated entirely automatically. This form of presentation is appropriate where events are of a continuously varying nature, where they can be observed by machines, and where the product can be presented graphically. The simplest form of this arrangement is the Webcam, a television camera which presents its most recent image(s) via a Web page. There are now hundreds of Webcams in existence on the World Wide Web, some of which can be directed remotely by the user. At some sites, you can pan the camera left or right and then receive the image it captures. While Webcams are curiosities for now, there are other more complex measurement engines on the Web with much more potential for creating understanding.

In this context, there are several experimental applications worthy of note. Firstly, there is the case of the array of sensors automatically measuring and reporting some phenomenon to a central computer which then prepares and presents a map or image of the complex process being measured. Some of the applications are clearly geophysical (for instance, the automated array of earthquake sensors which constantly measure and automatically report the current state of geophysical activity in real time to the Internet). Others present more complex social phenomena such as traffic patterns. The most complex display of this type is the real-time map of the LA freeway system. It presents traffic speeds at each segment of roadway such that the traffic slowdowns and stoppages can be easily seen. With this Web tool, Angelinos can plan their homeward or workbound trips to avoid congestion and accidents. When this system becomes available to motorists in their cars, it will be an even more valuable tool.

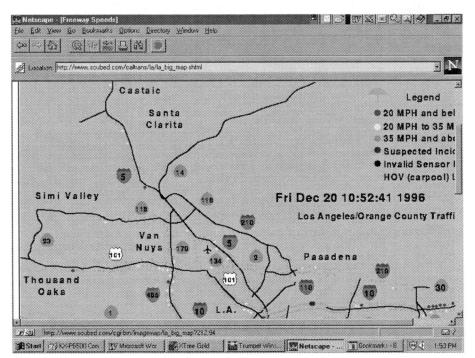

Figure 1 The northern portion of the LA freeway map which is updated every minute from buried sensors in each traffic lane. Note that the whole freeway system for the entire greater Los Angeles area appears on one map. Detailed intersection data is available in text form as well. The user just clicks on the intersection of interest and the detailed text information appears.

While the freeway map represents a macro analysis of a sort, microsystems can be studied as well. In some cases, a complete local system can be portrayed in one set of changing images. This can be one individual's office and whoever or whatever it happens to contain at the time a picture is captured and posted to the Web; or it can be the inhabitants of the fish tank at Netscape headquarters. The figure below presents the inhabitants of the Netscape corporate aquarium captured at one never-to-be-repeated moment in time.

Figure 2 The Netscape corporate aquarium, copyright 1996 Netscape Communications Corp. Used with permission. All Rights Reserved. This page may not be reprinted or copied without the express written permission of Netscape.

DIRECTORY SERVICES

As the number of e-mail senders and receivers in the world grew rapidly over the past few years, the necessity for directory services became obvious. However, these new directories could also be linked to other gigantic databases such as telephone directories, street maps, and other similar lists of civic data. Combined, these form a powerful new means of locating individuals of known name without any indication of their current location. While such services have been developed largely for Canada and the United States, they are now beginning to appear for other countries as well. Perhaps more ominously, it is now possible on several of these databases to do reverse record checks on addresses and telephone numbers to find out, for instance, who the registered user of a particular telephone number is, or who lives at such and such address. In the United States, these databases are also linked to a mapping service which will prepare an itinerary route from anywhere in the United States to any particular street address no matter where in the country it is located. Another service will then prepare a map of the local area surrounding the address in question with local street names and local features drawn in.

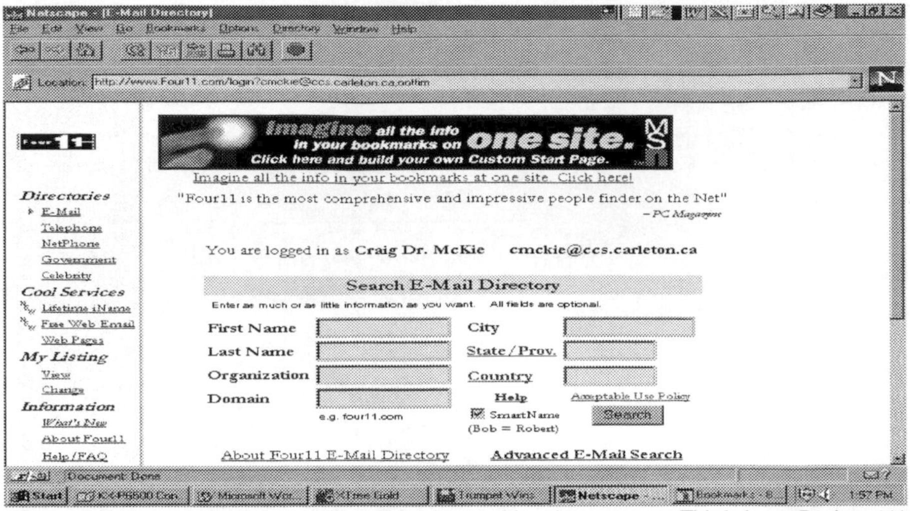

Figure 3 One example of an e-mail user database with enhancements. This is Larry Drebes 411 service, one of the first to appear on the Web.

Another example of a directory lookup activity is scheduling information. For instance, in the following figure the entire schedule of Canadian Airlines International is available for trip planning. At some point in the future it will probably be possible to actually reserve seats using such a system. This will require authentication of your identity (probably with a digital signature) to ensure that someone else does not make reservations using your name. A secure means of paying for the ticket using a credit card will probably also be required. These two issues (identity and secure payment) prove to be pivotal for the acceptance of electronic commerce. They will be discussed in more detail in the next chapter.

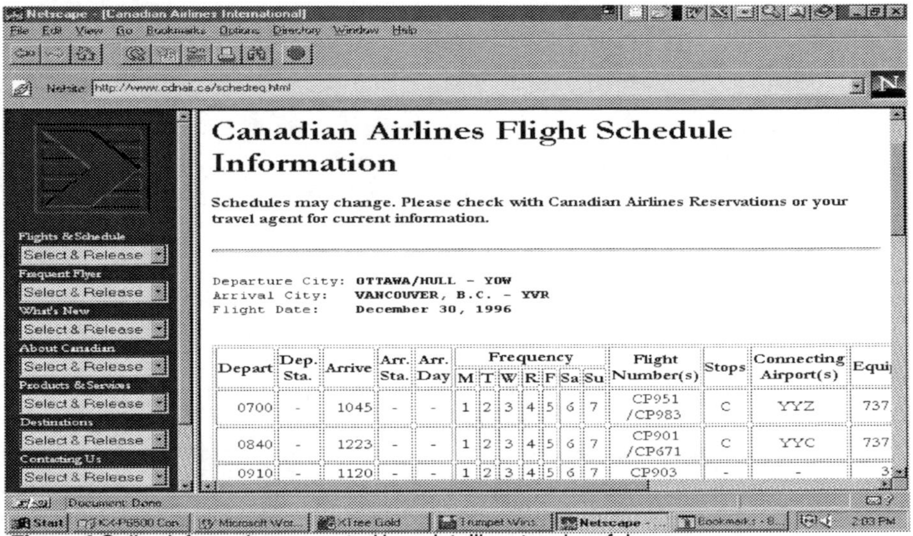

Figure 4 Online information presented in an intelligent and useful way.

TEACHING

Web pages can be used to present scholarship on line, that much is already obvious. The implications of doing so in preference to presenting it in the conventional manner in the scholarly journals are discussed in the final chapter. However, scholars can also use their pages in support of their teaching activities. Some few scholars have already jumped into this mode in a big way, one prominent example being Jim O'Donnell, the Augustine scholar at Pennsylvania State University. He has placed pretty much all of his classroom materials plus supporting readings on his Web page (he has an advantage in that many of his texts are no longer copyrighted!). In addition, he has other supporting materials, his vitae, most if not all of his scholarly publications, and other materials of possible interest. His primary page is presented in the figure below. It is adorned with attractive medieval or earlier artwork, making the page a visual as well as a textual experience.

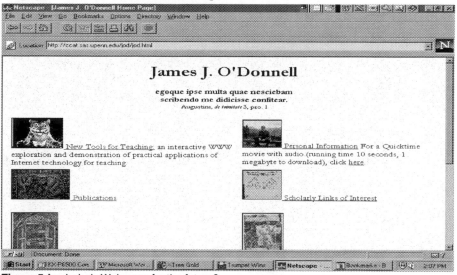

Figure 5 A scholarly Web page for the future?

It is likely that in the future, ways and means will be found to offer courses on the Web for credit. This could easily lead to strange situations in which people in other countries are registered at your university or college and maybe even complete whole degree programs without ever setting foot on campus, or in the country for that matter. Electronic assignment submission, mated with online required readings and CUSeeMe lecture delivery would seem to make this scenario feasible even today.

ONLINE BOOK STORES

Another research resource which exists in the form of a directory is the online bookstore. The most prominent of these is Amazon Books of Seattle, though another one called Bookstacks in Cleveland is also well used. These facilities allow browsing for book information by keyword search and they exist to take orders and ship books to your destination. Generally, a credit card number will suffice for placing orders, though again, sending your credit card number over the Internet involves a certain degree of risk at present.

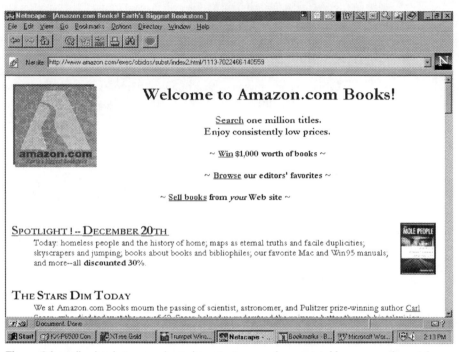

Figure 6 An online bookstore can be an important research resource. You can use the catalogue to do searches; and you can also place orders for mail delivery.

TALK

The talk utility can be used to establish a channel of direct keyboard text communication between two persons wherever they are located in the world provided, they both have an Internet connection. In general, the talk utility is an element of the UNIX system, and if you do not have a UNIX shell account you will not be able to communicate in this manner directly. There may be alternatives available, however.

To use talk, from the UNIX prompt you type "talk" and then the e-mail address of the person you want to talk to. If the person is logged on and wishes to talk to you (a message will appear on his/her screen saying you want to talk to them), they initiate their half of the connection. Once both parties are present, the screen is divided into two parts horizontally and each party types whatever they want in their half. The connection is bi-directional so both parties can be "talking" at the same time, a situation which can often lead to confusion and crosstalk. Nevertheless, such a session can be useful in establishing a dialogue with someone far distant who is an expert in matters of interest to you.

IRC

Internet Relay Chat is another popular means of having keyboard conversations with others connected somewhere to the Internet. In contrast to the case of the talk program, IRC is a forum for many people to communicate simultaneously. IRC channels have become extremely popular with children who can "meet" and discuss any issues they want. Necessarily then, the discussion on most child-oriented IRCs, MUDs and MOOs (for obscure reasons, role playing IRCs are called Multi-User Dungeons (MUDs); MOOs are an object-oriented variety) is juvenile, though they have proven to be of research interest in and of themselves, particularly in the context of the exchange of prohibited electronic objects such as some forms of pornography.

It is not impossible, however, to use the IRC technology to open a text-exchange conference call between collaborators for research purposes, and this use should be kept in mind. You would have to establish a new "channel" for your conversations and let all participants know where and when to join it. Though keyboard oriented, it does offer the promise of group collaborations. Without a doubt, future developments in this direction would facilitate collaboration between greatly dispersed scholars.

In order to use IRC, you need to have a connection to the Internet and some form of IRC client software. When you have these, you then join a pre-existing channel at an IRC server location somewhere on the Net. A list of "channels" is available at each IRC server.

A sound-based as opposed to text-based variation on this idea is the MBONE which is a multi-casting audio channel. It distributes a stream of audio from one source to many dispersed locations. It has been used for discussions and for the distribution of public events such as concerts. Though an attractive concept, for the moment MBONE requires specialized software, professional help in setting it up, and most importantly a very high volume connection to the Internet.

PGPFONE

The beginnings of long-distance voice communication within the confines of the Internet are also present in prototype versions already. For instance, the latest versions of Netscape were shipped with a voice communication program called CoolTalk. It is analogous to CB radio in its performance and suffers from several disadvantages. The quality of sound is generally poor. And, if you do not have a unique IP address for your computer, it may be difficult or impossible for someone to try to get in touch with you, since you do not have a stable address (your service host often assigns you an arbitrary one when you login under many present arrangements). Finally, your conversation is not secure and may be tapped and listened to by others.

One program currently in prototype attempts to address the latter problem by providing encryption to "scramble" your transmissions so that only the person you are talking to can "decrypt" and understand your conversation.

These programs are really still experimental. Still, it is quite possible that we will all talk to each other in this fashion in the future without having to consider long-distance charges at all. Think of a situation in which you could collaborate with scholars thousands of miles away through daily contact by voice and e-mail and could exchange drafts and working documents in a safe and secure manner and not be overheard by anyone else. This state of affairs is probably only months or at most a few years away from everyday feasibility.

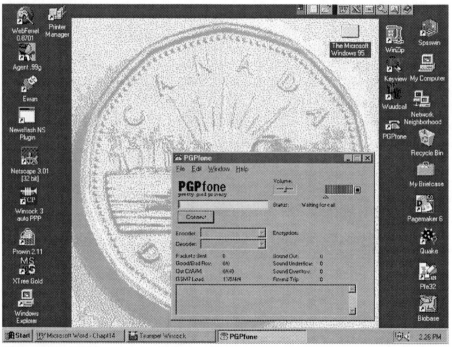

Figure 7 The PGPfone screen. This experimental program allows securely scrambled voice conversations across the Internet without the additional charges you would expect with ordinary long-distance telephone conversations.

INTERACTIVE SOFTWARE UPDATES

One final example of possible future lines of development should be noted in this chapter as a harbinger of things to come. Computer users often complain that their software (or hypothetically their databases) are out of date and in need of updating. Updating often means taking the time to download a new version of a program or database and reinstalling it. This problem has been addressed by the Norton software company with respect to their Crashguard program for Windows95. It contains a button which, if clicked while the user is online, automatically acquires any update software from the Norton site and then installs it without further intervention from the user.

In this same manner, it is possible to imagine an automatic database program updating itself from time to time, possibly many times a day, somewhat like the Pointcast screensaver now acquires news content from the Reuters news service by itself according to a preset interval formula, and a schedule of your news interests, and then presents the news for you to glance at if your screensaver is active.

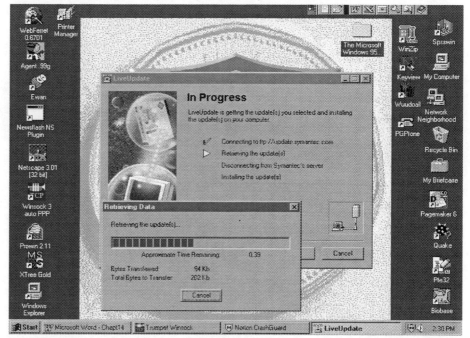

Figure 8 An example of automated software updating from Norton Crashguard. The update is acquired and self-installed with no intervention from the user at all. It even tells you what it is doing while it is doing it.

Sites shown in this Chapter...

Los Angeles/Orange County traffic map	http://www.scubed.com/caltrans/la/la_big_map.html
Netscape Fishcam	http://home.netscape.com/fishcam/fishcam.html
Four11	http://www.Four11.com/
Canadian Airlines	http://www.cdnair.ca/
James O'Donnell	http://ccat.sas.upenn.edu/jod/jod.html
Amazon Books	http://www.amazon.com/

CHAPTER FIFTEEN

Electronic Scholarship: Risks and Rewards

"Maximum prison term, in years, for possessing an unauthorized modem in Myanmar (Burma): 15."

Win Treese, Open Market Inc., the fifteenth **Internet Index**,
October 17, 1996

In this concluding chapter of the book, we will attempt to pick up some of the loose threads and then offer some summary interpretations of where the Web might be taking social science research and its students and practitioners in the future. We will also offer some thoughts on where the whole Web package of utilities is going and what it is likely to do to scholarship practices in the academy generally. It would appear that big changes are in store for the practices of both teachers and students and we will speculate a bit as to where these changes might be felt and where in the academic world they may find a part, a world which looks quite different from a contemporary student's point of view. There is a fairly clear indication now that students are obliged to learn how to use these new tools and skills if only for the purposes of finding post-graduation employment.

We will also have a look at some of the risks involved, and the so-called "dark side of the Web", the sordid and threatening part which is inseparable from the sum of all Web sites and not easily subject to control, if indeed control is possible at all.

I. RESEARCH METHODOLOGY IN AN AGE OF INFORMATION SUPERABUNDANCE

No one now knows how the transition to digital scholarship will work its way out - no one. All we have is informed speculation and hunch. Since to refrain from reflection is a disservice to everyone, perhaps some license can be allowed me at this point.

I now routinely glance through the electronic editions of several newspapers: the *New York Times* (two times because of the 1 pm update), the *Globe and Mail*, the *Toronto Star*, and the *Los Angeles Times* (often several times a day because it includes the Associated Press wire service and has a useful means of filtering its flow to my individual interests). In special circumstances, I can consult the *Washington Post* or the *Times of London*, though sadly not as yet the *Guardian,* the *Independent* or the *Observer* on the weekends. There are also the whole or partial contents of most of the quality news periodicals on offer as well. And all of this is delivered to me at any time, day or night, to wherever I am and without charge. None of this existed in 1994.

Taking this scenario a step forward, I can use the UnCover service in Colorado to do a literature search on any English-language periodical literature from about 1990 onwards and have obscure articles faxed to me for under $10US in less than 24 hours. There is also the *E-library* service in the U.S., shown earlier in this book, which delivers some whole text books to its customers for a modest charge, in addition to contemporary periodical literature.

I feel that the availability of these new services, virtually all of which have appeared in the last five years, is an immense boon to all of humanity. Still, a library without cellulose is a difficult transitional notion. This difficulty extends to the heart of contemporary professional scholarship practices, to the open accessibility of Web publishing and to the alternative reputational engine that is being established outside the bounds of traditional peer review and undergraduate essay-writing practices.

II. FIXITY, PROVENANCE, AND AUTHORITY

In traditional publishing terms, a book or an issue of an academic journal is fixed on paper once it appears. If there were errors included, and if they were detected early enough, perhaps an expensive errata sheet may have been included. But in many cases, the errors are known only to a few select readers. Now, with electronic publication, texts can be altered at will; they need never be fixed in content. The lessons are many for students and professional scholars.

Printed material is often deserving of being amended and updated. Criticism, alteration, rearrangement and adaptation lie at the core of the academic process and of course the scientific method as well. Economically this process is increasingly less feasible on paper, since it fills library shelves with material that is quickly superseded.

Publication of this additive and accumulating sort cannot be done in a timely and effective manner even in the best of circumstances. Therefore, a fully electronic text that is updated regularly is preferable for many reasons, but most importantly so since errors and omissions can be corrected. But then how does the student cite a shifting resource?

Further, one can never be sure one has the latest version, or even a version which comes from the ostensible author. It could have been doctored by somebody else. As a Web document, a book or influential journal article could be a rolling project. Its electronic file of scholarship will pass through many sets of hands in its lifetime. It will be broken up, expanded upon, commented on, excerpted, and so on. Excerpted material, even though from an early and incorrect source file, will take on a life of its own. The link of provenance is thus lost through excerpting. Many years later, people may still be trying to make sense, for example, of a flawed fourth edition, ignorant of the existence of a tenth corrected edition. Chains of sequential citations based on old sources take on lives of their own, and become legendary by repeated application, like urban myths and political party platforms. The requirement here is for a certification mechanism, a digital signature, which both fixes the document from tampering, states the date of revision, and alludes to a site where information on variants is available.

III. THE DARK SIDE OF THE WEB

The Web tools have the power to reveal all manner of information which is beneficial to humanity. But they are also able to deliver some of the very worst that humanity has to offer, apparently with impunity from national law enforcement agencies and their efforts. Distressing material abounds on the Web; on occasion it will leap out and confront the unsuspecting observer. For example, there is a USENET newsgroup (*alt.tasteless*) devoted, at least in part, to publishing disgusting stories and photos of dead bodies in various states of disarray, dismemberment, or decay. Also along these same lines, there is a Web site which presents photographs of human exhibits from 19th and 20th century traveling freak shows (*Dan's Gallery of the Grotesque*).

The presence of this material highlights the fact that the Web is largely unregulated. Occasionally, a particularly vicious Web site is shut down by a service provider following public complaints. One such site was shut down in Ottawa in 1996; it featured death threats against the current premier of the province of Quebec. But such terminations are few and far between and in the main, anything goes, up to and including laudatory commentary about the Third Reich, amateur photos of sexual behaviour, and so on. The presence of a large number of USENET newsgroups devoted entirely to exchanging photographs, and the large amount of traffic which flourishes in them, is both a cause for reflection on the human condition and an invitation for social science research to throw more light on these phenomena in order to better understand them. Is this Web behaviour supplanting other like-motivated behaviour which existed previously or does it occur in addition to pre-established patterns of behaviour?

We would be remiss here to neglect the underlife on the Web. Otherwise, the reader might get the impression that most of the content of the Web is seriously intended and generously conceived. While this may be true of the vast body of accumulated materials, it is certainly not true of all the material. The "other" material takes many forms and we will discuss some of these briefly in this section. It will briefly present a sample of the dark material to sensitize the reader to the full range of possibilities available on the Web. In one example, that of the unwarranted scurrilous attack on an individual's reputation, the victim is often totally unprepared for this sort of on-slaught which he or she may feel was completely unprovoked. And you may well actually find yourself the object of a text attack over the Net at some point; it happens to almost everyone sooner or later. It is best to understand the phenomenon before it happens to you so that you do not overreact.

This material might well be of academic interest to someone pursuing studies of some aspect of non-sanctioned behaviour on the Web. But beyond narrow studies, it is important to be sensitized to what is out there to be had, so that it can be recognized for what it is when it finally appears. None of these forms of abusive communication are unique to the Web; rather they have been transformed with the Web tools for use with a much larger potential audience.

Beginning with an obvious point, the amount of groundless nonsense available on the USENET newsgroups is indeed very large. Some of it is intended to deceive the gullible (Pierre Salinger was lead to believe in a missile attack on TWA 800 for in-stance), some of it to amuse by exaggeration, and some is merely deranged. Constant reminders to yourself that the basic principles of science remain in force are useful: demand evidence and independent corroboration. Belief is not something to be con-ferred lightly, no matter how many poorly informed citizens subscribe to a particular interpretation. Unless proven otherwise, Elvis is still dead, there are no flying sau-cers (nor are their infamous passengers, the greys, existent), Area 51 is an air force base, and life on Mars remains an intriguing hypothesis.

• Character assassination and abuse

There are individuals on the Web who seem to spend all of their waking hours posting to newsgroups and maintaining Web pages which advocate extreme causes and/or mount virulent attacks on opponents. Some of the individuals become well known by name and appear as posters in many newsgroups and memberships of listservs.

• Pornography: Common garden variety, and really nasty with sound effects

We are going to refrain from the obvious step of reproducing some particularly offensive piece of pornography here. Suffice to say that it exists in large quantity, perhaps even that it forms a large part of the USENET newsgroups flow of files. In part this is so because high quality photos make for very large digital files. These files tend to be broken into sequentially numbered uuencoded segments for posting to the USENET system. The interested viewer must somehow paste these pieces back together (generally, by designating a thread in order that the numbered pieces appear), then uudecode the reunited file. Most such still pictures are shipped in .gif or .jpg format. You may also encounter snippets of pornographic movies stored in the .mpg format. These movies, though short in duration, can be very large in file size, running to several megabytes in total for a few seconds of playing time.

Files of this sort are available in two ways. The first and most prevalent form is on a series of USENET newsgroups which contain the word *binaries* in their titles. Many service providers either do not carry these groups at all or carry only a selection. The reasons for not carrying such newsgroups may be potential legal liability, but the huge flow of data in such newsgroups also stresses the service providers online storage facilities. Notwithstanding the fact that a service provider does not provide access to this group of files, anyone with a valid service account and browser software or even USENET reader software like Free Agent can obtain the files from any one of dozens of public USENET sites around the world. It is this redundancy which makes simple censorship of the USENET impossible.

The second and less prominent way to obtain such materials on the Web is through sites dedicated to this purpose. These tend not to be common because their presence is quickly noted and their operators are then deluged with requests for the files. For this reason, private dial-in databases dispensing pornographic files completely outside of the Internet are also to be found if looked for. Access to these sites tends to cost money.

Pornography is not necessarily restricted to pictures either. There are binaries groups devoted to sounds, and some movie formats now come with sound components.

• Conspiracy theorists: the misguided and the seriously deranged

For some reason, many people in this world seem drawn to simplistic explanations of complex events which fly in the face of the laws of physics, common sense, and all previous experience. The Web provides a perfect place for these explanations to put down roots and grow. Conspiracy explanations have recently adduced to explain the crash of TWA flight 800 (Navy missile), the appearance of crack cocaine in central Los Angeles (CIA plot), various aspects of the Whitewater scandal (Vince Foster was murdered) and many, many other events of public interest. It is not hard to find this material. A search on "Area 51" or "Groom Lake" for instance will locate Web sites which would have you believe that the U.S. government has been storing crashed flying saucers for decades. These tales are interspersed with the appearance of mysterious black helicopters overhead, and so on. Even more prolific are the USENET newsgroups, especially *alt.conspiracy* and others devoted to Whitewater, the Central Intelligence Agency, and the National Security Agency. Some of this material is evidently offered as a spoof; some though is intended to be taken seriously.

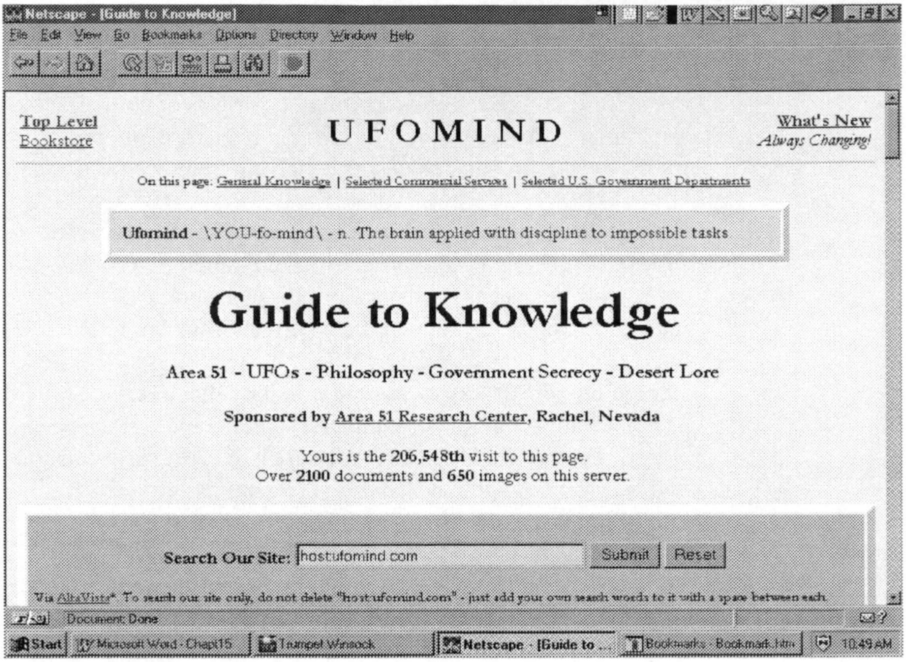

Figure 1 An example of a UFO conspiracy page.

• Pernicious politics: neo-nazis and skinheads

The extreme right wing in the Western World has populated the Web with information sites of all sorts. In addition, there are dedicated newsgroups for the exchange of views on such matters. Possibly the most famous of these sites is the Ernst Zundel site. It was mirrored by various other disinterested parties when a concerted but unsuccessful attempt was made to suppress it. That attempt has not worked because there is no international regulatory framework for censoring Web sites. There follows one example of vigorous right-wing activity on the Web.

Figure 2 A comprehensive right-wing activist page. This one also plays a complete synthesized rendition of the tune "I fall to pieces" while you browse it.

• Hacking of Web sites

Part of the vulnerability which Web site operators assume when they mount Web pages is the possibility that some individual or group of individuals may gain unauthorized access to their account area and then begin substituting bogus pages on their site. This sort of activity is usually undertaken in the spirit of juvenile pranksterism, but it need not be. For instance, the main sites of the Central Intelligence Agency and the U.S. Department of Justice were invaded in this manner and bogus pages full of insults and nose thumbing inserted in the place of the real pages.

Figure 3 When the official CIA site was hacked, this page was put in its place. This embarrassing episode has subsequently been repeated at other nominally high security sites.

• Predators in Cyberspace

If you choose to connect directly to the Internet, or if you rely on your service provider to safeguard your security interests, you are exposing your Network activities, your online files, and your electronic communications to some degree of risk from the "outlaws" of the Internet. While your site and your files are unlikely to be of great interest to this sort of interloper, it is nevertheless wise to keep in mind that intruders remain a threat, if only as a nuisance. While hackers are likely to be much more interested in the sites run by governments and large corporations, you too might be embarrassed by this type of covert attack.

There are many types of attack or threat from unknown players on the Internet. A very large amount of ingenuity and effort have gone into perfecting techniques which exploit the weaknesses of computer systems operating as members of the Internet. If you are interested in pursing this topic there is a modest but growing literature on the topic of hacking, cracking and associated predations. Attack and countermeasure strategies have engaged the wit and talents of some of the most ingenious of Net citizens. Since there is money to be made and lost in this battle of wits, it forms the basis for new occupational categories in the service sector.

LITERATURE ON HACKERS

If you are interested in pursuing this topic, you might wish to read:

Clifford Stoll, ***The Cuckoo's Egg***, New York, Pocket Books, 1989; *an account of what it took for one intrepid system administrator to catch a wily espionage-for-money intruder and the obsessive process it took to do so. In this process he lost everything else of value in his life; not for the weak of heart.*

Michelle Slatella and Joshua Quittner, ***Masters of Deception: The Gang that Ruled Cyberspace***, New York: Harper Collins, 1995. *An account of the epic battle between two "gangs," the Masters of Deception versus the Legion of Doom, fought out in the telephone switching computers of America with arrests as the reward for the losers.*

• Fraudulent advertising and sale and dealing in stolen goods

Many goods are for sale on the Web now. Just a few years ago, the informal rules of the Internet forbade commerce, but these rules have gone by the wayside now as more and more users, and more and more vendors have established themselves on the Web. Doubtless, the potential for Web-based flim flam and fraud has occurred to many individuals independently around the world.

Once upon a time, pawn shops were the place to take things you stole for conversion to cash. Nowadays, the forsale USENET newsgroups seem to be carrying this load. These newsgroups tend to be local since there is no point in trying to sell an item to somebody thousands of miles away. On your local forsale newsgroups, you can find all manner of goods for sale, undoubtedly many advertised by legitimate owners in what amounts to an electronic garage sale. Cars, stereos, even houses are advertised. Where questions tend to arise however is on the groups devoted to low-weight, high-value products like computer memory chips, central processor chips, or even whole computers at suspiciously low prices. If a vendor wishes to sell you a product still in its shrink wrap, for cash, and at a local coffee shop, and gives a cell phone number as a contact location, you might be well advised to give the deal a miss. At the very least, be aware that the transaction may not be completely above board.

• Dealing in illicit skills: telephone hacking

Likewise, stealing of telephone services is an activity avidly pursued by the technically inclined. There is a whole newsgroup devoted to these interests, *alt.2600,* named after the central exchange number of many big organizations' central telephone switches (e.g. 520-2600). The volume on this newsgroup is enormous, running to hundreds of posts a day. It caters to those wishing to exchange technical tips on defeating the telephone companies' security procedures, gaining access to trunk lines for free long-distance calls and so on. Since the volume is so heavy, and because there is so much noise on the group, there is also a moderated version called *alt.2600.moderated* which attempts to impose some order and rational categorization on the material presented.

• Multiple personalities and presenting as someone else

Literary pseudonyms are as old as literature. There have always been people who wish to write as an anonymous observer, or as a member of the opposite gender, or as a non-citizen, or as a member of another social class. The Web gives great latitude for such persons to realize their aims. It is relatively easy to construct new identities through the manipulation of sender addressing in the e-mail and USENET systems. By dint of fictitious presence, your new identity takes hold as a real Web presence, much in the same way that nicknames in chat rooms have a tendency to become "real". But one is not restricted to having one other identity. It is possible to have several, and then to concoct an argument between the various entities or tentacles. Quite raucous "arguments" of this sort have disrupted listservs in the past.

This section has shown a limited range of examples of slightly or greatly off-centre activities on the Web. It has by no means been an exhaustive tour and the opportunity for much further research and interpretation is abundantly obvious. It is to be hoped that much more effort is put in the future into gaining an understanding of how the contemporary telecomputing universe is evolving in its *sub rosa* aspect. It makes for fascinating and at times unsettling insights into human behaviour.

IV. PRIVACY ISSUES

Also in this concluding chapter we must raise the general question of eavesdropping in the context both of darkside risks, and of prevention through the use of strong encryption meant to defeat attempts at message interception. There is at present a vigorous discussion of the preemptive rights of the state to read your e-mail and peruse your transactions. While the technical means to defeat such scrutiny exist, your ability as an individual to use these means freely is very much the subject of debate. More and more commerce will be conducted electronically in the future and the governments of Western countries, and in particular that of the United States, wish to continue passive surveillance of these modes of communication. Vigorous government efforts have been mounted for instance to keep strong encryption out of the "international" version of Netscape while providing it for authenticated U.S. citizens resident in the United States. Such a distribution policy does not augur well for the privacy concerns of non-U.S. citizens everywhere else in the world.

If the privacy of e-mail transactions is of concern to you (and frankly it probably should be since without encryption your messages travel through many machines and are open to many system operators should they wish to record or look at them), you can take active steps to invoke the protection of encryption for your messages and files.

Encryption is the substitution, in the textual content of a message, of seeming nonsense for plain text by means of a complicated encoding scheme. The same substitution principal can be employed to encrypt any digital file, text-based or not, of any size up to and including the entire contents of a hard disk in your computer. There are any number of substitution coding techniques or algorithms in existence, some more secure than others. What they have in common is a formula (or in many cases several used sequentially) which is used to transform a text file, or any other kind of file, from a document which can be read to one which cannot be read without the application of a counterpart decoding formula or formulas. Coding in this fashion has been going on for at least hundreds if not thousands of years. Indeed some written languages which involve pictographs or phonetic symbols are themselves codes for natural spoken languages.

A more extended discussion of encryption in the context of actually invoking its protection for your e-mail transactions is included in the Technical Appendix.

V. WEB KNOWLEDGE

Without indulging in McLuhanesque hyperbole, it is clear that with the advent of the Internet, and of World Wide Web content on it, the potential has been created for a new and much less determinate knowledge-creation and dissemination environment in that part of the world which is wired. The realization of this vision of connectedness is taking place with breath-taking speed. For the social sciences, its realization means that an unprecedented richness of data, literature, current commentary, imagery and sound is being made available at little or no direct cost to all students and academics, and indeed to anyone, schooled or not, in possession of the right of electronic access. To this assemblage is also accorded the unfettered right to publish anything they want in whatever form they want without any form of review or scrutiny whatsoever. In thoroughly unfiltered fashion, the digital information and scholarship resources of the world are spilling into homes, classrooms and offices in the First World. For many, the very presence of these resources has changed the way in which the learning process itself is conceived of.
But without the ability to locate, evaluate and organize these resources, and without the possession of the skills to use these resources as they are found, it is as if they did not exist.

The overwhelmingly English-language nature of the Net is obvious to all users, new and old alike. What now happens to other languages and cultures whose products either do not exist in electronic form or which cannot be viewed in English-language browsers? Are we prepared to let heritage languages of greater or lesser presence simply depart the scene in scholarship? In order to preserve their living utility, a certain amount of investment in electronic tools which can render these languages on the screen would be necessary.

Further, since the Web exists for proliferating perfect copies of digital files without logical limit as to size and number, how can copyright persist in its present form? How could royalties be collected cross-jurisdictionally? The new World Intellectual Property Organization (WIPO) in Switzerland is attempting to devise wording for a new international treaty which would cover copyright on electronic databases, for instance. But how would new rights be enforced across jurisdictions? At present, no one knows the answers to these questions.

Peer review emerged in the medieval academy to ration scarce paper and text reproduction resources. It also imposed a conservatism and a time delay in scholarly exchange of views. Reputation in an academic sense was based in a rather direct fashion on one's ability to publish in this restricted zone of official culture. Acceptance of writings signified augmentation of reputation amongst one's peers. Publication was also thought to signify the soundness of your expressed views and your use of evidence. None of this apparatus has any apparent place now[1]. Personal Web publication of documents, whether peer reviewed or not, forces the onus of assessing the merits of documents back onto the reader, with uncertain results.

There are at least three dimensions to the introduction and application of the Web tools to the scholarly academy. There are direct impacts on the role of the teacher, on the nature of the curriculum, and on the organization of instruction. With respect to the first question, the role of the teacher, the Web-based model of scholarship clearly favours a learner-centred, activity-based type of instruction that is profoundly threatening to older teachers. Since texts from which to learn can be acquired on an as-needed basis, and since searches are likely to turn up pertinent material unknown to the instructor, individualized programs of instruction become unavoidable and they are no longer under the direct control and supervision of the instructor.

These are some of the questions for which I have no easy answers that come to mind about the processes of change in which I now find myself embedded. Having grown up as a willing participant in the book culture, I find the present rapidly departing from the norms I absorbed in the past. In large measure, this process of conversion is cost-reduction driven. Further, I don't believe the digital conversion (or "convergence" in Bill Gates' terminology) now underway can be stopped. There is too much momentum behind it and too much capital investment as well. I find this transition deeply unsettling and yet fascinating at the same time; you just never know what new toy is going to turn up in your e-mail sock the next morning.

***

Together, nuggets of information gold and tons of textual gravel fill the World Wide Web. It is up to the user to decide for himself or herself what to retain and what to throw away. More and more of the responsibility for this decision, and for the related decision as to what to publish, rests with the individual student and professional. Neither is any longer subject to control by authority figures or by states. This may prove to be a mixed blessing, combining risks with rewards in a highly unstable mix.

Sites shown in this Chapter...

UFOMIND	http://www.best.com/~area51/
Conservative Right-Wing Radical Redneck Page	http://www.concentric.net/~jpiers387
CIA site hack	http://www.skeeve.net

[1] See, for example, Peter Applebome, "Profit Squeeze for Publishers Makes Tenure More Elusive for College Teachers," *New York Times*, November 18, 1996, electronic edition. It begins: "Michael Parkhurst knew that his doctoral dissertation on the German sociologist and philosopher Theodor Adorno would not compete for sales with Oprah and Dennis Rodman. Still, he was stunned that when the Cornell University Press said it was not interested in publishing his book, it cited its lack of marketability."

PART FOUR

APPENDIX: TECHNICAL DETAILS AND INSTRUCTIONS

"as more multimedia titles come out, as more information is on-line, as we make these things easier to use, we start to draw in more and more people. Now, once you get in for one application, the hurdle to learn a second one is fairly low. My dad wanted to do his taxes automatically. Then I got him doing word processing and electronic mail because everybody in our family is connected."

Bill Gates, Microsoft Gazillionaire,
*in **Time Magazine**, June 5, 1995, Volume 145, no. 23, electronic edition.*

Unavoidably, we have had to gloss over a lot of technical detail in this book. This was inevitable because the book is directed to understanding end uses as opposed to technical processes. Nevertheless, some of the most puzzling problems facing Web users today lie in all too explicable failures to understand the complex underlying data communications processes. In general, these processes as embodied in software must <u>all</u> be correctly configured for <u>any</u> of them to work properly. The amount of fault tolerated in most configurations approaches zero. Also in general, most users of the Web do not understand what they are doing at the engineering level when they search for, acquire, and use World Wide Web resources. No one need know this detail provided everything is working properly. However, when it is not working, or when a new computer and modem must be set up without assistance, there is a compelling logic to acquiring some of this technical detail.

A. MODEM MECHANICS

Frankly, one the most frequent requests for advice that I receive from students has to do with getting their home computers, modems and software working properly together. Because of the extreme complexity of what is going on, it is easy to inadvertently do something wrong, causing the whole arrangement to sputter or not work at all.

Making your modem work properly is often a challenging task. Right out of the shipping materials, a modem is an unimposing piece of electronic equipment. It must be connected physically to your computer either internally in an expansion slot or externally connected to a socket at the back of the computer by means of the correct form of cable (there are different ones for IBM compatible and Apple equipment). In each case, a telephone cable (or a more sophisticated high-speed connection cable) must then be connected to the modem. Generally, modems come with a quite detailed instruction book on how to install and use the product. The manufacturer may also provide 1-800 help-line service as well. It should be understood, however, that many problems can occur. There are many settings which may need to be made correctly, both physically on the modem, and in the terminal and/or TCP/IP software in your computer. While full understanding goes much beyond the scope of what we are attempting here, this initial stage of making your modem work as advertised requires a certain understanding of how computers communicate. Retaining and reading the manual may be necessary, together with some experimentation[1]

In order to make use of a network connection, your personal computer must have special software which interprets the products of a connection between modems and creates messages which appear on your screen. This software comes in several varieties. There is terminal software (for example, *Procomm* in its many variants) which is almost exclusively text-oriented and there is *HyperTerminal* which comes with Windows95. There is also browser software (for example, Netscape) and its attendant and necessary SLIP/TCP/IP stack for presenting graphic materials and text. Finally there are helper programs which interpret and present sound files, photographs, movies, and even voice and television pictures if your machine has the hardware components (such as a good video card, sound card and speakers) to sustain these features. Much of this software must be purchased but some is freeware (meaning that some programs can be acquired free of charge on the Network itself). But if your modem is not set up properly in your home computer, none of the Web software will work properly!

As indicated above, the technical limits of using the ordinary telephone line for this purpose are in sight and it is unlikely that further large advances in modem speed can be made without additional technical modification to the telephone systems we have grown used to. TV cable systems on the other hand, if made to operate in both directions to and from the home, school or office, can carry a great many more impulses per second. But this kind of connection is not widely available to households

A NOTE ON MODEMS

Modems work by converting your keystrokes into tones which pass through the telephone system as sounds which are then converted back to keystroke characters at their destination, the service provider's modem at the other end of the telephone line. A rather large number of tones per second can be made to pass through a telephone line with contemporary modem equipment. Modems for sale today routinely pass 28,800 bits per second through such connections and the most recent of modems can pass 33,600 bits on a good-quality noise-free telephone line. Further improvements in transfer rates are provided by coding schemes which compress the information before it is sent and uncompress it at the receiving end. There is a theoretical limit to how much data can be passed between a modem pair, the so-called "Shannon Limit." While there have been announcements of future 56,600 bits per second modems for sale in 1997, it is unlikely that they will function at anywhere near that speed given the noise on most domestic telephone lines.

Modems no longer need be very expensive to purchase. A good internally-installed 14,400 bps modem would now usually cost less than $75 unless it is miniaturized to fit inside a notebook computer, in which case it might cost $175 or more. Faster modems will be much more expensive. The miniaturized version of a 28,800 bps modem for instance would usually cost at least $300, while the normal-sized version would only be about $175.

Two modems when connecting to each other over a telephone line automatically "negotiate" a common speed and information exchange protocol without further human intervention. If you were to listen in, the actual negotiation sounds like short periods of scratchy noise interspersed with very short periods of silence. The negotiated speed is often less than the maximum rated speed because of line noise on your telephone company's lines. Sometimes, if you can convince the company of this fact, they will replace the cable to your house and test the local distribution equipment in order to improve your service.

right now. Installation of such connections to most households, educational institutions and places of work will require an enormous capital investment, so such links, though fast and effective, would likely be more costly to use.

B. OBTAINING DIAL-UP SERVICE

In order to use the many research resources of the World Wide Web in particular, and the communications channels and information resources of the Internet as a whole, it is necessary to make and maintain a stable communications connection between your computer and the Internet. Access to World Wide Web resources in all their glory requires an Internet connection, minimally one which sustains text-based interaction with Web documents and other resources, but ideally one which sustains full multimedia browsing. Some agency or institution must provide this connection service to you at home.

I. FINDING A SERVICE PROVIDER

The technical considerations in finding a service provider for your home computer and configuring it for Internet use are unavoidable. Working over these hurdles is often disagreeable but it is necessary. Well informed colleagues are a very valuable resource in accomplishing this task since a solution which works for one person can be copied by others at the same location. Recently, the task has been made easier by service providers who install and configure the necessary Internet software at the same time as the computer is purchased. But for those in the academic environment, it is often necessary to accommodate the characteristics of the service your institution offers. Typically, there is not much help available for you in making the necessary changes and adjustments, particularly so in the present strained financial environment when the budgets for helpers and advisors are under severe fiscal pressures.

Thus, to be clear, your good intentions notwithstanding, and even with the best of personal computers and software, it is impossible to access the many useful things the Web has to offer if an appropriate connection between your machine and the Internet has not been made. Without such a connection, a personal computer is hobbled and unable to function as part of the Network world. While your computer may still serve you in such solitary pursuits as word processing, without an Internet connection it is about as useful for communication as a telephone in the middle of a desert. And making such a connection at the present time is probably the most difficult single aspect of computer use. It remains challenging even for the most experienced, though, in truth it has become easier with the passage of time due to the spread of the arcane black arts of telecommunication.

II. CONNECTION BASICS

In order to communicate with the wired world, your computer must be connected to the Internet by some means, and it must also have suitable software to make use of the connection. The software must either support text-based activity such as sending and receiving e-mail and using Web resources with the Lynx client (Lou Montoulli's 1993-era text oriented browser), or a graphics-oriented "browser" such as Netscape Navigator or Microsoft Explorer (display programs for viewing the "pages" of the World Wide Web) and also the other more text-oriented information sources such as data archive sites. While your ultimate goal is to move freely and acquisitively through these rich information resources, your first task is to arrange for a Network connection. This is an essential first step.

III. WHAT IS A CONNECTION?

Large organizations such as universities and big corporations purchase high-speed, high-volume direct connections to the Internet. They make use of these connections by developing ways in which hundreds of their users at a time can share that single high-speed central connection. Users may be physically dispersed throughout many buildings in labs, offices, and classrooms and also in remote locations such as their homes. Everyone is connected by some technical means to a central server or host which has control of the organization's Network connection and its architecture. The connections may be made by means of copper wire, fibre optic cable, local area network, or by telephone line with special devices called modems (modulator-demodulators which turn text and other characters into sounds for transmission over a telephone line. There must be one modem at each end of such a telephone connection).

The server, or host, handles all of these types of local connections between users in their homes, offices, or schools and the Internet.

Commercial service providers take this arrangement a step farther and make connections to their central server available for a fee to anyone in the general public who can establish a telephone connection with modems between their personal computers and the service provider's Internet-connected computer. It is not necessary for customers of commercial services to be members of a particular organization in order to be a user. You should expect to pay at least $10 a month for modest use of such a service and there may or may not be hourly usage charges on top of the basic charge. Heavy use of such services will cost $30 per month or more depending on the volume of activity.

A simple diagram of the sharing of a service host's facilities is shown below:

All information passes between the *Server/Host* of your service provider and the Internet using the *Transmission Control Protocol/Internet Protocol* or *TCP/IP* for short. This protocol governs the way "packets" of information are broken up, packaged, labeled, transmitted and received. It is the universal language of the Internet. You as a user do not have to deal with it directly; software programs do that for you.

You do have some choice, however, in the way in which your personal computer communicates with the server/host. There are basically two types of connections. *The first sustains only textual communication* and is often referred to as a shell account or a UNIX shell account. In this type of connection, only text content flows between the server and your personal computer, which has a terminal program such as *Procomm Plus* installed to handle your computer's end of the connection. A somewhat less capable text-only type of account is available on the many *freenets* discussed later in this Appendix.

However, *there is a second type of account service which supports the graphics browsers* such as Netscape, which now has at least 75% of the browser "market" (a misnomer since Netscape is given away free, at least for the moment). The difference between the two types of account (text and browser) is that the second sustains a TCP/IP connection all the way to your personal computer. In essence, this second type of connection links your personal computer to the Internet as a full participant, enabling it to request and receive TCP/IP packets from remote servers and present their contents to you in full colour on your graphics monitor screen, once they are reassembled after delivery. In addition, such connections also provide all the text-oriented services such as electronic mail (e-mail) as well as the colourful multimedia content.

Between your personal computer and the service provider's computer, you must either have a local connection through a *local area network* (LAN), or telephone service and a modem connection, and the faster the sustained data transmission rate of that connection the better. Modems for sale today routinely pass data at a rate of 14,400 or 28,800 bits per second. There are four types of browser-compatible connections in this context: SLIP (serial line Internet protocol), CSLIP (SLIP with data compression), and PPP (point to point protocol, with or without data compression). All four work at roughly the same level of efficiency to pass TCP/IP packets between your personal computer and the service provider's computer. In order to make full use of the speed and efficiency of this kind of connection, your personal computer must have installed within it a serial port controller chip capable of sustaining the data speed *inside* your computer. The part required is called the 16550 UART chip (UART stands for universal receive/transmit).

In addition, the software which drives this particular chip must also be capable of high speed. The driver software which comes with Windows95 is up to this task. But unfortunately the driver originally shipped with Windows 3.1 for this purpose (*comm.drv*) must be upgraded in a manner described later to do this. Some new modems now come with this software upgrade (such as *cybercom.drv*), but if neces- sary you can acquire the driver software at no charge from an Internet software distribution. Generally, install-inside modems (as opposed to external modems which have to be plugged in to your computer on the outside) now come with the 16550 UART chip as an internal component. If you have a plug-in external modem, the port you plug it into may need a hardware upgrade to be effective.

In order to establish the second type of connection (**TCP/IP** – a requirement for using a graphics browser) to the Internet, you will need: 1. A high speed modem and associated serial chip, and appropriate software; 2. A SLIP, CSLIP, or PPP account with a service provider; 3. TCP/IP and SLIP software (which may be integrated or be provided as separate software packages). Or alternatively, you may substitute for number 2 above with a UNIX shell account with TIA or SLiRP (described later) available to make your SLIP connection.

In the Windows 3.1, Windows95 and Windows NT environments, you may obtain a shareware program called Trumpet Winsock which handles the requirements of number 3 above. The cost of an individual license is currently $25US. Or you may purchase instead a program called Netmanage Chameleon or Chameleon Sampler. In addition, commercial services such as AOL and Compuserve now distribute packages of both browser and TCP/IP software to their customers. Windows95 comes with its own TCP/IP software as part of the optional installation package. The dialer and scripting system which come with it are not as friendly as those which come with Trumpet Winsock, so many people prefer the Trumpet product. It is important to note that the Microsoft TCP/IP program files and the Trumpet program files are incompatible and you can't have both operating at the same time in Windows95. Indeed, the installer program which configures the latest version of Trumpet Winsock for Windows 3.1 and Windows95 (Version 3) goes through your files looking for competing programs and will disable them if found.

In the Macintosh world, you will need a copy of a program call MacTCP (which is included in the System 7.5 and later operating system distributions). You will also need SLIP/CSLIP/PPP software such as MacPPP or InterSLIP to work with MacTCP.

INFORMATION YOU NEED TO USE A TCP/IP CONNECTION...

From your service provider, you need:

your user login name and your password
your IP number (the Internet Protocol number is the address of your machine) unless you are using TIA in which case you can always use the IP number 1.1.1.1 Your service provider may, in place of giving you a unique IP number, use a system in which a temporary IP number is assigned as you login each time.
The IP address of the Domain Name Server (DNS) you are assigned to use; it is necessary to look up the IP address which corresponds to the text name of the machine you wish to send a request to.
The IP address of your gateway machine (or the gateway machine to use for sending e-mail and obtaining USENET newsgroups). This is necessary in order to send electronic mail and receive newsgroup postings.
The MTU or the maximum packet size to use in your connection; and any other technical addressing information (such as a Subnet Mask address) that your service provider may want you to use.

MAKING A SLIP LINE ON A UNIX SHELL ACCOUNT...

Besides text-only and TCP/IP service accounts, there is a **hybrid type of connection**. Software products such as *The Internet Adapter, SLiRP,* and *Slipknot* can transform a text-oriented shell service account and, in the case of the first two programs, generate a TCP/IP type connection for you to use without in any way disrupting the server/host's operations. (In the case of *Slipknot*, the browser in effect is running on your personal computer by turning requested http (Web) files into graphics of a sort).

This method of forging a TCP/IP connection has become a very popular means of using a browser in the university environment, which today typically provides students and teachers with UNIX shell accounts only. *The Internet*

Adapter (TIA) was until mid-1996 available for licensing at a modest fee. It is no longer for sale because its vendors have decided against further development of the product. Nevertheless, TIA continues to be available on many university UNIX-based systems. Both Windows computers and Macintosh computers can use a TIA connection.

One of the reasons TIA is no longer a living product is that another program called SLiRP is available free of charge for anyone to copy and install. In addition, SLiRP provides both a SLIP connection or a PPP depending on the user's choice. It is a UNIX program which runs on your service host. It can be obtained from an FTP site in Australia at *blitzen.canberra.edu.au* in directory */pub/slirp/*. Installing SLiRP can be easily accomplished if you have some UNIX experience. The installation package diagnoses the host characteristics and makes up the unique blend of features necessary for your host computer and then makes and installs it in your account area. Starting it up is then just a matter of typing slirp [Enter] at the service prompt for a SLIP connection, or "slirp -P" [Enter] for the PPP version.

There is another, less satisfactory solution to the connection problem called *Slipknot.* It is easy to set up in contrast to the previous two utilities but is much more limited in usefulness. The latest version is available at the following FTP site: *ftp.netcom.com* in directory */pub/pb/pbrooks/slipknot.* The file you need is *slnot111.zip.* Netcom is a busy site, so you might have to try a number of times. Once installed on your Windows personal computer, you will run a setup program which will collect information about your service account then dial-up the service host and install some UNIX code in your account files area.

IV. MAKING A CONNECTION: SOME CHOICES IN QUALITY AND PRICE

How then is a high quality connection made? There are a number of answers to this question and each of the service options outlined below could be used if circumstances warrant. To each is attached a different pricetag and a different measure of performance. Many commercial service providers have a full range of products available. Your choice will reflect your assessment of your requirements and your ability to pay the charges associated with the different levels of service.

Though each form of connection helps you achieve the same purpose, interaction with Internet information and services, the price of the alternatives vary widely. The price differences usually depend on several factors:

- whether or not the connection is full time,
- the number of users per available connection,
- the speed at which information exchange occurs, and
- the quality of the connection (which can be understood as the relative absence of extraneous noise in the connection).

In order to receive the highest quality types of connection, you must have appropriate hardware for your personal computer and this equipment can be very expensive. If cost is no object, then extremely high rates of reliable information exchange can be sustained in most communities. For most people, and most purposes however, it is not at all necessary to make these investments. Even slow, telephone-based, text-oriented connections can be of immense value for research purposes, and personally valuable as well if the necessary navigational skills are learned. First though, some further comments on the types of connections that are available and how they differ from one another.

TYPES OF CONNECTIONS: SOME WAYS OF MAKING A CONNECTION TO THE INTERNET...

- by ordinary telephone line and modem between a personal computer and a remote service-providing host, connected only when needed.
- by modem and ordinary telephone line leased for 24-hour-a-day use from the local telephone company.
- by personal computer through a local area network (LAN) server, for example in a university computer lab setting, and then to a host by one of the above means.
- by a special leased telephone line designed for high-speed computer use (e.g. ISDN) to a host,
- by "frame relay" in large bursts of information accumulated by the client and the server and sent when filled over a leased line charged by the number of "frames" sent. Frame relay services are available commercially as services sold by the telecommunications companies.
- by a direct satellite two-way communications link to a host.
- by a special two way cable TV connection provided by a local cable TV company.
- by giving your personal computer a direct connection to the Internet over a dedicated wire or fiber circuit, thus making your computer a full Internet participant with its own name or identifying IP (Internet Protocol) number. IP numbers are four groups of numbers between 1 and 999 separated by periods. They are an individual Internet computer's "name."

V. WHAT YOU CONNECT TO: THE INTERNET

The Network your personal computer communicates with, once you have a connection and once you are logged in, exists as a very large interconnected web of millions of computers which exchange information with each other from wherever they might happen to be in the world to wherever their information-seeking counterpart is. The connection they make is indirect, transitory, and free of direct charge since there are no long distance tolls of any description on the Internet.

WHY HAVE ACCOUNTS AND PASSWORDS?

In part, this requirement is for your own protection. Unless some authentication is required to logon to the Internet, you could never be sure that the people you are communicating with on the Network are legitimate users of some other server computer on the Internet. Identification is important in order to be sure that someone else will not logon as yourself and misbehave using your identity. For this reason, a password challenge is a routine procedure as well. This sort of authentication is a routine requirement around the Internet world before you or anyone else will be permitted to use the Internet information services.

Once you have a connection, you may use it to acquire other potentially more useful logon accounts at other computers on the Internet to which you can logon remotely using the Telnet tool. Some sites offer free user accounts to visitors, as do most freenets. You might use these user accounts to disguise your identity effectively.

Because pseudonym accounts are possible to acquire, you should be a bit cautious about the ostensible source of postings and e-mail, since the individual you are corresponding with via e-mail may in fact not be the person whom they purport to be. Pseudonymous conversations are common in some forums, particularly the Internet Relay Chat (IRC) forums discussed in a earlier chapter for instance. But each Internet user must have an authenticated home base connection from which to venture forth. Unfortunately, there are technical means to steal someone else's authentic login name and password. We will consider this and related security problems in a later section of this appendix.

VI. INTERACTING WITH THE NETWORK

The telecommunications infrastructure of the world ties any two computers together indirectly by means of a sequence of point-to-point links *through* other computers carried by telephone lines, microwave relays, communications satellites, and fibre optic links or any combination of these technical means. The arrangements of these links does not have geometric regularity; they can be quite anarchic and complex. There are multiple point-to-point linkages with such great redundancy that should one particular link go down (except the one that leads to your computer), there need be no worry concerning interruption in service.

A message or request from you is broken into TCP/IP packets or identifiable chunks with addressing data added as an "envelope." For instance, a simple request from you (*send me the map of Nigeria*) is translated into appropriate machine language, broken into packets of information which taken together contain your request (though each chunk has its own addressing envelope), and the packets are then dispatched to the Network. The packets may then proceed as separate messages from your location to their destination by whatever pathway is allocated to each, ultimately to be reassembled when they arrive into a coherent request. If some do not arrive, their absence is noted and retransmission will be requested, although this would seldom if ever come to your attention as a user. The requested information (the map you want) is sent back to you in exactly the same way.

VII. HOW YOUR INFORMATION PACKETS TRAVEL

The quality and carrying capacity of an Internet connection is analogous to a pipe. Pipes come in various diameters and thus carrying capacities. Think of a Network connection as the hose connecting your garden sprinkler to your municipal water supply or well. The volume of water that is delivered at the sprinkler end is a function of: a) the pressure in the providing system, and b) the smallest internal diameter of any section of the hose (or in other words, the carrying capacity of your particular hose). The direct analogy in the Network world is to the amount of attention that a service provider's computer is devoting to your instructions, and the speed at which it is functioning to provide the information you have requested.

The level of service your provider can devote to your needs is like the pressure available to you from your municipal water supply. Your provider may have many customers online simultaneously making requests. This contention can degrade over-all performance from the individual user's point of view. Also analogous is the carrying capacity of the connection to the useful interior diameter of your hose. If your modem is slow, it won't matter how much information the provider is capable of sending you in a second because your modem and personal computer cannot absorb information any faster.

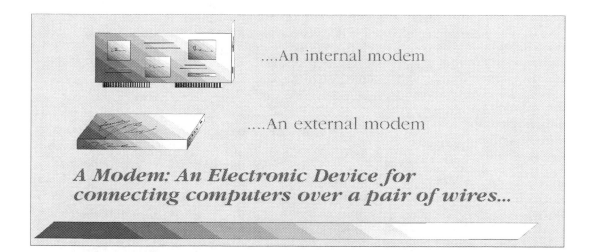

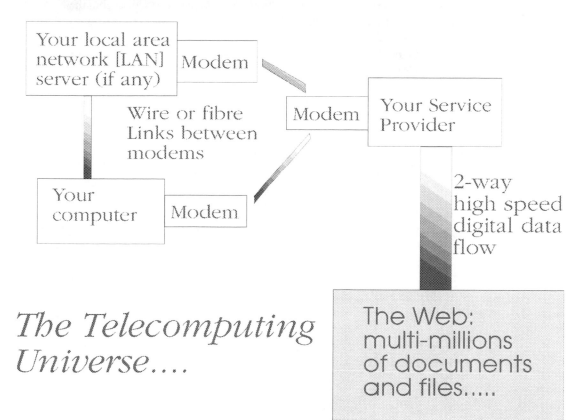

Figure 1

Clearly, the two aspects (speed and volume devoted to your purposes) are related to each other. For instance, if you were to connect your lawn hose to a fire department pumper, the hose might well disintegrate from the high pressure applied to its inside surface. It would be unable to contain the pressure and would cease to work as a hose. Similarly, if you borrowed a fire hose from the pumper and somehow connected it to your domestic water supply, very little more water would come out in comparison to the case when you were using the garden hose. In general in the Network connectivity world, you must pay for the level of performance you choose in terms of speed and carrying capacity. Once this decision is made, you must acquire the hardware for your personal computer or terminal in order to achieve this objective. Having enormous carrying capacity at your disposal may not make much sense if you are running only one machine with which to read from. After all, there is a limit to how fast you can read or observe too. But if you are running a large lab of machines each of which is drawing on a single Network connection (through a local area network or LAN for instance) it makes great sense indeed.

The redundancy of potential pathways and the unregulated nature of the Network is one of its greatest strengths. For instance, during the 1994 Northridge earthquake in Southern California several major trunk lines went out of service, but the Network as a whole continued to function throughout the event precisely because of its redundant pathways. The same cannot be said for the telephone systems which suffered understandable failures, overloads and shutdowns of long-distance services. This left at least some Californians with the Internet and its electronic mail service as their sole means of communicating with concerned relatives elsewhere in the world. The authorities in Southern California used this facility to communicate news and instructions to affected communities with great success[2].

It seems clear that in the future, management of disaster sites and the provision of emergency services will routinely involve the creation of *ad hoc* Internet information distribution and coordination sites. These will be located well outside the disaster zone yet will be accessible to the affected citizens. This novel use is ironic in light of the fact that the Internet owes its existence to preparations for preserving the thermonuclear war fighting command and control functions of the United States government.

VIII. ALTERNATIVE PROVIDERS OF SERVICE

Your Internet provider (referred here to as the provider, the host or the server — your machine is the client) need not be your university or college or even a local concern. Many providers make local access telephone numbers available to their clients but in fact provide their services from hundreds if not thousands of miles away. Some are international in scope, like the big commercial services such as America Online and CompuServe. These services are provided commercially and are for-profit concerns. But comparable services are also provided by most colleges and universities to members of their communities, by large organizations for the use of their employees on and off the premises, by local "freenets" or user cooperatives, and by a wide range of lesser choices which may provide electronic mail but little else.

Another aspect of Net activity must be addressed at this stage. We are accustomed through watching television and listening to the radio to being passive consumers of information and entertainment. On the Internet, one can be both an active consumer and an active producer of information among other things. By having an account on a full-service host, one can easily become a provider of information services. Because this is so, the Internet has seen an explosion of little "publications" which never reach paper but which nevertheless have considerable influence. Sometimes referred to as "zines" (such as *Phrack* and *2600*), they and the newsgroups can take many forms and deal with many subjects. Some, such as ***alt.2600*** for example, deal with the finer points of misusing the telephone system, giving the reader some sense of the freedom from censorship and controls which is a basic hallmark of the Internet. There is a flourishing trade in pornographic images as well.

In order to participate as a provider of Web materials, it is necessary to learn how to write HTML files (Hypertext Markup Language – a notation system common to all Web sites) and how to arrange them correctly on your server's host machine in order that others may browse them. Most such resources are now located on computers running a UNIX operating system. For this reason, learning some UNIX commands is more or less essential if you wish to maintain your own Web sites.

IX. FREENETS

For you, as a prospective Internet user, it is thus invariably the case that a service provider connection is needed at the outset. In general, these services exist in the private sector and access and usage charges are routine. There are some exceptions to this rule, though. In many urban communities in North America, there exist cooperative organizations known generically as *freenets*. These cooperatives offer Internet connections, almost always by dial-in telephone modem connections. These telephone ports are often fully utilized. Thus, rapid automatic re-dialing is a very desirable feature when considering the purchase and installation of a new modem or terminal software. It may take 30 or 40 dialing attempts to get a connection at a heavily used freenet, especially during the daytime or early evening.

Though of limited usefulness and presently text-only in format, an account on a freenet may be of considerable value for doing routine activities such as receiving and sending electronic mail which can be done in off-peak periods late at night and early in the morning, and for which TCP/IP software is not required. A freenet account has the singular advantage of being free of charge. However, for purposes of using advanced Internet tools, for extensive or prolonged use, or for time-sensitive use, it is necessary to obtain higher quality services than can usually be obtained from a community freenet.

THREE COMMON PROBLEMS WITH FREENET SERVICES:

1) There is heavy competition for dial-in access. The more popular the freenet is, the heavier the contention becomes. The consequence is that you cannot assume that a connection can be made when you need it. This obviously makes planned use of Network services problematic and frustrating.

2) The quality of service (in general, the speed at which information can be delivered to your personal computer) is slow, largely because the freenet organizations do not have the financial resources which are necessary either to guarantee access or to provide high-speed access.

3) Freenets often constrain the types of activities which members can actually carry out. These restrictions may involve curbs on tools available for use (for example, access to World Wide Web services may be limited or non-existent) or the permitted time use quota may be too limited.

C. WINSOCK MECHANICS

Readers who have access only to lab computers which are already set up for Netscape and other TCP/IP programs, or those who already have a computer with browser access to the Web, need not dwell on this section. This material is rough sledding for anyone and not for the faint of heart. It is intended for those who, through the force of necessity, must configure their personal computers either for use with a modem and a dial-up Internet host, or for those whose computers are connected to the Internet by means of a local area network (LAN). While the arcane mechanics of making such a TCP/IP connection may be of little or no interest to many readers, they are a vital concern for students and professionals who find themselves on their own in either of the above two common situations.

I. THE MAGICIAN'S REALM: TRUMPET WINSOCK AND CONSTRUCTING A TCP/IP STACK

From the very beginning of the graphical browser era, with the appearance of the original Mosaic Web browser client, users needed a program which would connect a personal computer to the Internet in such a way that IP packets of information would flow directly, and in an orderly way, into and out of their machines. This need was met with the development of Trumpet Winsock by Peter Tattam in Tasmania. Winsock is short for Windows Sockets. Winsock opens this sort of connection, sometimes called a stack, which can be used by several programs at once: a browser, a TCP/IP e-mail program, a Telnet client such as NetTerm, and so on.

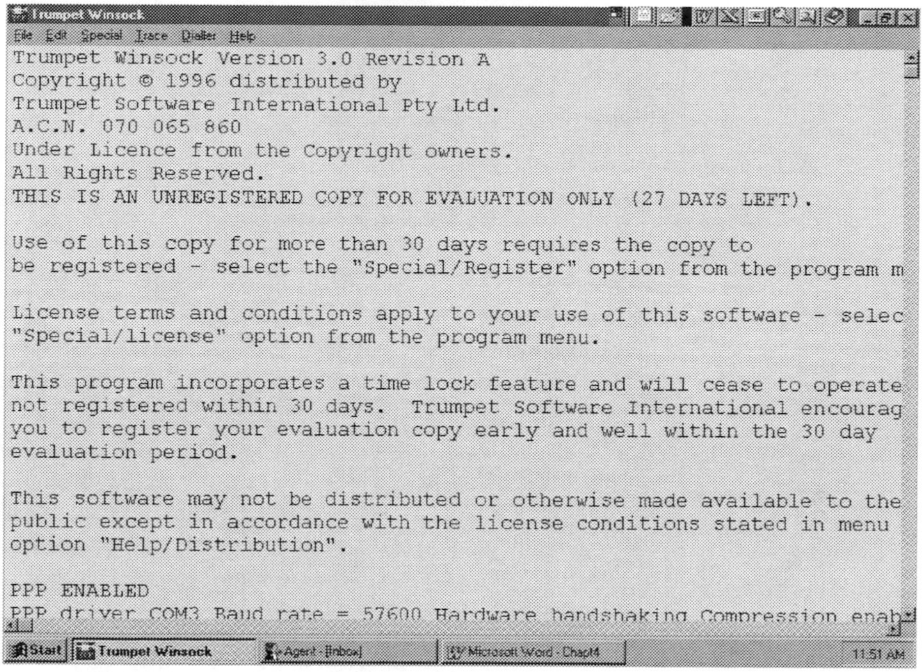

Figure 2 The Trumpet Winsock Version 3 screen

Trumpet Winsock has gone through many revisions and total rewrites and is now in its third major release, one which is capable of working in both Windows 3.1 and Windows95. In its Windows95 incarnation, it handles "data words" that are 32 bits long (as opposed to 16 bits in the original). It is this complexity which allows Netscape in its Windows95 version to handle the complex Java "applets" or programs which are downloaded to and then run on your machine. Windows95 does come with its own Microsoft TCP/IP software (its own winsock if you will) and you may choose to use it. However, Trumpet Winsock has superior automation software which allows complex scripting. This is important because often it takes many phone calls to establish a modem connection to your service host. Often there is heavy contention for these lines. Thus, having a script that will rapidly redial the number when it encounters a busy signal and then, when you finally do get a line, supply all the login information and start the SLIP or PPP connection without further intervention on your part is a valuable asset.

The current version of Trumpet Winsock (Version 3) comes with an install program which walks the user through a series of installation steps. In the Windows95 environment, the essential element of these steps is to replace two files in the Windows directory with Trumpet's versions, and the install Wizard will do this for you.

The files are named *winsock.dll* and *wsock32.dll*. This substitution can be done manually if you wish by first renaming the two files as *winsock.ms* and *wsock32.ms* (with a file manager such as Xtree or Windows Explorer) and then copying the Trumpet versions of those files to the Windows directory on your hard drive. It is easy to make mistakes when doing this substitution manually but the new install Wizard handles this aspect for you. In the Windows 3.1 environment, this new version works right from installation without further modifications or file substitutions.

II. TIME OUT: UPDATING WINDOWS 3.1 FOR TCP/IP USE

Most home computers in the world still use Windows 3.1 or 3.11 as their basic operating system and will continue to do so for some time into the future. This is simply an obvious empirical fact. But one of the nastiest aspects about using Windows 3.1 or 3.11 as a basis for Web browsing is that, out of the box as it were, it is *not* equipped to support Winsock/Netscape browser use. It is deficient in two major respects. The first of these is the slowness of the COM port driver (*comm.drv*) which must be replaced with a faster, later port driver (*cybercom.drv*) if you are intending to use a modem moving data at 14.4 kbs or faster (which is now just about everyone). The process of replacing *comm.drv* with *cybercom.drv* is not difficult[3]. If you do not do this, you will encounter the dreaded *Com Overrun* error which occurs when the modem actually overpowers Windows 3.1.

The other deficiency in Windows 3.1 and 3.11 is a lack of support for the special purpose windows handling software necessary to support browsers like Mosaic and Netscape. Since Microsoft's Internet Explorer only works with Windows95, for it the question is moot. But if you do have a computer that runs Windows 3.1 and you wish to continue on this basis, you have to secure and install a large augmentation package of code by means of the network itself from an FTP site. The good news is that this additional software is free. The addition is called *OLE32S13.EXE* (note the uppercase). This package has been through several generations with slightly different names, but supposedly development has ceased with the release of this version.

The Windows update is obtainable from many sites including Microsoft's Web site, and that for the Mosaic project[4]. Once a copy is obtained by FTP by using the text-based Lynx Web client to get a copy, or by getting a copy from a friend, place it in a temporary directory and "run" it to unpack the files. When this is done the *setup.exe* program (one of the several files in the package) is run from within Windows. This sequence of events will install all the additional Windows software you require. Nothing obvious changes in Windows; but it is now smarter (and larger). If you try running Netscape without the alterations, it will tell you to stop and install the *OLE32S13.EXE* package before proceeding. It is an absolute requirement for Windows 3.1 and 3.11 users who still form the majority of all computer users in the world.

III. BACK TO WINSOCK

Trumpet Winsock functions for 30 days after it is installed, after which a license is supposed to be obtained from the vendors. It is possible to reinstall the program every month to avoid this fee but in fairness, the software is so useful and the fee so modest ($25 US) that registration is a wise course of action.

Both manual installation and the install program create a directory for Trumpet Winsock on the hard drive called Winsock into which a number of files are deposited by default. Key among these is *tcpman.exe* (the central Winsock program and the one which you start using the icon when network connection is desired). The other key programs are *winsock.dll*, *twsk16.dll* (the 16-bit interface) and *wsock32.dll* (the 32-bit interface).

Trumpet Winsock also comes with an automatic login program which you customize to automatically dial the phone, login to your account, then start your Internet connection (whether that is by SLIP or PPP). Some aspects of the customization are carried out by the program itself while others must be inserted with a text editor such as that which comes with Windows, the editor in *Xtree*, or preferably, an excellent and free text editor called Programmers Favorite Editor (*PFE*), available from many freeware sites. Winsock also writes a startup file called *trumpwsk.ini* which can also be customized for the automatic login process. The two, *login.cmd* and *trumpwsk.ini* work together. Another supplied program *bye.cmd* hangs up the phone when you are done.

IV. WINSOCK ON AN ETHERNET NETWORK WITH WINDOWS 3.1 OR 3.11

You may well have access at a college or school to an Ethernet network connection for your computer. This is a typical situation now in large office complexes and college residence rooms. An Ethernet network delivers a high-quality connection to your office, dorm room or work area by means of a special cable which connects many computers including your own to a local area server. A special network interface card is inserted into your computer into which the Ethernet cable is plugged, in much the same manner that a domestic telephone connector is inserted into a wall outlet until it snaps into place. The plastic connectors at each end of the cable look like the familiar modular telephone plug but they are thicker and wider. The other end of the Ethernet cable goes into a facilities wiring socket in the wall. The socket must be turned on by local technicians before you can use it.

Making Winsock (and thus the Internet and the Web resources) work with an Ethernet local area network connection is not difficult. None of the COM port information which is necessary for modem use is important when you are using an Ethernet connection. In Windows 3.1, the crucial ingredient is the loading of a small packet driver program called *winpkt.com.* It is loaded by a line in your *autoexec.bat* file after the regular packet driver line required by your local area network. This all occurs when you start up your computer but before you start Windows. The *winpkt* program used to be included in the Winsock distribution package and now is considered a generic helper program. Copies are readily available in software archives. If you don't presently have a copy of this program and can't find one to use, you can probably acquire one from your local area network systems administrator. To use *winpkt.com* you add a line to the *autoexec.bat* file as follows so that the packet driver loads before the winsock program starts from within Windows. It should appear on the line *after* the line which loads your local area network's driver:

c:\winsock\winpkt 0x65

(where the program *winpkt.com* is to be found in directory winsock; it can of course be stored in any other directory and this line altered accordingly.)

You also have to make a space in memory for this packet driver program in your *config.sys* file by altering the emm386 line as follows:

device=c:\windows\emm386.exe /noems x=c800-cbff

Since an Ethernet local area network has rules about how users connect, you should confirm this information with the network administrator. You will also need to be told which IP address to use to identify your computer, along with a Netmask address (you can use 255.255.255.0) and gateway address to insert into the setup screen of Winsock. On the setup screen, under the drivers heading, choose the Packet Driver option, and fill in the appropriate information in the Vector box (it may work with 00 if your autoexec.bat has been modified as shown above but try 65), the Netmask box (an IP number supplied by your administrator or the one listed above), and the Gateway box (this will be the IP address of your Internet service host). Once this is all done and tested, you might also want to set your copy of Winsock to load when you start your computer. You do this by placing the Winsock icon in the startup group. That way your TCP/IP stack will be ready to roll when the installation of Windows is complete.

One thing to watch for concerns the sequence with which computer cards such as the network card for using Ethernet are added to your computer. Network cards are added after your machine is set up. It may have a sound card already installed. Care must be taken that when the network card is added that the logical settings it uses are not already taken, for instance by the sound card. Speaking from personal experience, this sort of conflict can be very difficult to solve.

Other than these few steps and alterations, there is little else to do. IP information packets can now use the local area network to make the trip to your computer.

V. BLACK MAGIC: MAKING SLIP CONNECTIONS IN UNIX ACCOUNTS: SLIRP (AND ITS PREDECESSOR TIA)

For many in academic settings, Internet service is provided by means of a UNIX account administered by the college or university's computer centre. Today's UNIX account is a lineal descendant of the first academic computer accounts which first appeared in the late 1960s for remote job entry.

Typically, the user first logs on, either through a modem service or through a lab or Ethernet connection. Once having logged on, the user lands in a personal account area with little or no guidance as to what to do next, aside from a blinking cursor and a prompt for commands. The experienced UNIX user then proceeds to perform tasks with the common UNIX utilities such as the e-mail programs *Elm* and *Pine*, using UNIX editors such as *Emacs* or *Pico*. This is text-only territory and the Internet services are well hidden from view and generally accessible only through command line versions of common Internet programs such as *Lynx* for text-based Web browsing, *FTP* for acquiring software located with *Archie*, *Tin* for reading the USENET newsgroups, and so on.

Some universities and colleges now offer SLIP or PPP connections (a requirement for graphics-oriented use of Internet services) through their dial-up services directly, but this is still uncommon. Increasingly it will be available to users through a simple text menu which appears after you log in asking in which direction you wish to proceed, graphical or text only. More common now is the situation in which there is a desire or requirement on the part of the user to exploit the resources of the graphics-oriented Web and Internet tools, but no obvious way of fulfilling that wish. Since Web service is and must be based on a SLIP or PPP connection to transfer TCP/IP packets to and from your computer, you simply must find a way to make such a connection. But this type of service is not usually available within a UNIX account. While most commercial service providers now routinely provide a SLIP and/or PPP type of connection in their dial-up services, the situation in the academic world has not yet reached this level. And typically, there is little help, guidance or supporting literature to help academics and students get around this potential roadblock. In part, the retention of the text-based university service is necessary because many students and faculty will continue to need text-based data processing services such as SPSS, SAS, or other heavyweight statistical packages running with huge computer centre resident databases such as Census microdata samples, which cannot easily be copied to student computers, if possible at all.

In order to solve this problem of conflicting requirements in UNIX shell accounts, a program called TIA (which stands for The Internet Adapter) was devised in 1994 to forge SLIP or PPP connections entirely from within a UNIX shell account of the type typically offered academics and students. TIA is still in widespread use in academia though it is no longer being developed or supported. To find out if you have it, at the prompt just type tia (followed by the carriage return Enter key) and see if anything constructive happens. If it does, your problems may be solved. Hang up and phone back from within a copy of a Winsock program, log in, type "tia" [Enter] and then press the escape character on your keyboard. If all is well, TIA will provide a SLIP connection from your UNIX account to your computer via the Winsock program, a topic discussed earlier in this appendix.

In place of the now defunct TIA, there is a shareware alternative called *SLiRP*, written and supported by Danny Gasparovski in Canberra, Australia. It is a freeware TCP/IP emulator which converts ordinary shell accounts into SLIP/PPP accounts, which can be then be used as a base for the use of graphical browsers, off-line news and e-mail readers such as Pegasus, Eudora, and Agent, and telnet clients such as Ewan. Several such programs can be open simultaneously on a single SLIP or PPP line. For instance, you can start an e-mail reader such as Agent and have it check for new email or newsgroup postings every ten minutes while you use the line for other purposes such as searching for research resources with Netscape, downloading a new piece of software, or loading recent news into a TCP/IP news presenter such as Pointcast. While simultaneous use may appear to be going on, the applications are in fact sharing the same SLIP or PPP line which can be physically carried over one telephone line from your personal computer to your service's modem bank.

In order to use SLiRP, you must first acquire a copy of the SLiRP archive file and then install it in your UNIX account. Complete instructions for doing this are available at SLiRP's home site at *http://blitzen.canberra.edu.au/slirp*.
A brief overview of instructions for unpacking and installing SLiRP follows:

    1. With FTP or in some other fashion such as using *Lynx*, acquire a copy of the latest version of SLiRP and deposit it in your UNIX account. The file you are looking for will have a name like *slirp-10c.tar.gz*

    2. Unpack this copy with the following (quasi-magical) UNIX command from the prompt:

gzip -dc slirp-VERSION.tar.gz I tar xvf - [Enter]

(Where VERSION is the number of the package version you acquired, at the time of writing it was called **10.c**). The contents of the package will be deposited in a sub-directory called slirp-VERSION, again where VERSION is the number of your package. In this example the sub-directory would be called **slirp-10.c**

In the "package" is also a manual called slirp.doc you can consult.

    3. Change directories to that sub-directory with the command

cd slirp-VERSION/src

4. Compile SLiRP with two commands from the prompt. They are:

```
./configure     [Enter key]
make            [Enter key]
```

These commands will start a long series of acts and activities which run by themselves and which culminate in the production of a single executable file called *slirp*. If the compilation fails, there are some suggestions in a help file in the sub-directory, but assistance should probably be sought from your system administrator.

5. Copy the file *slirp* to the highest level directory in your account area (the level in which you find yourself when you log in).

6. Once you have compiled your copy of SLiRP (and it is configured specifically for your UNIX host machine), you can delete all the other files that are not the executable *slirp* file.

Using SLiRP after these steps have been completed is relatively easy in comparison. The file *slirp* simply sits in your account and can be summoned to start whenever you want a SLIP or PPP connection. Any documentation you may have which tells you how to connect to a SLIP/PPP account now also applies to your UNIX shell account. Usually this means dialing and connecting with your UNIX server, or otherwise connecting to it by wire, using a Winsock program on your personal computer or lab computer. Once you have logged in, you start the SLiRP generated SLIP or PPP connection with a simple command, either

```
slirp       [Enter key] for a SLIP connection
or
slirp -P    [Enter key] for a PPP connection (note the uppercase P in the command)
```

Once this magical activity is done, and your login scripts perfected, logging on is one click of the mouse away. The whole sequence of dialing with Winsock, logging in and then starting SLiRP can be automated using a Winsock script (example shown earlier as a sample file called *login.cmd*). After it is written and perfected, the script will handle the entire process with a single click of the mouse.

Of the two protocols, PPP is widely believed to be marginally superior in practice though the difference is in the details. PPP is intended to work better with noisy telephone lines, a common situation. Both SLIP and PPP can use data compression to increase the velocity of information transfer to and from your computer in TCP/IP information packets.

You can also use a normal terminal program such as *Telix* or *Procomm* to dial your service and log in. After logging in, you then start *slirp* then exit from the terminal program without hanging up, picking up the connection with your Winsock program. This can take some dexterity however as some Windows programs don't like to share a single COM port.

Should you wish to cease using SLiRP but want to remain logged on to use the shell account, type five zeroes (0 0 0 0 0) with a 1 second gap between each zero. This will put you back textwise in your shell account service.

If you have trouble, and your system administrator can't help you, there is a USENET newsgroup called *alt.dcom.slip-emulators* you can post your question to. Use of newsgroups was discussed in an earlier chapter.

TRUMPET SETUP FOR SLIRP

The only other aspect of using SLiRP which might cause trouble concerns the settings for Winsock on your computer which may need adjusting in order to work well with your modem connection with SLiRP. The setup menu in Winsock is accessible through the file pull-down menu. When you choose setup, a series of setting choices is presented. The following settings will work:

IP: use the IP address which the host server offers you; if none is offered use 10.0.2.15
Netmask: 0.0.0.0
Nameserver: whichever IP address your host server recommends: phone the computer if necessary; if nothing else works you can try 134.117.1.1
Gateway: leave as is (usually 0.0.0.0)
Time: leave as is (usually blank)
Domain suffix: leave blank
Packet Vector: 00
MTU: 1500
TCP RWIN: 4096
Demand Load Timeout: 5
TCP RTO MAX: 60
Internal SLIP: checked on
SLIP Port: same as your COM port number your modem talks through (usually 2)
Baud Rate: 57600 (if you don't have a UART 16550 chip, use 19200)
Hardware handshaking: checked on
Van Jacobsen Compression: checked on
On-Line Status detection: none

VI. A SPECIAL CASE: CREDIT CARD CALLS WHEN YOU ARE TRAVELING

One of the most irritating situations which can occur when you are traveling is trying to use a friend's computer to connect long distance with your service back home, or to negotiate the switchboards at hotels while trying to use your computer and modem to phone your regular service provider long distance in order to pick up and send e-mail messages (or anything else you can do with a TCP/IP or standard UNIX shell account login). The problem lies in the practice of many hotels of charging much higher rates for long-distance calls than would accrue if you were phoning long distance from a residence phone. The way around this is to obtain a calling credit card from your home phone company. Using it from a hotel phone with your computer and modem can be an adventure, however.

When making a credit card call from a hotel phone, you are generally instructed to dial 8, leave a short pause, then 0, then the area code followed by the local number you are trying to reach. After you do this, a cyborg voice comes on the line and tells you to enter your credit card number. It is not always clear that after you have done this you also have to enter the 4 digit PIN number which appears on your card. This usually works fine when you are making a voice call but it is a little more difficult with a computer and modem. I have found the following works with my notebook making a credit card call.

*   Make sure your modem is connected to the hotel phone line and so is the voice telephone – <u>you need both</u>. Arranging this might take some engineering.
*   Open Winsock and choose manual dial. If you are using a terminal program such as Procomm, essentially the same sequence described below will work fine.
*   Using commas to create pauses, enter the destination dialing sequence as in atdt 8,0,666-521-1000 (where the number you are trying to call is area code 666 and the local number is 521-1000), <u>but don't press enter.</u>
*   Pick up the handset and hold it so that you can listen.
*   Press the Enter key; you should hear the modem dialing its string of numbers. <u>Do not hang up the handset!</u>
*   Wait for the cyborg voice; use the telephone handset keypad to enter your credit card number and the PIN. After a recorded cyborg expression of gratitude for your business, the destination number will ring and hopefully your service's modem will answer. <u>Do not hang up the handset but do cover the mouthpiece with your hand.</u>
*   Allow the handshaking exchange of bleep tones to take place until you clearly hear your modem making bleep tones in the exchange (at least two seconds of handshaking). Then, and only then, gently hang up the handset. The handshaking bleep tone sequence need not have been completed before you hang up the handset but <u>it must have started!</u>
*   Most of the time the connection proceeds to a login sequence. You do the login/ password challenge and start SLIP, PPP, TIA, or SLiRP or whatever you normally do, and then start your session. It goes without saying that preparing your messages for

sending in advance of dialing is a good cost-reduction strategy if you can. TCP/IP e-mail programs like Forte Agent make this accumulation of messages to send easy. Once you have posted the messages, it will then check for and download new messages to you. You can read and prepare replies to these after you have hung up. This exchange of messages with the server should take a minimum period of time and the charge will not be augmented to suit the interests of the hotel, since the charge will be to your credit card.

Sometimes, the extraneous noise from the handset messes up your connection and you have to try again. But whatever charges you incur in the second attempt will likely be more than offset by the savings you gain by using your credit card.

D. E-MAIL DETAILS

I. CLASS 1 E-MAIL — UNIX SYSTEMS

This type of e-mail exists in standard UNIX shell accounts. If you have another type of service, for example full TCP/IP privileges, you can skip over this section.

The following examples are drawn from a standard UNIX-based Internet host, a Sun Microsystems workstation with a direct Internet connection. This is a standard service provider arrangement referred to as a UNIX shell account. Though different in appearance, underlying all mailer applications will be programs operating in the same general fashion.

If you have already composed a text file you wish to send to somebody, you either have to send it as a file, or include the file in a new e-mail message. In the first case, the message may be sent to your recipient with a single command which in *Elm* would look like this. You need not even start the *Elm* mailer program first.

> **elm fred@system.com < yourfilename** or, *elm destination address < file to send*

When you start the *Elm* mailer program from a menu or a prompt (by typing *Elm* and the prompt and then pressing the Enter key for instance), you will see the type of screen shown previously in Figure 3 of Chapter Three. In the following examples, there is one incoming message for you to read:

Mailbox is '/usr/spool/mail/username' with 1 messages [ELM 2.3 PL11]

1 Jun 20 Bill Robinson   (43)   Re: cse web

You can use any of the following commands by pressing the first character;
d)elete or u)ndelete mail, m)ail a message, r)eply or f)orward mail, q)uit
To read a message, press <return>. j = move down, k = move up, ? = help

Command: <== elm is waiting for your command

When you start Pine from a menu or from a prompt (with the typed command Pine and the Enter key), this is what you see:

PINE 3.91 MAIN MENU   Folder: INBOX 1 Messages

        ?   HELP   - Get help using Pine

        C   COMPOSE MESSAGE   - Compose and send a message

        I   FOLDER INDEX   - View messages in current folder

        L   FOLDER LIST   - Select a folder to view

        A   ADDRESS BOOK   - Update address book

        S   SETUP   - Configure or update Pine

        Q   QUIT   - Exit the Pine program

You select folder list and the following appears on your screen:

   1 May 30 Aaron Barnhart   (3,486) About the TOPTEN mailer
? Help   M Main Menu P PrevMsg   - PrevPage   D Delete   R Reply
O OTHER CMDS V [ViewMsg] N NextMsg   Spc NextPage   U Undelete   F
Forward

Here is an example of how you would compose and send a message using the E*lm* mailer and the *Emacs* editor (an alternative is the simpler to use *Pico* editor). Again, text editors like *Emacs* and *Pico* are built in to the UNIX operating systems; you use them normally from within the mailer program of your choice. They are also useful for general file editing purposes unrelated to electronic mail. You start the mail program with the typed command *Elm* and the Enter key.

Mailbox is '/usr/spool/mail/username' with 1 messages [ELM 2.3 PL11]

1 May 30 Aaron Barnhart   (76)   About the TOPTEN mailer

You can use any of the following commands by pressing the first character;
d)elete or u)ndelete mail, m)ail a message, r)eply or f)orward mail, q)uit
To read a message, press <return>. j = move down, k = move up, ? = help

[Responding to the prompts you supply the command m (for mail),
an address (blogger@nowhere.com,
a subject line text (this is optional, copy addresses (null in this example)).
Elm then invokes the editor you use, in this case emacs]

Command: Mail   To: blogger@nowhere.com
Subject of message: just another message
Copies to:
Invoking editor...

[you add your text; if you have a signature (sig) file, it is added to the end of the
text. Signature files are covered later in this appendix]

This is a silly example of an important principle
--
Your signature file goes here. They will be explained in a later section of this
appendix.
Please choose one of the following options by parenthesized letter: **s** < = =
save option chosen

The message will then be sent to its destination. There are many variants of the process, for example for including other files of various sorts, but essentially these examples demonstrate typical cases. Receiving and displaying messages is quite simple as well. You start your mail program (*Elm, Pine,* etc.), select the message you wish to view by moving the cursor or highlighted line to the chosen message, and then press the Enter key on your keyboard. The message will be displayed in "pages" which can be scrolled through, usually with the use of the space bar. Once read, you may delete the message, leave it where it is, or save it by using the appropriate key strokes. An example of the process of reading a message appears below:

Mailbox is '/usr/spool/mail/username' with 1 messages [ELM 2.3 PL11]

O 1   July 4 (65) DEMONIC Mailing List <kidsphere@sitrep.edu>   Useless facts

   You can use any of the following commands by pressing the first character;
d)elete or u)ndelete mail, m)ail a message, r)eply or f)orward mail, q)uit
   To read a message, press <return>. j = move down, k = move up, ? = help

Command: Display message

Message 1/1

From kidsphere@sitrep.edu Tue Jul 4 19:21 EDT 1996
Date: Tue, 4 Jul 1996 19:14:07 EDT*[this is information on the time the message was received]*
From: DEMONIC Mailing List <kidsphere@sitrep.edu>
Subject: Useless facts *[this is the subject line]*
To: DEMONIC Subscribers <kidsphere@sitrep.edu>   *[this is your address]*
Errors-To: <demonic-request@sitrep.edu >
Warnings-to: <demonic-request@sitrep.edu >
Reply-to: <DEMONIC@sitrep.edu >*[this is the address of the sender; useful for sending return replies]*
Message-id: <Pine.3.88.9507041508.A10516-0100000@svpal>
Content-Type: text
Content-Length: 673

Date: Tue, 04 Jul 1995 15:15:06 -0700 (PDT)FRFrom: Eduard L Furbling

From: Eduard L Furbling<furbling@svpal.org>
Subject: Useless facts and procedures

Dear all,

I am at a loss for words.

Command ('i' to return to index):
[The command i will return you to the index page where all your mail can be accessed]

Mailbox is '/usr/spool/mail/username' with 1 messages [ELM 2.3 PL11]

D 1 July 4 (65) DEMONIC Mailing List <demonic@sitrep.edu >   Useless facts

You can use any of the following commands by pressing the first character;
d)elete or u)ndelete mail, m)ail a message, r)eply or f)orward mail, q)uit
To read a message, press <return>. j = move down, k = move up, ? = help

Command:**d**   **<== delete option chosen**

This message will be deleted when you exit the program because the option d
for delete was selected.

You may save an incoming e-mail message for later re-reading or for decoding by choosing the save option [the *s* command in *Elm*] and choosing a location in which to store it. Usually, a default storage "folder" location is offered to you for storage but you may change this name by overtyping the offered option. That is, if you wish to accept the default folder, just press the Enter key. But if you want to save it with a different name, you simply type in the alternative name and press Enter.

II. CLASS 2 E-MAIL: TCP/IP PROGRAMS

A full featured TCP/IP e-mail program such as Forte Agent is not only much more capable than the older style UNIX programs like *Elm* and *Pine*, it is much easier to use as well. The main screen was shown previously in Figure 4. As a user, you can set many options to suit your needs and then drive around the menu surfaces with the mouse. Aside from typing new messages, there is really little that is not directly addressable with a mouse. Care must be exercised with one particular option though: the question of whether or not to delete messages from the server when they have been copied to your computer. Opinion is divided on this; leaving the messages on the server does give you a chance to undo mistaken deletions, but if you don't have direct access to your server mail file, it is probably better to delete the messages from the mail server as they are downloaded to your computer. This decision is to be found under the mail preferences options box in all major full-featured e-mail client programs, including that built into Netscape itself.

In complex programs such as Agent, you are required to know the name of the computer where you mail file resides, the name of the computer where your new messages are sent, and also (because Agent is also a newsgroups reader), the same addressing information for your provider's newsgroup computer. There will be an account/password challenge as well but the program will "remember" this information once supplied for the first time if you set the option for this feature. All of this information is all available from your service provider. Note that Agent provides virtually automatic decrypting of MIME attachments and filtering for posts and e-mail from specified undesirable sources. A later version of Agent which, it is promised, will appear in the coming year will have embedded e-mail encryption as well, once the MIME standard for this aspect is agreed upon. Encryption, dealt with sparingly in a later section of this Appendix, is currently cumbersome because encrypting and decrypting must be done off-line and thus off the e-mail reader's desktop.

All in all, if you do have access to TCP/IP service, this is the way to go. It is a pleasure to peruse and respond to both e-mail and newsgroup postings from the same graphic "desktop".

III. CLASS 3 E-MAIL: FREENETS

Freenet e-mail programs are text-oriented front ends for the same old UNIX e-mail functions described above in the first class discussed. The menus are designed in such a way that is impossible to break out of them. Literally, what you see is what you get. An example of this type of menu screen was shown in Figure 5 in Chapter Three.

What you loose in this process is direct access to your files. Saving and printing of files becomes very difficult in comparison to the other two modes of e-mail in which printing is feasible (UNIX) and easy (TCP/IP mailer). Persons who use this type of system quickly become frustrated at the rigidity they impose and thus move on to another service provider. Nevertheless, as a starting point, freenets have drawn a great many people into the Internet world and for some, no further facilities are required.

IV. CODING AND DECODING BINARY FILES

Occasionally, you will receive a file attached to or embedded in an e-mail message that is encoded in its entirety for passage through the e-mail system. Nowadays, it is more likely to be appended to an e-mail message as a MIME attachment, a process discussed in a later section of this Appendix. If you receive such a file, it must be decoded (or likely *uudecoded* since *uuencoding* is a common way of converting word processor files for e-mailing). Briefly here, such files must be converted back to word processor files before they are useful to you. Shareware for uuencoding and decoding, as well for another kind of coding called zip compression are available at many shareware sites on the Web free of charge.

If the message needs uudecoding (that is if someone has sent you a file which has been uuencoded, perhaps a WordPerfect file for instance), you will need to save that message with a unique name. You will recognize that uuencoding has been used if, when you attempt to read the e-mail message, all you can see is a square of seamless letters, numbers, and symbols. Once the uuencoded file has been saved, you will need to remember that unique file name in order to locate the message for subsequent uudecoding purposes, after which you will probably want to download the WordPerfect file to your personal computer. Alternatively, you can download the uuencoded file to your personal computer and uudecode it there. Either way, the fully marked up WordPerfect file will be recovered for your use. Uuencode/decode is a most useful utility to get to know. For instance, virtually all photos posted to the USENET newsgroups are now uuencoded to pass through the e-mail system intact.

Once you have learned how to send and receive e-mail easily, you might then like to learn about mailing other types of files which have to be encoded for transmission such as graphics files, WordPerfect or Word files, or other special types of files in binary format. These types of files have to be converted from 8-bit to 7-bit format for passage through the e-mail system. It is not necessary to understand this process, only that it is necessary that files be in the right file format to transit the Internet without being damaged.

Some files are both compressed with Pkzip, a ubiquitous shareware program and then uuencoded. Upon receipt, the process must be reversed by appropriate software. A compression program called BinHex is used on Macintosh computers sometimes in place of Pkzip.

V. INCLUDING TEXT FILES IN UNIX SHELL E-MAIL USING ELM

If you want to send an existing text file using *Elm* in a UNIX shell account by including it in a new message, you type **ctrl-x** and then **i** (while pressing down the control key, press **i**). You will then be prompted for the name of the file to include in the message. If you then supply the name of the file you wish to send, its contents will be included in the text of the message.

VI. MIME ATTACHMENTS

Sooner or later you will see the word **MIME** used in connection with attachments to e-mail. The need for such attachments arises from the fact that contemporary e-mail systems use only 7 of the potential 8 bits in a network computer "word" or byte. The reasons for this lie in the dim past[5] and need not concern us here were it not for the fact that word processor files, and all manner of binary files including pictures and sound files use all 8 bits. This is awkward because they cannot therefore be sent in ordinary e-mail without modification. The MIME rules (or Multipurpose Internet Mail Extensions to be exact) govern ways in which native 8-bit files can be attached to e-mail. This is particularly relevant for everyone who uses a complex word processor such as WordPerfect or Word. Documents written in these "8-bit languages" cannot be sent via e-mail without modification. Further, collections of documents bundled in a compressed archive by Pkzip or BinHex cannot be directly e-mailed either. Early e-mail programs allowed the user to attach these 8-bit documents in the form of MIME attachments. These worked by encrypting 8-bit words into 7-bit format using a public formula called base-64. Upon arrival, they could be decrypted by base-64 to recreate the original 8-bit word files. The text-based UNIX e-mail program called Pine could do this very well for instance.

Another initial attempt to solve this problem was an encryption program called uuencode which was discussed in a previous section of this Appendix. Uuencode is still in wide use on the USENET newsgroups, especially for encoding binary files of photographs. It is still useful therefore to have a uuencoder/decoder program on your computer as a "helper" application. You can also uuencode word processor files for e-mailing. Uuencode will if requested, break up very large files into independently mailable chunks for reassembly upon arrival. Because uuencode folds 8-bit words into 7-bit format, processed files enlarge by at least 12 percent in size. Again, on the binaries newsgroups, photographs are typically broken into two or more chunks. Some e-mail systems will not accept very large files, so this segmentation is a standard requirement. Uuencoder/decoder programs for most computers and most software systems are available at shareware sites free of charge.

The MIME standard seeks to solve the general problem of moving any kind of digital "object" from any computer platform to any other computer platform on the Internet.

It is a core convention of the Multimedia Web because the pictures and the sounds flow through the Network in formats governed by the MIME conventions. MIME rules are the emergent grammar of the Web. A given type of file will have a standard three character filename extension which will both tell the user which type of information is contained, and also tell the browser program which type of helper application is required to decode its contents and present them in a cogent manner.

Moving into the present, full-featured e-mail packages and the graphics browser can handle a wide range of MIME attachments, either on their own or with the help of assisting programs. In Netscape, "helper applications" are acquired, installed and designated to handle the various MIME formats. For instance, Netscape itself can handle images in the GIF and JPEG formats. But for other formats, for instance the pages the *Adobe Acrobat Distiller* produces in PDF format, you need a helper, in this instance the *Adobe Acrobat Reader*, to decode these files in order to view them. This particular program renders a full-colour fully detailed version of a printed page on your screen and is also free of charge to the personal computer user. Many publications are available on this basis now, including the short summary of the daily *New York Times*. These pages, after decoding, may be printed on most printers and are a faithful representation of the original printed page.

The same potential is now found in contemporary full-featured e-mail/newsgroup read/write programs such as Forte Agent.

VII. SIGNATURE FILES

With electronic mail one can also append a special file automatically to all messages sent which gives (sometimes) important information about the sender. Often this signature file is also a personal stylistic statement which might convey the writer's point of view or philosophy of life. This material is composed by a text editor and stored in whatever location the mailer program expects to find it. (in *Elm*, it is stored as a file called signature in the directory *.elm*) There are very few rules about what should or could be included in signature files (universally referred to as *sig files*). The first rule is that the first line should be composed of two dashes '—' followed by a divider line '_____' as in the following example:

—_____   *[first line of a sig file, the divider]*

The two dashes are important since some automatic processing programs on the Internet will take these dashes to be an indication that a sig file follows. In some circumstances, for example where the sig file should be removed, the two dashes will trigger this deletion. In the normal sig file, there follow approximately 6 lines of text about the sender. Perhaps, name and address, telephone numbers, fax numbers, contact information plus a favourite quotation or observation on life in general. Sig files which dwell past 6 lines sometimes attract negative attention and especially in the early Internet days, long sig files were viewed as uncivil. Though this convention has largely been abandoned as the Net has filled with novices, extra long sig files, or extraneous cleverness such as pictographs composed of letters and numbers used to form images can be annoying. But on the other hand, some of the pictographs known collectively as "ASCII art" can be very engaging. There are collections of such efforts in special archives.

You may also encounter something in sig files called a "public key" or a "footprint" of a public key. These chunks of letters and numbers are the beginnings of the digital signature which in future will be used in electronic transactions of all sorts. They are used to authenticate the identity of the senders of e-mail and are also employed in the encryption of messages in such a way that only the intended recipient of the e-mail message can read them, even though they pass through public Internet space on their way to that intended reader.

Here is an example of a sig file:

Rosa Luxemberg
Smith University
Department of Phrenology
Lobe Building Rm. 666   "If I can't stay up all night then
{319} 820-2600 ext. 7456   it's not my revolution..."
{319} 762-9034 fax
{319} 709-5678 cell

e-mail: rluxembe@smith.edu

As with all other Internet utilities, electronic mail can be used in a disruptive manner. Sending out messages about personal grievances to strangers for example, or offering inappropriate services for sale are both regarded as an "offences" referred to as *spamming* after the infamous canned pork product sometimes called the "devil's toothpaste". System operators sometimes receive complaints when such offences occur and the ultimate sanction if warnings fail is revocation of e-mail privileges or loss of account. It is possible to commit an abuse of this nature unwittingly when one is a novice. If you are unfortunate enough to violate one of these informal rules, you may well receive abusive responses for you violation of Netiquette, the subject of a later section in this appendix. Such abusive responses, often referred to as "flames" should not be taken literally but rather as helpful indications that you have transgressed some informal Net rule in some specific way. The rhetoric of flames is one of intemperate and ill-disguised aggression. This is the way behaviour modification occurs on the Net.

Notwithstanding the sanctions, there are individuals in the world who pointedly and persistently violate the norms and appear to get away with it. Persons with a strange mission in life seem to crop up everywhere, in all social contexts and Net milieux. You will undoubtedly see some of them in action from time to time and you may well become the object of their unwanted attentions. There is no simple solution to this sort of problem but deleting messages on the basis of who sent them is the usual response. Deleting disruptive and unread e-mail messages is not rude nor a breach of Netiquette and is sometimes an instrumental necessity. Some of the better known "net loons" have multiple pseudonyms and tend to pop unexpectedly anyway. One particular gentleman appears to want to discuss the Armenian genocide on an almost continuous basis for instance.

VIII. SMILIES AND EMOTICONS

One of the intrinsic difficulties of Internet use in its text-only mode of communication is the inability to convey nuance, facial expression, and body language to augment and cast the literal content of the text. One means of getting around this shortcoming is the use of Emoticons or Smilies which qualify the sense of a remark. Smilies are constructed of text characters arranged is such a way as to convey the missing context. They look like this:

   :-) for a smile or   **:-(** for a frown or   **;-)** for a wink

There are endless variations of this icon set. Some are more transparent in meaning than others but all are intended to convey an ironical self view of the author or his or her state of mind when the statement was typed. One cannot assume however that this rendition of emotive content is not itself a manipulation of the audience at a certain level.

A complete dictionary of Smilies and Emoticons is available at a French Web site. Its address is *http://olympe.polytechnique.fr/~violet/smileys*.

IX. NETIQUETTE

There is no code of conduct for the Internet largely because there is no possible enforcement mechanism. This being the case, we are left with a series of forceful suggestions relating to behaviour. We have already addressed "spamming" or the unwanted flooding of Netspace with inappropriate and offensive messages of a self-serving or deranged nature. There are a number of less obvious rules as well, some of which may not be intuitively obvious to the newcomer. Some but by no means all of these "rules" for e-mail and posting are:

Sig files should not be verbose. No large ASCII art montages, don't give all of your e-mail and other addresses, phone numbers, date of birth etc. Most often, this rule is honoured in the breach if at all.

Do not include all of previous post(s) in the thread. Mail editor programs will habitually include all of the previous message to which you are responding for your annotation and commentary. Delete unnecessary parts. This injunction is honored in the main.

Don't post personal responses to the list. It is tempting to dash off a quick reply to the author forgetting that it will also go to everyone else on the listserv or who reads a newsgroup. Can be very embarrassing if forgotten; has happened to others.

Don't cross post to all possible groups. Close to spamming in gravity. Confine your remarks to centrally important lists or newsgroups.

Never post a message with the subject: test please ignore. The height of intrusive boorishness. Try the group alt.test instead.

Do not provide textual exegesis of all mistakes made by all posters. Self-evident waste of time.

Do make your point in a polite, reasoned and to the point fashion.

Do make your descriptive subject lines accurate and concise. It may be the difference between being read and being ignored.

Do check the frequently-asked-questions files (FAQs) before posting the same simple question for the 15,000th time.

Avoid "me too" responses. Basically your opinion carries little or no weight when expressed in this manner.

Don't report the news. If it happened and it's important, chances are your local TV and radio will be reporting it long before your news post reaches Nepal in five days on the USENET.

In your own user account, *do delete unwanted messages*, *don't waste storage space on junk files*, and *do assume that others will be able to read your files* and thus *do not keep confidential materials on a public system,* which might be thought of as any machine of which you are not the exclusive user. Consider encrypting sensitive material.

E. ENCRYPTION AND PRIVACY

Encryption in the world of telecommunications and computers is used to ensure that no one other than the person or persons intended as readers of your files or messages actually does read them. To other potential readers, encrypted files are meant to be opaque, unreadable chunks of seemingly random characters in a huge squared array. Alas, things are seldom that simple. Governments possess the technical means to decrypt almost any type of encrypted file (but not all) through the use of extremely powerful special-purpose computers. They maintain the right to make such attempts in the interests of collective security, fighting crime, or other worthy motives. Hypothetically, persons interested in stealing your money could also be interested in your computer message traffic if you are in the habit of supplying a VISA number to purchase items electronically, for instance. As more and more commerce is conducted electronically, from personal banking to investments to routine purchases of good and services, this type of exposure must increase. Not surprisingly, most Canadians wish to protect the integrity of their transactions, the privacy of their electronic conversations, and the personal details of their lives. To accomplish any of these ends, strong encryption is a requirement.

I. GENERAL INTRODUCTION TO ENCRYPTION

Strong encryption is not yet easy to use. Several factors have retarded its development and adoption. While sophisticated encryption algorithms exist which are so difficult to break that it's not even worth the effort to try, these methods seldom find their way into the hands of ordinary computer users. This is not an accident. Those concerned with national security and law enforcement have resisted attempts to place routine encryption at the disposal of e-mailers and those conducting commercial transactions through the Web. For example, most Web browsers now have provisions for encrypting commercial transactions such as finding out what your bank balance is through the Internet. The algorithms used however, while strong enough to defeat casual thieves, are of little practical use against the organs of the modern state. This is intentional.

The limitation imposed on Netscape users (of the international version) is a secret key 40 bits long. For domestic U.S. users, the length of the key rises to 128 bits. It is widely believed that governments have the technical ability to recover (guess) a 40-bit key in a matter of minutes using powerful computers, and further that they may be able to recover 128 bit keys, albeit in a significantly longer period of time[6]. The ability of governments or technically proficient crooks does not however currently extend to recovering 2048-bit keys. If these were routinely used, and the more people that used them the better, the prospect of anyone ever viewing your files or transactions would approach zero.

A second reason why strong encryption is not available to average users of the Internet is that given the stated intention of governments to suppress its use, software companies have not yet integrated its routine use into everyday use, in e-mail programs for instance. Since encryption is not integrated, the user wishing to encrypt a message for someone else must hop out of the email program, do the encryption, then paste the resulting encrypted file into the e-mail and then send it. Further, such a user must maintain a file with the public keys of the intended recipients. This assumes of course that the recipient has gone to the trouble of generating a public/ private key pair and then posted the public half in some prominent public location. Though sites exist on the Internet for holding such public keys and then dispensing them to all comers, their existence is not well known.

It is possible to imagine an e-mail program which would automatically check a "public key library" for the name and e-mail address you have indicated on a completed piece of outgoing e-mail, and if found, acquire a copy of that person's public key, add it to your local public key ring for future use, automatically encrypt the outgoing message for that person's public key, then send the now-encrypted text as a regular e-mail message. This <u>could</u> be a routine series of events in the future, as would be the routine automated decryption of incoming e-mail. Unfortunately, all major suppliers of e-mail programs have declined to this point in time to include integrated encryption for reasons alluded to above. This is a commercial decision based on specific instances of threats and intimidation which have entered the software culture and act as a drag on adoption of strong encryption techniques. No one wants to be prosecuted for exporting strong cryptography (a crime) nor do they want their products ordered off the shelves as a security risk. Even the threat of years of costly litigation is a sufficient threat to stop development cold.

Another aspect of this situation is the creation and use of digital signatures. These can be used to authenticate both non-encrypted and encrypted messages or transactions. In effect, the affixing of such a digital signature to a message attests to the incontrovertible fact that the message is from you, and also that the integrity of the message remains intact during its passage from you to the intended recipient. Any attempt to tamper with a signed message would trigger a warning to the recipient that it is not an authentic message; an electronic "tilt" sign lights up in the same way that pinball machines cease to function if you lift them physically to influence the course of a game ball. These digital signatures do not appear to pose a perceived national security threat (or at the least there has been no public discussion of ways in which they might do so). Digital signatures are now available for a small fee from commercial services such as Verisign. You can acquire one of these and install it in the security section of your browser with no difficulty at all. But until more people and more companies start using these facilities, routine use will not occur. In the future however, routine electronic banking will require the equivalent of a signature, especially if loans and security purchases and sales are involved. Therefore, the arrival of digital signatures for everyone seems just a matter of time.

II. PGP ENCRYPTION EXAMPLES

1. A plain text message

Bring 60 pounds of cocaine to the square at midnight. Why don't you throw in a gross of dirty pictures and a few slaves as well. You will be richly rewarded. Regards, Blacknet Enterprises.

2. The same message with a PGP digital signature attached:

```
——BEGIN PGP SIGNED MESSAGE——
Bring 60 pounds of cocaine to the square at midnight. Why don't you throw in
a gross of dirty pictures and a few slaves as well. You will be richly rewarded.
Regards, Blacknet Enterprises.
——BEGIN PGP SIGNATURE——
Version: 2.6ui
iQBVAwUBMofv+iS1AkwDK9jJAQHUBQH/
fbgkiwAyM9xg7Z3yS5lDvraz9PCmLJUk VRbqzwnmeR5MWr3TcmHs/
yJrOE0FOVFDHPzdeeL+NFvQ/1vqSa7NHA==
=5tVk
——END PGP SIGNATURE——
```

3. The same message fully encrypted with PGP:

```
——BEGIN PGP MESSAGE——
Version: 2.6ui
pgAAAL5vyyXikfABoe45n3Qz5PulXv8GYjQcv/Aolemjo+tlA416NqoBECAosxFX
58fBU5090/HahzvpCbuP83lMlk7BU67KGZrJx+WWAwkB2BXK4d1ym1/
8b2BLn4xG    ea7dlukDeAJ2ebZIiMjakWBY5ej3SZMKAKztlvliN/
uvBvEGJ3ld8mNgWFA5rYlg
eKrlZJksV0Yi9JkxXNaR1nLu81vurusM6N4tvLjSeizdxz8HZFM8LYWsNwHWXeBY
YOiU
=f5mb
——END PGP MESSAGE——
```

It may not occur to you immediately that if you can encrypt messages you send or any content on your hard drive, so too can persons with hostile intent. In the familiar example, the pedophile can encrypt his image files in such a way that police cannot recover evidence without his permission. Likewise the money launderer can hide his accounts, the right-wing gun nut can hide plans for insurrection and murder, and the organized crime figure his plans. Encryption can serve any and all ends, both licit and illicit. This situation of the moral neutrality of strong encryption is often used by law enforcement and intelligence community representatives to justify either banning, limiting key length of, or sabotaging strong encryption. Sabotaging strong encryption would occur if there was included in the algorithm a secret "backdoor" for law enforcement, or mandatory secret key deposit (escrow of some sort). The first type of sabotage is precluded by the requirement of full public disclosure to the cryptography community of the algorithm used. Such scrutiny by the community would quickly reveal any "backdoor". The second type of sabotage (key escrow) would be imposed by legislation and would be known to and avoided by anyone with a serious interest in privacy.

When a new cryptographic product is announced, it is immediately subjected to close scrutiny for flaws. The 'attackers' are serious hobbyists or professionals for whom cracking a major encryption scheme represents attainment of Nobel laureate status in the encryption world. For example, the earliest versions of Netscape commercial transaction encryption were vigorously attacked by math students around the world and several flaws were quickly detected, one by a Canadian graduate student studying in California and another by a group of French students. The process was so useful to the Netscape company that it began offering cash rewards to successful attackers, the so-called "bugs bounty". It was useful because in the process of sustained attack by aficionados, revisions to the system firmly established its efficacy. In the end, no more successful attacks occurred. In this instance, sensationalized press accounts of the cracks had the effect of strengthening public confidence in the method since revisions were also publicly announced as countermeasures. However, for shoddy or poorly conceived encryption systems, the lack of adequate response to attack can condemn them to early death, and their sponsoring companies often accompany them into the long good-bye.

III. LEVELS OF PROTECTION

No form of encryption can offer perfect protection. This is true because irrationally large amounts of money have been spent by governments on defeating encryption, many devious techniques perfected, and many superb computers built for this sole purpose. One must also take human frailties into account: choosing guessable passphrases is one common example, writing a passphrase down on a piece of paper and storing the paper in your wallet is another.

PGP for instance is dependent on an individual's being able to conceal a secret passphrase necessary for encryption and decryption with their own pair of keys. Physical threats may be enough to elicit this phrase, which in turn can be used to unlock the encrypted material. One wonders in future whether such a passphrase might not be demanded as evidence in a legal case, failure to produce leading to contempt citations perhaps, as does now the failure of reporters to disclose sources of press stories. In part, the degree of security must be balanced against the potential risks. If you are intent on using the Internet to foment trouble or defraud others, your degree of risk is quite high. Thus your degree of security should be commensurably high. Most readers will not assess their risks in this way but certainly some kinds of political activity might occasion a high degree of scrutiny even though political expression enjoys nominal privileges. In the end, individual Internet users must make their own assessments of risk, adopt whatever tactics they feel are justified (and invest the time in learning how to use encryption tools), and then live with the consequences. Overall though, the levels of protection required will go up in complexity as more and more commerce is conducted on the Web. Both aspects are inevitable.

Strong encryption imposes time delay penalties and energy expenditure penalties on those who wish to acquire embedded information; they impose an entropy penalty on snoopers. One of the most effective ways of improving overall performance of encryption given this dynamic is to increase the workload facing your opponent. By encrypting many items, including grocery lists, and encouraging others to do the same, the workload of potential snoops is greatly expanded. No one would be able to assume that an encrypted message contained a item of special importance as they probably could now. As is the case in many other instances, there is safety in large numbers. In this case, ironically, the large number providing confidentiality of communications requires both a long key (a large number) and routine use by many e-mailers. Flooding the Net with strong encryption would probably spell the end of the ability of nation states to monitor the computer related activities of their own citizens and citizens of other countries they spy on. In the post-Cold War era, this might not be a bad thing at all.

F. MORE ON CONSTRUCTING YOUR WEB PAGE

Once you have acquired and then opened the software programs you will need for the task, you select a text file with which to start, for example a document you wish to make the heart of your home page, which you have previously written in Word or WordPerfect.

I. CONSTRUCTION PRACTICES AND PRINCIPLES

Without any HTML work at all, you may view your Word or WordPerfect generated files with the browser (load local file on the files menu) if you save them first in ASCII (text-only format). Once you see the result in your browser, you can start experimenting with the insertion of HTML code to indicate type style (bold, italic, etc.) and type size (H1 through H6). You can also introduce paragraph markers <P> and line breaks <br>.

If you have the Internet Assistant, the free HTML conversion program from Microsoft, installed in your copy of Word, within Word you can select the entire document, globally reformat it into HTML, then save it as an .htm file. You then can view that htm file with your browser, and look at the code the Internet Assistant has produced and deposited in that .htm file with PFE to see which commands do what. Experimenting with this auto-layout product can show you what command in HTML does what. HTML files nearly always have the extension .html or .htm in order that browsers can recognize the files for what they are. The shorter form of .htm is necessary on personal computers which are limited to three character file extensions.

Adding images can be done later. Again, the best way to learn how to use images is to look at the underlying HTML code in Web pages you admire. Source codes can be viewed with Netscape; and you may save a copy of the code which creates that admired site for yourself by using the "save as" command on the Netscape file menu. This and other similar activities require that you alternate between the window that has Netscape and the window that has PFE. This is obviously easier to do if you size your windows to leave a small strip across the bottom of the screen so that you can get to the icon of the non-visible program window easily to maximize it when you need to. Another solution to this problem is a shareware program for Windows 3.1 called *Barclock.* It allows you to run a bar with tiny program icons across the top of your screen and floating above all applications. It shows all the programs that arc open at that moment and any can be maximized with a single click.

HERE IS AN EXAMPLE OF A SHORT HTML FILE, IN THIS CASE, A CONSTITUENT PART OF MY RESEARCH PAGES:

```
<title>Online Institute Segment: Craig McKie</title>
<BODY BGCOLOR="8000FF" BACKGROUND="pap3.gif" TEXT="#000000"
LINK="#3333FF" VLINK="#3333FF" ALINK="3333FF">
<h3>ONLINE COMMUNITY RESOURCES ON THE NET</h3><br><br>
<LI><a href="http://www.sscnet.ucla.edu/soc/csoc/"><EM>The Centre for the
Study of Online Community </EM></a><br>
<LI><a href="http://www.fis.utoronot.ca/mcluhan/"><EM>McLuhan Program
in Culture and Technology </EM></a>  : at the University of Toronto. Marshall
McLuhan's old institute on Queen's Park Crescent in the heart of beautiful
downtown Taranna.
<Li><a href="http://www.well.com/user/hlr/vircom/index.html"><EM>Virtual
Communities Resources (Howard Rheingold) </EM></a><br>
<LI><a                          href="http://sunsite.unc.edu/dbarberi/
communications.html"><EM>The Communications Archive at Sunsite </
EM></a><br>
<LI><a href="http://eerie.eerie.fr/~alquier/cyber.html"><EM>AJL Cyberculture
Web Pages: Net Tribes - Cyberculture </EM></a><br>
<LI><a href="http://www.york.ac.uk/~jjrk1/index.html"><EM>Travels in
Hypermedia </EM></a>
<LI><a                          href="http://www.clas.ufl.edu/anthro/
Seeker1_s_CyberAnthro_Page.html"><EM>Seeker1's Anthropology Page </
EM></a>
<LI><a href="http://www.rpi.edu/~decemj/cmc/center.html"><EM>Computer
Mediated Communications Studies Center </EM></a>
<LI><a href="http://valley.interact.nl/megacities"><EM>Megacities 2000 Dig-
ital Village </EM></a>
<LI><a href="http://oak.cats.ohiou.edu/~aw148888/"><EM>Center for Utopian/
Dsytopian Studies </EM></a>
```

You will see in this short example file, most of the basic HTML formatting conventions plus a few more advanced ones as well. You will first notice a large number of angle brackets [< and >]. All the HTML formatting commands are enclosed with sets of the angle brackets. The first line for example is a title line: <title>Online Institute Segment: Craig McKie</title>. The contents of this line appear across the top of the browser window when this page is loaded. In general, HTML commands come in pairs. In this line, the first command is <title>, then comes the text to appear as a header, then the command is completed by taking off the title line (or bringing it to an end) with the matching command </title>. Note that the forward slash terminates the command. The general syntax is <command> ....</command>. The pair brackets the content of the command.

Here is what the finished product looks like:

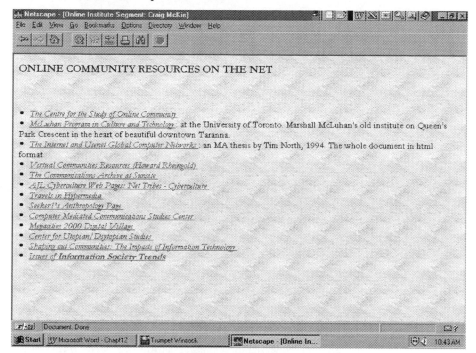

Figure 3 The simple example Web page created by the code listed above.

More properly according to HTML style standards, each HTML document should start with the <HEAD> command which is missing in this example. Thus the general syntax for an HTML Web document would be:

```
<HEAD>
<TITLE> Online Institute Segment: Craig McKie</TITLE>
</HEAD>
and then:
<BODY>
your Web page content goes here
</BODY>
```

It seems to matter little whether or not your HTML commands are entered in upper or lower case though you are encouraged to use upper case for these formatting commands. Spaces between command lines and at the end of text lines are generally ignored by browsers. Paragraphs are formatted continuously with wrap around imposed by the browser used to view the file. If however you want to have a carriage return at the end of the line (perhaps you want the next sentence to start at the left edge), you can terminate the previous line with a break using the <br> symbol. Paragraphs start with the <P> symbol. These commands in HTML are generally referred to as tags.

In this example, the second block of HTML code governs the appearance of this page when viewed in a graphical browser. For text-only lynx browsers, this segment is ignored.

<BODY BGCOLOR="8000FF" BACKGROUND="pap3.gif" TEXT="#000000" LINK="#3333FF" VLINK="#3333FF" ALINK="3333FF">

In this set of code, the background colour is set to a particular colour "8000FF". This is hexadecimal code for a particular colour. In addition, a background pattern is set to load a particular background file "pap3.gif" which resides in the public files area of my account. Then, text colour is set, as is the colour of various aspects of the active links on the page. These tend to change colour once you have visited them. The browser keeps track of these visits for you.

Next comes a line which establishes a heading on your page:

<h3>ONLINE COMMUNITY RESOURCES ON THE NET</h3>

It has formatting tags which indicate to the browser to use size 3 type for the heading. Heading type sizes vary from H1 (the largest available) through H6 (the smallest available). Note that this heading is followed by two line breaks to create space under the heading before the entries of data start. These data entries have the same format. Here is a sample entry:

<LI><a href="http://www.sscnet.ucla.edu/soc/csoc/"><EM>The Centre for the Study of Online Community </EM></a>

The entries start with the <LI> tag. It stands alone and inserts a "bullet" at the beginning of the entry. Next comes the address of the active link. Note that this part is not portrayed on the visitor's screen. Note as well the full address of the Web site you are linking to is enclosed in double quotes.

<a href="http://www.sscnet.ucla.edu/soc/csoc/">

The text that appears on the screen follows immediately thereafter, bracketed by <EM> tags for emphasized typeface, followed by the anchor tag </a> and a linebreak <br>:

<EM>The Centre for the Study of Online Community </EM></a>
Other link entries follow until the end of the document....

It is wise to also remember the lowly text-oriented Lynx browser user and to check how your page looks in text-only format. For each image you load, you should provide a text alternative for the image as a courtesy to the Lynx user using the *alt* command in HTML as in the example below:

<IMG SRC="sitelogo.gif" alt="Site Logo" HEIGHT=55 WIDTH=62>

The alt command inserts the indicated text (e.g. Site Logo) when the image cannot be loaded. Neglecting to do this can produce pages which are entirely blank in the world of the Lynx browser. Remember that a large percentage of Web users in the world today use text-only browsers with slow Network connections and that this situation is likely to persist for some time. You may even consider creating a separate version of your page specifically for Lynx text-only users and putting a link to it on your principal graphics-oriented page. Even some graphics-equipped visitors may not wish to spend the time acquiring a graphics heavy page. Especially if online time costs them money, users may opt for text only in the interests of economy of loading time. If the resource is a newspaper for instance, most visitors may opt for the text version in spite of a well-designed graphics version which takes a long time to load, is difficult to capture and print, or to forward to a friend by e-mail. This reservation about graphics-heavy pages is true in spades concerning pages that use the Netscape "frames" capability. Frames are not visible in other browsers and total confusion at the receiving end may result from the ill-advised use of complicated frames-based pages.

Colours can also create confusion. Many users of graphical browsers have their colour palettes set to 16 or 256 colours out of ignorance that their video cards can produce 65,000 colours or more. With limited colours, images may appear unattractive, grotesque, or worse. Coloured backgrounds may obscure text in the limited colour world and make otherwise useful pages unreadable. Generally, and from personal experience, if your page produces illegible images, visitors will tell you about this. It is wise to include a return e-mail address in your page so that visitors can tell you about what aspects of your page are not working well. They will do this. Assistance in selecting colours (and selecting their corresponding hexadecimal code number) can be found at a number of sites.

You can learn much from examining the HTML code on pages already in existence which you admire. Use the "view source" feature of your browser to examine how they were created and then copy their features.

II. THE WORLD WIDE WEB: ADVANCED SKILLS AND APPLICATIONS

There are many guides and references works available on the Web concerning the HTML "language", the basic encoding and tagging system of the World Wide Web. Some of those available on the Web (and thus locatable with an active search engine) are: the www.w3.org information page, Werbach's Guide to HTML, and the HTML Quick Reference Guide. A summary of the available HTML tags is available at http://www.sandia.gov/sci_compute/html_ref.html. For the purpose of improving your design skills and execution finesse, there is no better way of learning than examination of and experimentation with the code written by others. All browsers have the ability to show you the coding which underlies the pages you are looking at.

In addition, there are special enhancements involving the Java and Javascript languages which can add animation and other special effect to your pages, or special forms which can be used to capture respondent answers from questions listed on a Web page, and so on. Learning how to use these "languages" is clearly beyond the abilities of the average Web user. In truth, these effects are based in programming languages and they have to be learned like any other programming language. While there are many books available in bookstores which purport to teach these skills, it is probably not realistic to hope and expect to add these enhancements to your personal Web page without taking instruction in their use.

But you do not need these enhancements, especially at the beginning of your career as a novice webmaster. Once your page or pages have been perfected in the closed loop between your browser and your editor programs on your own computer and offline, you must then upload all the necessary files to the public area of your Internet service, or to a designated area in your own files area. Of necessity this takes you typically into the realm of UNIX file systems. It is for this reason that I often say that you can run but you cannot hide from UNIX forever. Sooner or later you have to face its rules directly and learn enough to be getting on with your projects. Again, many UNIX books exist and may be of assistance to you. Nothing however takes the place of a short course of instruction.

Your Internet service may be located at a university or college server, a freenet, or a commercial service. Each site has different rules about how such Web site files will be mounted and how permissions for access to the files will be set. You simply must ask the system administrator for detailed instructions or alternatively (and perhaps better since common English is more likely to be involved), ask someone you know who already has a Web site on your server how to proceed.

The procedure is not likely to be very difficult to follow if it is described to you as a set of stepwise instructions. In the generic case, you have to establish a directory in your account "area" where your files reside which is open to all Web visitors, then put your perfected files in it, and then make all those files readable by all visitors as well. Remember that HTML files must end either with the suffix extension .html or .htm in order that visiting browsers know what to do with them. Supporting binary files (such as pictures or graphics of various sorts) should have their appropriate extensions as well (such as .gif for GIF image files). If your service host allows multiple public directories (and many just allow one with a specific name in each account, though it may have public sub-directories), you can store the various types of files in use at your Web page in different directories. If only one public directory is allowed, then of course all the files will have to go in it.

One other small point: when a browser visits a Web site, and no particular file has been requested, the browser will automatically look for an HTML file with the name *index.html* and acquire it if it is there to be found. Therefore, it is good practice to make such an HTML file called *index.html* and put some basic information about your site in it, together with a list of the major components of your site listed as active links. That way, the naive visitor can actually find your real page content directly without stumbling around in the dark from file to file.

To upload your files to the public files area wherever it turns out to be, you can use one of two main methods. If you have a TCP/IP connection to the server, you can use FTP to "put" the files to your account. If you have a UNIX shell account, you can use *zmodem* (or any other transfer protocol) to transfer them to your account area. For instance, with zmodem, you log in to your account, change to the directory where you want the files, type **rz -b** and then press [**Enter**] at the server end, then start the upload of files with whatever commands your terminal program requires (often pressing the PageUp key works) and then specifying the location and names of files to be transferred. Keep in mind that binary files are often in the group of files to be transferred and that there the binary switch has to be set [-b in zmodem; -i in other protocols].

Try to keep a backup copy of all the files in your public directory in some other protected non-public area of your account or on your personal computer. The easiest way of doing this is to make a zipfile archive of all the files [zip archive * in UNIXland] and then move the archive to your root directory [mv archive.zip ~/ again in UNIXland]. Should anyone, through some security breach, get in and mess with your public files you should be able to restore them from the archive. Even better, download a copy of the archive to your personal computer and keep it there.

A FINAL ENCOURAGING WORD

If you feel that the material in this Appendix is arcane, indigestible, and confusing, you are not alone. The day in which you simply "plug and play" on the Internet has not yet dawned. It **is** difficult to gain a understanding of the technical aspects of telecommunications. In accepting this proposition, you will perhaps be more tolerant of yourself for making mistakes, incurring the stifled sneers of advisors of several age groups, and feeling foolish on occasion. This is normal. If to err is human, than embarking on Net use for the first few times is a humbling human experience for virtually everybody, even those who eventually come to understand the process and its many levels of transactions and display.

Notwithstanding the initial problems and frustrations, the effort will be well worth it.

NOTES

[1] With IBM-compatible computers, the difficulties principally lie with logical port selection and the speed at which serial ports are capable of operating. Some upgrading of the serial port drivers may be necessary to get high-speed modems working properly. Many of these problems can be avoided by purchasing and installing an internally mounted modem. One useful Web site which deals with these questions is located at the following Web address: http://www.intellinet.com/CustomerService/FAQ/AskMrModem/

[2] In fact, logs of network news activity surrounding this earthquake event form an important research resource for the study of disaster events and human response to them. The logs of interactive discussions which occurred during the Northridge event may be viewed at the following address: *http://sunsite.unc.edu/pub/academic/communications/logs/94-earthquake/EQ.log*

[3] You can obtain a copy of the new driver at http://www.carleton.ca/~cmckie/programs.html as *cybercom.drv.*. Once you have downloaded the copy to your computer (remember to use binary transfer options), move *cybercom.drv* to c:\windows\system. Edit file c:\windows\system.ini from comm.drv=comm.drv to comm.drv=cybercom.drv. Then check the file system.ini in c:\windows directory under [386 enh] for the following lines (change them if necessary):
COMnFIFO=1[where n stands for the com port your modem is using, e.g. most commonly 2]
COMnTXSize=8[where n stands for the com port your modem is using, e.g. most commonly 2]
COMnRXSize=8[where n stands for the com port your modem is using, e.g. most commonly 2]
Check the file win.in, also in c:\windows directory for the following line and change it if necessary:
COMn=57600,n,8,1,p[where n stands for the com port your modem is using, e.g. most commonly 2]
Then restart Windows.
Finally, in the Windows Control Panel, in the Ports icon section, set the COM port you are using, in this example 2 to a speed rate of 57600.

[4] ftp://ftp.ncsa.uiuc.edut/Mosaic/Windows/Win31x/Win32s/OLE32S13.EXE

[5] The most restrictive of Internet e-mail systems use only the first 128 characters of the 256-character ASCII computer alphabet. Thus the entire system of e-mail exchanges operates on this lowest common denominator.

[6] In November 1996, an Israeli company announced the release of a new product called SecureScape which is to be retrofitted to international versions of the Netscape browser to bring it up to 128-bit strength. At the time of writing, only an experimental version of this program, available for Windows95 only, is being dispensed. The company may be found at the following address: http://www.SecureScape.com/secscape/

GLOSSARY[1]

address
There are three types of addresses in common use within the Internet. They are the e-mail address; the IP, internet or Internet address; and the hardware or MAC address.

agent
In the client-server model, the part of the system that performs information preparation and exchange on behalf of a client, or server application.

alias
A name, usually short and easy to remember, that is translated into another name, usually long and difficult to remember.
racter-to-number encoding widely used in the computer industry.

anonymous FTP
Anonymous FTP allows a user to retrieve documents, files, programs, and other archived data from anywhere in the Internet without having to establish a userid and password. By using the special userid of "anonymous" the network user will bypass local security checks and will have access to publicly accessible files on the remote system.

application
A program that performs a function directly for a user. FTP, mail and Telnet clients are examples of network applications.

archie
A system to automatically gather, index and serve information on the Internet. The initial implementation of archie provided an indexed directory of filenames from all anonymous FTP archives on the Internet. Later versions provide other collections of information. See also: archive site, Gopher, Prospero, Wide Area Information Servers.

archive site
A machine that provides access to a collection of files across the Internet, An "anonymous ftp archive site," for example, provides access to this material via the FTP protocol.

bandwidth
Technically, the difference, in Hertz (Hz), between the highest and lowest frequencies of a transmission channel. However, as typically used, the term refers to the amount of data that can be sent through a given communications circuit.

binary
Information represented in code as a string of zeros or ones, e.g. 11001001; the basic language of data transmission and exchange between and among computers.

bounce
The return of a piece of mail because of an error in its delivery.

checksum
A computed value which is dependent upon the contents of a packet. This value is sent along with the packet when it is transmitted. The receiving system computes a new checksum based upon the received data and compares this value with the one sent with the packet. If the two values are the same, the receiver has a high degree of confidence that the data was received correctly.

client
A computer system or process that requests **a** service of another computer system or process. A workstation requesting the contents of a file from a **file** server is said to be a client of the file server.

client-server model
A common way to describe the paradigm of many network protocols. Examples include the name-server/name-resolves relationship in DNS and the fileserver/file-client relationship in NFS.

dialup
A temporary, as opposed to dedicated, connection between machines established over a standard phone line.

distributed database
A collection of several different data repositories that looks like a single database to the user. A prime example in the Internet is the Domain Name System.

Domain Name System (DNS)
The DNS is a general purpose, distributed and replicated data query service. Its principal use is the look-up of host IP addresses based on host names. The style of host names now used in the Internet is called the "domain name" because it is used to look up anything in the DNS. Some important domains are: .COM (commercial), .EDU (educational), .NET (network operations), .GOV (U.S. government), and .MIL (U.S. military). Most countries also have a domain. For example, US (United States), UK (United Kingdom), AU (Australia).

dot address (dotted decimal notation)
Dot address refers to the common notation for IP addresses of the form A.B.C.D; where each letter represents, in decimal, one byte of a four byte IP address,

Electronic Mail *(e-mail)*
A system whereby a computer user can exchange messages with other computer users (or groups of users) via a communications network. Electronic mail is one of the most popular uses of the Internet.

***e-mail* address**
The domain-based or UUCP address that is used to send electronic mail to a specified destination. For example an editor's address is "gmalkin@xylogics.com".

encryption

Encryption is the manipulation of a packet's data in order to prevent any but the intended recipient from reading that data. There are many types of dat2 encryption, and they are the basis of network security.

Ethernet

A 10-Mb/s standard for LANs, initially developed by Xerox, and later refined by Digital, Intel and Xerox (DIX). All hosts are connected to a coaxial cable where they contend for network access using a Carrier Sense Multiple Access with Collision Detection (CSMA/CD) paradigm.

FAQ

Frequently Asked Questions. FAQs exist on most important topics dealt with on the Net.

File Transfer Protocol (FTP)

A protocol which allows a user on one host to access, and transfer files to and from, another host over a network. Also, FTP is usually the name of the program the user invokes to execute the protocol. It is defined in STD 9, RFC 959.

finger

A program that displays information about a particular user, or all users, logged on the local system or on a remote system. It typically shows full name, last login time, idle time, terminal line, and terminal location (where applicable). It may also display plan and project files left by the user.

Freenet

Community-based bulletin board system with e-mail, information services, interactive communications, and conferencing. Freenets are funded and operated by individuals and volunteers - in one sense, like public television. They are part of the National Public Telecomputing Network (NPTN), an organization based in Cleveland, Ohio, devoted to making computer telecommunication and networking services as freely available as public libraries.

internet address

An IP address that uniquely identifies a node on an internet. An Internet address (capital "I"), uniquely identifies a node on the Internet.

Internet Relay Chat (IRC)

A world-wide "party line" protocol that allows one to converse with others in real time. IRC is structured as a network of servers, each of which accepts connections from client programs, one per user.

IP address

The 32-bit address defined by the Internet Protocol in STI) 5, RFC 791. It is usually represented in dotted decimal notation.

listserv
An automated mailing list distribution system originally designed for die Bitnet/EARN network.

Local Area Network (LAN)
A data network intended to serve an area of only a few square kilometres or less. Because the network is known to cover only a small area, optimizations can be made in the network signal protocols that permit data rates up to 100Mb/s.

Lurking
Inactive participation on the part of a subscriber to a mailing list or USENET newsgroup. A person who is lurking is just listening to the discussion. Lurking is encouraged for beginners who need to get up to speed on the history of the group.

Gopher
A distributed information service that makes available hierarchical collections of information across the Internet. Gopher uses a simple protocol that allows a single Gopher client to access information from any accessible Gopher server, providing the user with a single "Gopher space" of information. Public domain versions of the client and server are available.

hacker
A person who delights in having an intimate understanding of the internal workings of a system, computers and computer networks in particular. The term is often misused in a pejorative context to denote someone who attempts to access computer information systems without authorization, where .,cracker" would be the correct term.

header
The portion of a packet, preceding the actual data, containing source and destination addresses, and error checking and other fields. A header is also the part of an electronic mail message that precedes the body of a message and contains, among other things, the message originator, date and time.

host
A computer that allows users to communicate with other host computers on a network. Individual users communicate by using application programs, such as electronic mail, Telnet and FTP.

IMHO
"In My Humble Opinion" dropped into *e-mail* as self-evident expression.

internet
While an internet is a network, the term "internet" is usually used to refer to a collection of networks interconnected with routers.

Internet
(note the capital "I") The Internet is the largest internet in the world. A free store-and-forward scheme whereby the message is received from one system completely before it is transmitted to the next system, after suitable translations.

Multipurpose Internet Mail Extensions (MIME)
An extension to Internet e-mail which provides the ability to transfer nontextual data, such as graphics, audio and fax. It is defined in RFC 1341.

Multi-User Dungeon (MUD)
Adventure, role playing games, or simulations played on the Internet. Devotees call them "text-based virtual reality adventures". The games can feature fantasy combat, booby traps and magic. Players interact in real time and can change the "world" in the game as they play it. Most MUDs are based on the Telnet protocol.

netiquette
A pun on "etiquette" referring to proper behavior on a network.

network address
The network portion of an IP address. For a class A network, the network address is the first byte of the IP address. For a class B network, the network address is the first two bytes of the IP address. For a class C network, the network address is the first three bytes of the IP address. In each case, the remainder is the host address. In the Internet, assigned network addresses are globally unique.

packet
The unit of data sent across a network. "Packet" is a generic term used to describe unit of data at all levels of the protocol stack, but it is most correctly used to describe application data units.

Packet InterNet Groper (PING)
A program used to test reachability of destinations by sending them an ICMP echo request and waiting for a reply. The term is used as a verb: "Ping host X to see if it is up!"

packet switching
A communications paradigm in which packets (messages) are individually routed between hosts, with no previously established communication path.

protocol
A formal description of message formats and the rules two computers must follow to exchange those messages. Protocols can describe low-level details of machine-to-machine interfaces (e.g., the order in which bits and bytes are sent across a wire) or high-level exchanges
router
A device which forwards traffic between networks. The forwarding decision is based on network layer information and routing tables, often constructed by routing protocols.

Serial Line IP (SLIP)
A protocol used to run IP over serial lines, such as telephone circuits or RS232 cables, interconnecting two systems. SLIP is defined in RFC 1055.

server
A provider of resources (e.g., file servers and name servers).

signature
The three- or four-line message at the bottom of a piece of *e-mail* or a Usenet article which identifies the sender. Large signatures (over five lines) are generally frowned upon.

Simple Mail Transfer Protocol (SMTP)
A protocol, defined in STD 10, RFC 821, used to transfer electronic mail between computers. It is a server to server protocol, so other protocols are used to access the messages.

talk
A protocol which allows two people on remote computers to communicate in a real-time fashion.

TCP/IP
The basic data transfer protocol of the Internet.

Telnet
Telnet is the Internet standard protocol for remote terminal connection service. It is defined in STD 8, RFC 854 and extended with options by many other RFCS.

Usenet
A collection of thousands of topically named newsgroups, the computers which run the protocols, and the people who read and submit Usenet news. Not all Internet hosts subscribe to Usenet, and not all Usenet hosts are on the Internet.
people shows a person's company name, address, phone number and *e-mail* address.

Wide Area Information Servers (WAIS)
A distributed information service which offers simple natural language input, indexed searching for fast retrieval, and a "relevance feedback" mechanism which allows the results of initial searches to influence future searches. Public domain implementations are available.

World Wide Web (WWW or W3)
A hypertext-based, distributed information system created by researchers at CERN in Switzerland. Users may create, edit or browse hypertext documents. The clients and servers are freely available.

Notes

[1] Exerpted from "Network Working Group Request for Comments:RFC1392 by G. Malkin, Xylogics, Inc. and T. LaQuey Parker, UTexas, Editors, January 1993. " Status of this Memo: This memo provides information for the Internet community. It does not specify an Internet standard. Distribution of this memo is unlimited". Other terms added by the author.

Acknowledgements

CHAPTER 2

Figure 1: This screen is produced by the Norwegian Social Science Data Services (NSD). Reproduced with permission.

Figure 2: Reproduced courtesy of Datastorm Technologies.

Figure 3: Reprinted by permission. Imageseek, Infoseek, the Infoseek logos, iSeek, "Proof of intelligent life on the net," Quickseek, Ultraseek, Ultrashop, and Ultrasmart are trademarks or registered trademarks of Infoseek Corporation which may be registered in certain jurisdictions. Copyright 1995-1997 Infoseek Corporation. All rights reserved.

CHAPTER 3

Figure 1, 2: Reproduced courtesy of WhoWhere.

Figure 4: Reproduced courtesy of Forte Inc.

CHAPTER 4

Figure 1: Reproduced courtesy of Adobe Systems.

Figures 2-5: Reproduced courtesy of Nexor, Ltd.

Figure 6: Reproduced courtesy of FTP Software.

CHAPTER 5

Figures 1-3: Reproduced courtesy of Carleton University Library.

Figures 4, 5: Reproduced courtesy of the Library of Congress.

Figures 6, 7: Reproduced courtesy of the Institute for Scientific Information.

Figure 8: Reproduced courtesy of Torstar Electronic Publishing.

Figure 9: Reproduced courtesy of Enews.

Figure 10: Reproduced courtesy of *The Atlantic Monthly*. *The Atlantic's* web site publishes essays from the print magazine as well as an array of exclusive online-only features, including web-site reviews and commentary on digital culture.

Figure 11: Copyright 1997. Reprinted with permission of the *LA Times*.

Figure 12: Reproduced courtesy of the *Electronic telegraph*.

Figure 13: Reproduced courtesy of FoxNews.

CHAPTER 6

Figure 1: Reproduced courtesy of Stephen Burnett, Ohio State University.

Figure 2: Reproduced courtesy of Jonny Goldman.

Figure 3: Data and graphs courtesy of Statistics Canada and CHASS, University of Toronto.

Figure 4: Reproduced courtesy of Carleton University Library.

Figure 5: Reproduced courtesy of GNS.

Figure 7: Reproduced courtesy of FerretSoft LLC.

Figure 8: Reproduced courtesy of HotWired.

Figure 9: Reproduced courtesy of AltaVista Software.

Figure 10: Copyright 1996 Lycos, Inc. All Rights Reserved. The Lycos "Catalog of the Internet" Copyright 1994, 1995, 1996 Carnegie Mellon University. All Rights Reserved. Used by permission.

Figures 11-14: Reproduced courtesy of The UnCover Company.

CHAPTER 7

Figure 1, 2: Reproduced courtesy of Scott Southwick.

Figure 3, 4: Reproduced courtesy of Deja News.

Figure 6-9: Reproduced courtesy of Infonautics Corporation.

CHAPTER 8

Figure 1: Copyright 1996 Netscape Communications Corp. Used with permission. All rights reserved. This page may not be reprinted or copied without the express written permission of Netscape. Netscape Communications Corporation has not authorized, sponsored, or endorsed, or approved this publication and is not responsible for its content. Netscape and the Netscape Communications Corporate Logos are trademarks and trade names of Netscape Communications Corporation. All other product names and/or logos are trademarks of their respective owners.

Figure 7: Reproduced courtesy of University of Michigan Library Documents Center.

CHAPTER 9

Figure 2, 3: Reproduced courtesy of Nottingham Trent University Library & Information Service.

Figure 4, 5: Reproduced courtesy of Dr. Cecil Greek, Florida State University.

Figure 7, 8: See credit chapter 2, figure 3.

Figure 9: See credit for chapter 6, figure 8.

Figure 10, 11: See credit chapter 6, figure 9.

Figure 12: See credit chapter 6, figure 2.

Figure 13, 14: Reprinted with the permission of the National Library of Canada.

Figure 15: Reproduced courtesy of the Department of Justice.

Figure 18: Reproduced courtesy of Matthew Ciolek.

CHAPTER 10

Figures 1-5: See credit for chapter 5, figures 6, 7.

Figure 7: Reproduced courtesy of the *Electronic Journal on Virtual Culture*.

Figure 8-10: Reproduced courtesy of the Inter-university Consortium for Political and Social Research (ICPSR), University of Michigan.

Figures 11-14: Reproduced courtesy of The Data Archive, Essex University.

Figure 15-17: Reproduced courtesy of Carleton University Library Data Centre.

Figure 18-21: See credit for chapter 6, figure 3.

CHAPTER 11

Figure 1: Screen shot reprinted by permission from Microsoft Corporation. Microsoft PowerPoint is a registered trademark of Microsoft Corporation.

CHAPTER 12

Figure 1, 2: Reproduced courtesy of Mark Blair.

Figure 4: Reproduced courtesy of Kayhan Boncoglu.

Figures 5, 6: Reproduced courtesy of Candice Bradley, Lawrence University.

Figure 7-9: PsychREF (tm): Resources in Psychology on the Internet. Reproduced by permission.

Figure 10, 11: TradeWave Galaxy is copyright 1993-1997, TradeWave Corporation. All rights reserved. TradeWave is a trademark of TradeWave, Inc. Reproduced with permission.

Figure 12: Reproduced courtesy of RAND organization.

Figure 13, 14: Reproduced courtesy of Dr. James Bolner, LSU.

Figure 15: Reproduced courtesy of Information Resource Centre, Canadian Forces College, Copyright 1997.

Figure 16: Reproduced courtesy of Joan Korenman, University of Maryland, Baltimore County.

Figure 17, 18: Reproduced courtesy of Academic Information Technology Services, University of Maryland.

Figure 19: Reproduced courtesy of Mike Hammer.

Figure 20: Reproduced courtesy of Ben Granger, Colorado State University.

Figure 21: Reproduced courtesy of A. Simon Mielniczuk.

Figure 22: Reproduced courtesy of Mediapolis.

Figure 23: Reproduced courtesy of the Dept. of Media & Communications, University of Oslo.

CHAPTER 13

Figure 1: Reproduced courtesy of Maxwell Information Systems.

Figure 2: Reproduced courtesy of Netscape. See credit chapter 8, figure 1.

Figure 3: Reproduced courtesy of 411.

Figure 4: Reproduced courtesy of Canadian Airlines.

Figure 5: Reproduced courtesy of James O'Donnell, University of Pennsylvania.

Figure 6: Amazon.com site as of Dec 20, 1996; reprinted by permission of Amazon.com.

Figure 7: Reproduced courtesy of PGPfone.

Figure 8: Reproduced courtesy of Symantec Corporations.

CHAPTER 14

Figure 1: Reproduced courtesy of Ufomind.

APPENDIX

Figure 2: Reproduced courtesy of Trumpet Winsock International Pty Ltd.

Index

Symbols

411 200

A

abstract 170
accounts and passwords 230
Acrobat 42
Agent 30, 108
aliases 100
AltaVista 82, 138, 144
analysis 169, 170
animation 194
Anthropology 178
Apple Macintosh 20
Archie 10, 42
Archieplex 44
Arj 50
ASCII 27
AskERIC 102
Associated Press 66
attribution 5

B

BioBase 18, 24, 54, 78, 144
BIRON 160
bookmarks 122
Boolean searches 54

C

Canadian Airlines International
    200
CANSIM 22, 80, 86, 138, 164
CAPDU 86
CD-ROM
    18, 20, 36, 62, 86, 152
Census data 14, 62
Champlain search engine 82
character assassination 210
Claris Homepage 194
Clifford Stoll 214
coding and decoding binary files
    252
connection basics 224

conspiracy theorists 210
cookies 50
CoolTalk 100
copyright 218
credit card calls 244
Current Contents
    60, 86, 120, 138, 151,
    152, 154
CUSeeMe 10, 100
cybercom.drv 20, 226, 238
cypherpunks 66

D

dark side of the Web 207, 208
Data Liberation Initiative 62
dealing in stolen goods 214
Deja News 108
designing Web pages 194
dial-up service 224
digital convergence 6
Digital Equipment 20
digital files 17, 218
digital scholarship 208
digital signatures 258
directory services 198
document 6

E

E-Library 112, 114, 208
e-mail 2, 8, 10, 22, 27, 28,
    29, 30, 32, 246,
    250, 258
e-mail transactions 216
E-STAT 62
earthquake sensors 198
Edupage 70
electronic card catalogues 10
Electronic Newsstand 64
electronic scholarship 2
Electronic Telegraph 64
electronic text 208
Elm 22, 30, 32
Emacs 18, 22, 27, 30
encryption 216, 258, 260
Eudora 30, 32, 34
Excel 134
Explorer 124

F

Finger 128
Fox Network 66
fraudulent advertising 214
Free Agent 10
freenet 20, 32, 234
FrontPage 120, 194
FTP 10, 42, 50, 128, 159, 194
Futurenet UK 72

G

Gallup polls 80, 86, 162
gateway 126
generic e-mail address 36
Geography 182
Globe and Mail 208
Gopher 10, 42
graphics 172
graphics editors 194

H

hackers 214
hacking 2, 212
helper Software 50
HTML 12, 14, 80, 120, 194
http format 10
HyperTerminal 32
Hytelnet 58

I

IASSIST 86
ICPSR 86, 138, 158, 159
image maps 196
information packets 232
Infoseek 26, 138, 142
Inktomi 84, 144
Internet 8, 20, 99
Internet Assistant 194
Internet Explorer 18, 41
INTERNIC 12
IP address number 8, 12,16, 24
IRC 202

K

Keyview 14, 50, 52

L

LA freeway system 198
Laina Ruus 78
Library Data Centre
       80, 138, 162
Library of Congress Web site 56
Linux 20
listservs 2, 8, 10, 28, 100, 210
Liszt 34, 104, 106
Los Angeles Times 64, 208
Lotus Notes 100
Lview 44, 48
Lycos 84, 86
Lynx 18, 42, 64, 122, 124

M

MacTCP 226
Major-domo 100
Mass Communications and
       Journalism 190
Michelle Slatella and Joshua
       Quittner 214
MIME 27, 30, 34, 252
modem mechanics 222
modems 222
Mpegplay 48
multiple personalities 216

N

Nando News 68
National Library of Canada 146
Nautilus 10
neo-nazis and skinheads 212
netiquette 256
NetMeeting 100
Netscape
       10, 18, 24, 30, 32, 41, 100,
       108, 110, 120, 122,
       124, 140
NetTerm 41, 48, 50
New York Times 64, 77, 208
newsgroups 10, 210
NNTP 24, 106, 108
Norton Crashguard 204
NTU Electronic Library 138

O

Office97 194
OLE32S13.EXE 238
online book stores 200
opinion research data 14

P

PageMill 194
peer review 6, 218
Pegasus 30, 32, 34
PFE 194
PGP 260
PGPfone 10, 202, 204
Phil Agre 112
Pico 18, 22, 27, 30
Pine 22, 30, 32
Pkunzip 50
Pnews 110
Political Science 184
pornography 210
Powerpoint 134, 172, 194
PPP 22, 226, 240
predators in cyberspace 214
presenting as someone else 216
privacy issues 216
Procomm 24, 242
Profusion 138
provenance 208
Psychology 180

Q

QuickTime 48

R

RealAudio 66
RealVideo 66
reputation, 5
Research: a Generic Approach
       134
Reuters 66
review 172
role of the teacher 218

S

SAS 62, 80, 86, 159
scanners 54
scholarly journal 6

scholarship 5, 6
search engines 138
service provider 224
shareware 50
sig files 34, 36, 254
Silverplatter 60, 86, 152
SLIP 22, 226, 240, 242
SLIP connections in Unix
       Accounts 240
SLiRP 22, 240, 242, 244
slow scan television 8
smilies and emoticons 256
SMTP 24, 28
social science data archives 22
Social Sciences 1, 8
Social Work 188
Sociofile 60, 86, 120
Sociology 176
software setup 2
SPSS 14, 62, 80, 86, 159
Stuffit Expander 50
style sheets 78
Sun Microsystems 20
SUNSITE 102, 146
SVGA monitors 20, 24

T

Talk 202
TCP/IP 16, 41, 108, 222, 236
teaching 200
telephone hacking 214
Telnet
       10, 39, 41, 46, 48, 110, 152
The Atlantic Monthly 62
the document 6
The Research Page 136, 142
The Toronto Star 76, 208
the Web 8, 18, 24, 62,
       99, 120, 133, 136, 193,
       197, 218
TIA 22, 240, 242
Tim Berners-Lee 14, 17
Times of London 208
Tin 10, 18, 108
Tribnet 70
types of connections 230

U

UART chip 226
UnCover 86, 88, 120, 138,

151, 152, 208
UNIX 10, 12, 18, 20, 22,
        24, 27, 30, 32, 39,
        108, 194
UNIX shell account 120
updating Windows 3.1 238
URL 8, 14, 16, 122
USENET newsgroups
        2, 8, 10, 12, 24, 39,
        41, 99, 106, 110, 208,
        210, 214
uuencoding 50, 128
uuencoding 252

V

VDOPhone 100
visual basic 78

W

WAIS 80, 90, 146
Washington Post 208
Web document 6
Web Knowledge 216
Web page 2, 12, 193
Web publication 6
Web sites 14
Web Virtual Library 148
Webcam 197
WebFerret 82
Webmaster 194
Windows 3.1 20, 78, 226
Windows95
        18, 20, 32, 41, 78,
        84, 120, 226
Windweaver 82
Winsock 41, 48, 236, 238,
        242, 244
Winsock mechanics 236
Winsock on an Ethernet Network
        238
WIPO 218
Women's Studies 186
Word 27, 32, 34, 128, 194
WordPerfect
        27, 32, 34, 128, 194
World Wide Web
        1, 6, 10, 14, 17, 24,
        99, 197, 221
writing a research paper 170
WWW 17
WWW Virtual Library 148, 176

Y

Yahoo 66, 84, 138
Yankee News Desk 68

Z

zip 50